巴哈马农业历史沿革
1492—2012

AGRICULTURE IN THE BAHAMAS
Historical Development 1492-2012

第二版
Second Edition

[巴哈马] 戈弗雷·埃尼亚斯　著

邹卫宁　樊丽霞　译

中国海洋大学出版社
· 青岛 ·

图书在版编目（CIP）数据

巴哈马农业历史沿革:1492—2012/［巴哈马］戈弗雷·
埃尼亚斯著;邹卫宁,樊丽霞译 . —青岛:中国海
洋大学出版社,2018.8
书名原文:AGRICULTURE IN THE BAHAMAS:
Historical Development 1492-2012
ISBN 978-7-5670-1918-8

Ⅰ. ①巴… Ⅱ . ①戈… ②邹… ③樊… Ⅲ. ①农业史
—研究—巴哈马—1492-2012 Ⅳ . ① F376.89

中国版本图书馆 CIP 数据核字（2018）第 187854 号

出版发行	中国海洋大学出版社				
社　　址	青岛市香港东路 23 号		邮政编码	266071	
出 版 人	杨立敏				
网　　址	http://www.ouc-press.com				
电子信箱	1922305382@qq.com				
订购电话	0532-82032573（传真）				
责任编辑	邵成军		电　　话	0532-85902533	
印　　制	青岛国彩印刷有限公司				
版　　次	2018 年 8 月第 1 版				
印　　次	2018 年 8 月第 1 次印刷				
成品尺寸	170 mm ×240 mm				
印　　张	22.75				
字　　数	400 千				
印　　数	1—1 000				
定　　价	58.00 元				

Preface*

As a former Minister of Agriculture, I can speak with confidence about the policy positions outlined in *Agriculture in The Bahamas*: *Historical Development 1492–2012*. Indeed when I became Prime Minister of The Bahamas for the second time in 2012, I incorporated some of these same policy initiatives into the political agenda of my Government.

In his book, Ambassador Eneas provides us with a panoramic historical view of Bahamian Agriculture. It recalls that The Bahamas was the place of first arrival for Europeans in the New World. When they arrived, however, they found a functioning food production system, features of which have been retained in our present agricultural system utilizing a technology rooted in our indigenous pothole farming.

In more recent history, with the ascendency of Tourism, Agriculture in The Bahamas was relegated to an inferior place in our economy.

However, with the resurgence of Food and Nutrition Security as integral components of the global food agenda, it was necessary for my Government to revisit the role of Agriculture in our economy.

Agriculture in The Bahamas: *Historical Development 1492–2012*. provides a perspective which only an agricultural professional with an intimate knowledge of food production in The Bahamas and the Caribbean Region can provide. Ambassador Eneas has met this challenge with his customary erudition, and a deep-seated understanding of this industry.

I cannot commend him highly enough.

The Rt. Hon. Perry G. Christie, M. P.,
PRIME MINISTER
COMMONWEALTH OF THE BAHAMAS

* 本序作于 2012 年。——译者注

序 *

　　作为巴哈马前农业部部长，我认为《巴哈马农业历史沿革：1492—2012》一书对巴哈马农业历来的政策立场都进行了准确的描述。2012年，在我第二次当选巴哈马总理的时候，我就把其中一些政策举措纳入了我国政府的政治议程中。

　　作者埃尼亚斯是巴哈马驻世界粮农组织大使。他的这本书给我们全面地讲述了巴哈马农业的历史与现状。书中指出，巴哈马是欧洲人在新大陆最先到达的地方。当时的欧洲人就发现了我们这个运作良好的粮食生产体系，其中的一些特征保留至今，在我们植根于原生农业又结合了现代科技的农业体系中依然发挥着作用。

　　在最近的历史中，由于旅游业的崛起，农业在巴哈马经济中的地位退居其次了。

　　但是，随着粮食和营养安全重新成为全球粮食议程中不可或缺的组成部分，我国政府有必要重新审视农业在我们经济中的作用。

　　《巴哈马农业历史沿革：1492—2012》为我们提供了一个研究视角，这个视角只有对巴哈马和加勒比地区的粮食生产熟稔的农业专业人士才能提供。埃尼亚斯大使以其一贯的博学和对这个行业的深刻了解满足了这一挑战。

　　我对他的赞扬怎么都不过分。

巴哈马议员、总理

佩里·格拉德斯通·克里斯蒂阁下

中文版序

　　《巴哈马农业历史沿革：1492—2012》和《新加勒比：转型之地：1943—2005》两本书由巴哈马农业与海洋学院校长、巴哈马非常驻联合国粮农组织大使戈弗雷·埃尼亚斯先生撰写，将由中国海洋大学出版社翻译出版，这源于中国和巴哈马的教育合作。

　　巴哈马是加勒比地区一颗璀璨的明珠，拥有700多座岛屿和2 400多个珊瑚礁，具有得天独厚的自然资源、温暖气候以及丰富多元的历史文化。中巴于1997年5月23日正式建立外交关系，2013年12月19日，中巴签订《中华人民共和国政府与巴哈马国政府关于互免签证的协定》。两国关系经历了20多年的发展历程，经贸合作和人文交流持续加强，两国人民的友谊不断深化。

　　2015年1月，中国 - 拉美和加勒比国家共同体部长级会议在北京举行。习近平主席、李克强总理分别亲切会见加勒比国家共同体轮值主席国、巴哈马时任总理佩里·格拉德斯通·克里斯蒂。两国领导人长远规划了中巴各领域互利合作的方向。彼时，中国海洋大学于志刚校长专程赴京应约拜访佩里·格拉德斯通·克里斯蒂总理，商谈推动双边教育交流与合作，帮助巴哈马更好地保护生态环境并推动巴哈马农业与海洋经济的可持续发展，落实两国领导人达成的共识。

　　2015年7月，于志刚校长应邀率团访问巴哈马，在佩里·格拉德斯通·克里斯蒂总理和中国驻巴哈马大使苑桂森等中巴代表见证下，与戈弗雷·埃尼亚斯校长签署了中国海洋大学和巴哈马农业与海洋学院合作备忘录，双方将在人才培养、学术交流、合作研究及产业开发等多方面开展务实互利合作，积极为中巴教育交流及中巴友好做出贡献。在中国海洋大学代表团访问巴哈马期间，作为校际合作内容之一，双方商定由中国海洋大学资助在中国出版由戈弗雷·埃尼亚斯校长编写的两本书《巴哈马农业历史沿革：1492—2012》和《新加勒比：转型之地：1943—2005》的中译本，以加强两校的合作，增进两国的相互了解与友谊。

　　巴哈马农业与海洋学院成立于2013年11月，位于巴哈马最大的岛屿——安德鲁斯岛。巴哈马时任总理佩里·格拉德斯通·克里斯蒂是该机构的主要推动者。该机构的设置旨在通过教学、培训等形式培养农业与海洋资源领域技术人才，大力发展种植业、畜牧业和现代渔业。2014年9月，学院首个农业与海洋科学班开班，学生毕业后将授予副学士学位及证书。巴哈马农业与海洋学院正在快速建设中，学院计划占地2 400余亩，其中包括1 800余亩的教学实验用商业农场和多功能滨海实验基地。

　　我们希望通过本次出版，让更多民众认识和了解巴哈马，促进中巴两国人民之间的友谊。相信在中巴各界的共同努力下，中巴友谊之树将更加枝繁叶茂，结出丰硕果实，造福两国人民。

　　2013年至2016年我出任中国驻巴哈马大使。2015年1月我有幸参加了习近平主席和李克强总理同佩里·格拉德斯通·克里斯蒂总理的会见，受益良多。我也亲历了中国海洋大学于志刚校长拜访佩里·格拉德斯通·克里斯蒂总理以及对巴哈马的访问，目睹了两校扎扎实实地把双边互利合作不断推向深入。谨以此序感谢中国海洋大学领导的信任并祝福两校交流与合作继续迈向前方。

原中国驻巴哈马大使：范桂森

2018年7月1日

2015 年 7 月，本书作者（前排右二）陪同巴哈马时任总理佩里·格拉德斯通·克里斯蒂（前排中）会见到访的中国海洋大学代表团

中国海洋大学代表团考察巴哈马农业与海洋学院实习基地

巴哈马农场

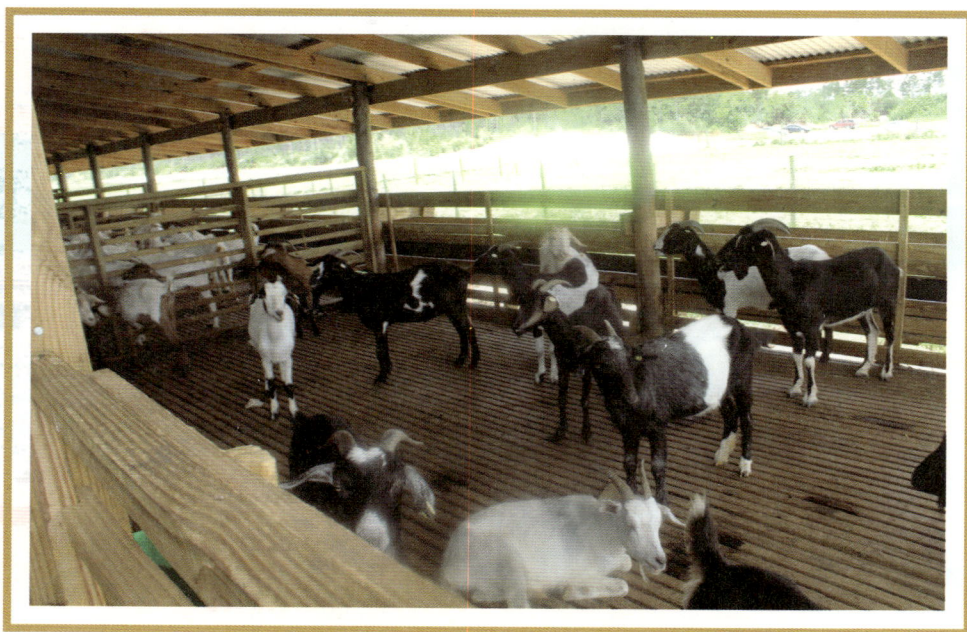

巴哈马养羊场

献　词

谨以此书献给我已故的母亲西尔维娅。她在我童年时给我读的一个个希腊神话故事，使我对历史这一学科有了最初的认识。同样把这本书献给我的父亲威廉，是他引导我一步步走进了农业这个领域。

我的妻子桑德拉在本书写作期间仔细阅读各章节并给出了审慎的建议。我的儿子戈弗雷以一名农业经济学家的身份为本书的最终呈现提供了很多帮助。我的小儿子蒂莫西是一名历史专业的毕业生，为我提供了实用的历史研究方法。我把这本书献给他们。

最后，我要把这本书献给我已故的叔叔克利夫兰·埃尼亚斯博士。他是作家、牙医，毕生坚持记录我们的历史。这种精神深深地激励了我，成为我写这本书的初衷。

致　谢

　　本书第一版是一种职业责任使然。作为第一版，它的产生充分调动了各方面的资源。因此，请允许我感谢参与第一版出版的所有人员。

　　第二版与第一版的不同之处在于，它需要为读者提供大量更新的数据。为此，我特别感谢农业部的莱斯利·明斯先生对我的大力帮助。

　　在过去的二十年里(1992—2012)，巴哈马的农业形势随着温室栽培等新兴技术的引进而发生了改变。这一领域的领军人物有卢卡亚热带农产品公司的提姆·豪伯先生、乔伊·斯威廷夫人以及勒罗伊·圣地亚哥博士，他们在农场主以及农业企业家中率先推广这种技术。他们都为这本书提供了有用的信息和照片。

　　第二版也给了我一个机会，让我可以为读者提供 20 世纪 70、80 和 90 年代这数十年间有关农业发展的更深入的信息，同时突出贸易自由化对农业产生影响的一些观点。

图：作者于 2003 年向世界粮农组织总干事雅克·迪乌夫递交大使文书。

　　我向这本书的关键出版商尼尔·赛利先生表示我的谢意。他持续不断的推动是我修订本书的一个因素。很显然，读者对这本书的需求增加了，尤其是教育工作者、农业研究人员以及具有各种学术水平的学生。

　　意识到农业在地缘政治中的重要性之后，巴哈马政府在 2003 年任命我为联合国粮农组织驻意大利罗马的大使。这是巴哈马政府首次对粮农组织进行这种任命。

戈弗雷·埃尼亚斯

2012 年 8 月

目 录

Chapter 1

Agriculture: Early Development in The Bahamas// 153

Chapter 2

Bahamian Agriculture and British Colonial Policy// 163

Chapter 6

Major Agricultural Projects (1965-2001)// 245

Chapter 7

The Impact of Tourism on the Agricultural Sector// 276

Chapter 8

Agriculture's Future // 285

引　言

　　巴哈马农业的情况从未得到过完整的叙述。本书试图从全新而又全面的视角来阐释这一话题。

　　巴哈马的农业在历史中的作用与其社会经济发展紧密相关。农业曾一度是巴哈马从业人数最多的行业，也是外汇收入的主要来源。大权在握的从政者试图控制农业，因为他们深知农业的经济实力及其对经济的重要性。

　　尽管巴哈马的物质资源极其有限，但是土地的收成还是产生了足够的财富来维持殖民经济。有了新的知识和技术，农业可以再次成为社会的支柱，但必须理解和明白其潜力才能实现这一点。

　　在21世纪，这种资源需要更多的关注和保护，才能实现其预期的潜力。要实现这一目标，新方向是最重要的。

　　农业被视为与环境和发展问题密切相关的主要经济活动之一。在此背景下，21世纪推动农业增长和发展的农业政策和计划必须考虑环境问题。

　　只有建立合作伙伴关系才能实现该目标。政府独自掌握决定一个行业国家发展方向砝码的时代已经一去不复返了。产业、政府、本地农业企业、小规模农场主、消费者、向我国农业部门投入原材料的外国实体，以及巴哈马和外国粮食进口者之间的对话十分重要。

　　农业正在发生着深刻的变化，没有哪个组织拥有能够解决21世纪我们将面临的诸多挑战的所有方案。大型国际机构正在发展中国家实施结构调整方案，市场的自由化和开放对第三世界国家未来的各类经济活动造成了威胁。农业政策的转向不仅出于能够感觉到的需要，也出于经济需要，如食品加工厂系统对巴哈马农民及其生活方式和收入的影响。

然而，许多政策和决策在制定时并没有与农业和农业企业群体经过任何形式的磋商。农民最接近自然环境这一事实无可争议，协助成功管理我们的自然资源符合农民的利益，因为这是 21 世纪农民生存的根本。

《巴哈马农业历史沿革：1492-1992》首次出版于 1998 年，2001 年稍作修订后重印。

在第二版中，增加了三处较长的实质性内容。在第三章"20 世纪 70、80 和 90 年代的农业"中，我认为应该注意到平德林政府在此期间的大量投资。

第六章强调了新技术的引进，主要是温室栽培技术，该技术由农业的主要投资方卢卡亚热带产品公司引进。与此同时，一些小规模农场主也采用了温室技术，从而使他们的技术能力得到了提升。

新增加的第九章涉及多种视角：全球性、地区性及国家性的食品生产问题相互交叉。插入这一章是因为我开始关注国际农业。在 2003 年 3 月至 2007 年 5 月，我被任命为巴哈马驻粮农组织（FAO）大使，加上 2005 年至 2008 年我被选为哥斯达黎加图里亚尔瓦热带农业研究与高等教育中心（CATIE）的董事，因而提高了对全球农业的关注度。

第 1 章 »»

农业:在巴哈马的早期发展

1492年哥伦布登陆巴哈马时,他遇到了一种与欧洲截然不同的文化。

作为巴哈马的第一批居民,阿拉瓦克人有自己的环境基础。欧洲人邂逅了有着丰富的海洋生物的亚热带气候,这里有绿海龟、海龟蛋、海螺(大凤螺)和有鳞鱼类;有各种各样的陆地动物:浣熊、草食龟(特别是象龟)、鬣蜥(特别是岩鬣蜥)、刺鼠、硬毛鼠、鸽子、白鸽、鹦鹉和几种仓鸮(包括巨型仓鸮(巴哈马仓鸮)),目前这些仓鸮已经灭绝。植物品种丰富,包括可食用的水果:西班牙青柠(美洲格尼帕树)、海葡萄、椰李、菠萝、松果和棕榈树;地下食物有木薯、红薯、花生和具有药性的植物群,如铁梨木(愈疮木)。

哥伦布和其追随者还发现了一个社会群体(在当地语言中名字叫卡西卡古斯),他们有着秩序井然并且世袭的等级制度——酋长世袭制(在当地语言中名叫卡西格),"哥伦布与这个群体进行了很多交易,并受到他们的尊重"(瓦特,1987)。阿拉瓦克人有生产食品的工具,有石头或燧石式工具和武器,精通制陶、纺棉、篮子编织、金属加工,能够制造长矛、标枪、独木舟,懂得用棕榈叶作顶建造房屋。生活在岛上的阿拉瓦克人,像在巴哈马的阿拉瓦克人一样,不了解黄金开采,而在大安的列斯群岛中较大岛屿(如伊斯帕尼奥拉岛和古巴)上生活的阿拉瓦克人却普遍开采黄金。

据瓦特1987年的研究,有证据表明,大安的列斯群岛的阿拉瓦克人之间进行过贸易。西班牙人登陆时,阿拉瓦克人村庄的人口在1 000人到2 000人之间,一般居住在远离海岸的内陆地区。关于岛上的阿拉瓦克人(阿拉瓦克裔巴哈马人),有两个有趣的事实需要注意:首先,据西班牙人记载,当地没有主要的传染病;其次,阿拉瓦克女性在社会中占优势地位,按母系继承财产(瓦特,1987)。

图 1.1　泰诺人的房屋结构（瓦特，1987）

泰诺人或卢卡亚泰诺人农业

在阿拉瓦克人时期，巴哈马的地势和欧洲各地都不同。陆地上主要是生长着松树和阔叶林的浅层石灰土壤。

基于与岩石类型和降雨密切相关的植被和产量，1971 年至 1976 年进行的土地资源研究对土地进行了分类。两个主要的群岛被命名为松树群岛和矮林群岛。

阿拉瓦克人在松树群岛和矮林群岛上都有分布，但居住在矮林群岛上的人数似乎更多，那里混合生长着阔叶林和灌木林，别具特色。这些岛屿本身狭长、崎岖，硬岩起伏。阿拉瓦克人或在"白色土地"的沙质土壤上耕种，或在壶穴和溶洞中发现的肥沃的黑土或红土上耕作。

在这种种植环境下，壶穴农业以阿拉瓦克人农业为基础发展起来了。阿拉瓦克人农业中的轮作或火耕技术、园地开发和家庭农场的建立是壶穴农业的基本方面。

西班牙人对岛上阿拉瓦克人发展的粮食生产体系印象极其深刻。阿拉瓦克人从一个体系中培育了几种粮食作物，他们在哥伦布登陆之前已经发展了该体系。西班牙人能够对该体系进行观察、评估、记录，在某些情况下，还能进行实践。

食物来源有三个：

（1）移耕农业：基于家庭农场的创建和维护，家庭农场中种植富含淀粉和糖类的食物。

（2）菜园子用来种植厨房型作物。

（3）狩猎野生动物、鸟类和捕鱼——这可以提供肉类,采摘野生植物和水果。

阿拉瓦克人农业系统的核心是发展家庭农场,使之成为保证粮食可靠来源的机制以及阿拉瓦克裔巴哈马人粮食生产循环的重要技术发明。

泰诺人家庭农场

如果土地不陡峭,也不低洼,有良好的排水和轻质土壤,阿拉瓦克人的家庭农场就紧挨着村庄而建。一旦选中地点,就会将大树环割(除去树皮),砍伐树林。树桩留在地里腐烂,砍倒的残枝则被烧毁。

瓦特写道:"就在播种前,家庭农场上部分烧毁的树干和树枝杂乱无章地缠在一起,土壤上是厚厚的灰层,中间混杂着腐烂的树桩。"(参见第5章)

把场地清扫后,这里就准备好播种了。播种使用的手工工具叫点播器,巴哈马的自耕农和壶穴农民从阿拉瓦克人时期一直沿用至20世纪。

作物借由生长力旺盛的插枝繁殖,主要包括淀粉块茎,如木薯和丝兰以及红薯(甘薯)、花生和利马豆(菜豆)。西葫芦也是岛上阿拉瓦克人的栽培品种之一。

旱季结束时播种。由于缺乏灌溉设备,阿拉瓦克人依靠季节性降雨来灌溉家庭农场,因此要在旱季结束时播种。

除了燃烧树林带来的养料,在哥伦布到达这里之前,岛上阿拉瓦克人还用粪便作为土壤的改良剂和肥料。

栽培的主要作物是木薯或者丝兰。在其两个品种中,一种苦,另一种甜。

苦木薯必须进行提取,该工艺由女性操作。提取后的残渣被烤成无酵面包,称为木薯面包。几年前,在第一次登陆的圣萨尔瓦多人们发现了岛上阿拉瓦克人用来烤木薯的一个很大的陶制烤盘的碎片。

阿拉瓦克人将甜木薯作为蔬菜煮熟烘干,西班牙人将红薯作为甜点食用,因为它很甜。阿拉瓦克人则喜欢不太甜的品种。

农场管理(或家庭农场管理)的基础是进行分工。男人负责挑选和清理场地,种植庄稼。女人从事日常的劳动,如除草、饲养动物和收割庄稼。只要家庭农场没有洪水威胁,这些随时都可以完成。

家庭农场的耕作活动于黎明开始,通常在中午前结束。

家庭农场的农事是一项长期的活动，因为一个地方的生产可以坚持 15 至 20 年。在此之后，家庭农场会被遗弃，休耕 30 年。在此期间，植被会再生，土壤的养分会再次积聚。

在哥伦布首次登陆后，西班牙人只用了二三十年就消灭了巴哈马岛上的阿拉瓦克人。阿拉瓦克裔巴哈马人被送往古巴和伊斯帕尼奥拉岛的金矿工作，最终导致其灭绝。

泰诺巴哈马人被迫离开这些岛屿后，巴哈马的历史几乎中断了。直到 1647 年，伊鲁萨拉岛探险者重新将巴哈马群岛开拓为殖民地，巴哈马才开始了新的历史。

伊鲁萨拉岛探险者

伊鲁萨拉岛探险者来自百慕大，由清教徒组成，主要是农民和渔民。他们来到开放的新大陆寻求宗教自由。他们在百慕大前总督威廉·塞勒的领导下起航，但航船撞到了伊鲁萨拉岛北部海岸的礁石。航程因此结束，他们就在此安顿了下来。

在巴哈马生活对于伊鲁萨拉岛探险者来说并非易事。1649 年，他们上岛没多久，就开始遭受颗粒无收带来的恶劣影响。所幸的是，他们能够从马萨诸塞州殖民地获得供应。

这批货物包括价值约 1 000 英镑的玉米和其他必需品，靠销售巴西木挣来的钱支付。巴西木是这一时期的主要染料木。1650 年，10 吨巴西木被运往波士顿出售，挣的钱中有 124 英镑捐给了哈佛学院（现为哈佛大学），以表示感谢。有份报告指出，这是当时数额最大的捐款之一。

伊鲁萨拉岛探险者每年都会前往特克斯群岛耙盐、捕捉海龟以及收集鲸鱼的龙涎香。他们还通过营救失事船只增加收入。

在此期间，有建议发给领主，据说领主是殖民地严格意义上的所有人。第一次建议是 1670 年写给领主的一封信，信中称，巴哈马可以种植出比美国大陆质量更高的烟草。然而，似乎没有任何迹象表明当地居民开始为商业市场种植烟草。

另一次向领主提建议是在 1671 年 12 月，建议是关于引入保护措施。人们认为，有必要保护和规范巴西木的砍伐，同时还要保护海龟。

保皇党人

美国独立战争（1775—1778）后，许多英国保皇党人离开美国，开始在巴哈马进行殖民；来自美国南方的人带来了他们的奴隶。保皇党人也带来了农业创新技术，这在当时改变了巴哈马的农业面貌。在他们到来之前，这里没有大规模种植过任何农作物。这些人来自美国农业发达的地区，带着奴隶，因此能够引入规模化种植。他们熟悉美国南部的棉花，所以棉花是他们的不二之选。

保皇党人涌入巴哈马对解释人口增长很重要。他们于1783年到达，这一举动也刺激了农业的发展。他们得到大片土地，开垦后种植棉花。

棉花成为这些岛屿上种植最广泛的作物，在矮林群岛更是如此。一份报告指出，崎岖岛共有40个种植园，种了2 000～3 000英亩棉花。长岛约有4 000英亩。据报道，1703年到1785年之间，从长岛和伊克祖马斯岛每年出口约600吨棉花。棉花种植持续了约20年，直到作物因虫害、土壤贫瘠和不良的耕作方法而开始歉收才停止种植。

这些岛屿上土壤的厚度自保皇党人时代开始大幅下降，当时岛屿上森林密布。土壤厚度下降的原因是不停收割、砍伐和燃烧植被使土壤失去保护，导致大量的土壤被侵蚀。

显然，王室意识到了水土流失和土壤贫瘠的危险。1787年，王室购买了巴哈马原始领主的权利，进行转让，出售地块。其目的是鼓励人们停止不断地焚烧土地，转变为耕种几年后再移到另一个地区，以消除移耕。

该计划并未被完全接受，但如今从猫岛上当年修建的石墙、纤路和人行道中可以看出一些成功的迹象。

从18世纪后半叶到20世纪初，巴哈马农业成为世界市场上成功的竞争者。在此期间，除棉花外，主要农作物还有剑麻、菠萝、柑橘类水果和番茄，巴哈马农民与佛罗里达州、古巴、波多黎各、夏威夷以及后来的加州的农民进行竞争。

20世纪20年代农业的衰退被赋予了多种解释。官方报告认为原因在于土壤侵蚀和土壤贫瘠、加在巴哈马出口产品上的高关税以及巴哈马的高劳动力成本。不可否认的潜在问题是，农民仍然采用传统的耕作方法，而不是紧跟最新的科技进步。因此，巴哈马农业开始停滞不前。

出口农业

巴哈马一直在展示为国内和国外市场生产大量产品的能力。在19世纪的后半叶，巴哈马产品和农产品参与了世界市场竞争。

据记载，1860年至1877年间，每年有542吨柑橘出口到英国。在1879年达到顶峰，有1 241吨橘子和166吨柚子出口国外，运往欧洲（英国）和北美（美国和加拿大）市场（马丁，1981）。

柑橘出口业到 1920 年已萎缩，原因是经营不善、劣质水果运往市场以及蓝灰色蝇破坏果林。柑橘产量恢复其出口潜力需要近 60 年的时间。

如今生产的菠萝主要供当地消费。早在 1720 年前后，德国难民将其引入巴哈马。1844 年，大量菠萝被运往英国。1855 年至 1864 年间，菠萝每年出口量约为 2 000 吨，成为巴哈马出口的主要农产品。一直到 1900 年，菠萝都是重要的出口作物。1907 年，出口的菠萝价值相当于 30 000 英镑。殖民地报告记载，菠萝是主要的出口作物，但在 1907 年之后，菠萝产业仅限于国内市场。

该行业的衰败是由于其无力参与国际竞争、管理不善和缺乏可靠的运输方式。到 1920 年，菠萝出口几乎完全停止。

到 1920 年为止，柑橘类水果和菠萝种植主要是针对本地市场；这时番茄名列前茅。1920 年至 1927 年间，向美国市场出口的番茄几乎翻了一番，从刚过 2 000 吨达到约 4 000 吨。

这样的生产能力主要是在伊鲁萨拉岛和猫岛发展起来的。伊克祖马斯岛和长岛等其他岛屿也有生产，但产量没有伊鲁萨拉岛和猫岛大。

虽然失去了柑橘和菠萝的出口市场，但巴哈马农民仍为国内市场生产各种热带水果和蔬菜。因为是群岛，农民面临的限制因素之一是使产品以可接受的状态进入拿骚市场。直到 20 世纪 60 年代初，拿骚都是唯一的城市市场。

剑麻于 1845 年由殖民地大臣 C.R. 内斯比特先生从尤卡坦半岛引入，但推广该作物的是巴哈马当时的总督安布罗斯·谢伊阁下。到 1929 年，剑麻出口量已下降到勉强为 10 年前的 1/10 的地步。1931 年，剑麻产业已经边缘化，因为出口盈利不佳。其失败的原因是劳动力成本高，这有碍种植园和工厂的运作。剑麻检验及海产品局制定了《1931 年修正法案》，以规定更好的分级和剑麻的包装，但这项立法措施为时已晚。

如今，伊鲁萨拉岛仍是菠萝的生产中心。猫岛的产量也很高。1964 年，一家离岸公司为出口开始种植 500 英亩菠萝，到 1965 年旺季，菠萝的出口价值为 3 900 英镑。1966 年，出口值更加惊人可观。新鲜菠萝在出口市场卖出 8 000 百慕大元，菠萝果脯则卖出 135 000 百慕大元。菠萝业的后续失败是由于存货变质和土地歉收。化学物质等创新技术的采用，为复苏针对国内消费的菠萝生产做出了贡献。

一直到 1900 年，柑橘类水果大批出口到美国。佛罗里达州开始大规模生产柑橘后，美国政府对巴哈马柑橘征收每磅 1.5 美分的税，这迫使巴哈马退出了美国市场。巴哈马无力竞争的另一个原因是蓝灰色蝇的入侵。

1965 年,柑橘生产受到了挫折,飓风贝琪对正在恢复的柑橘行业造成了重创。但几乎所有地区都恢复了元气。到 1966 年底,当地水果供应充足。

柑橘生产对国内市场至关重要,每年 11 月到次年 2 月产量很高。由于缺乏灌溉设施,该产业在矮林群岛的扩张受到了限制。相反,松树群岛有利的生长条件推动了该行业的发展。

近年来,农业部已着手从佛罗里达州引进优良的柑橘类水果品种。结果非常振奋人心。1995 年柑橘占作物总出口额的 86%。

20 世纪 20 年代,番茄成为巴哈马最重要的出口商品之一。在该产业的发展初期,出口额约为 39 000 英镑,并在短时间内达到 10 万英镑。在此期间,佛罗里达农学家发现,他们可以生产早熟番茄,这对巴哈马构成了威胁。然而,番茄一直保持大量的供应;1965 年,有 9 万蒲式耳 ① 的番茄出售给当地的罐头厂,还有少量作为新鲜水果在当地市场上销售。出口市场由安德鲁斯和阿巴克斯的大型离岸公司供应,巴哈马的小规模农场主无法参与出口市场竞争。小规模农场主种植的番茄的主要出路是食品加工厂和当地的新鲜水果、蔬菜经销商,经销商再向超市、酒店和餐馆供货。

离岸公司

第二次世界大战后,巴哈马的经济发展进入了新时代。旅游业成为推动经济的动力。随着新农业系统的逐步引入,农业摆脱了停滞不前的状态。

18 世纪后期,保皇党人移民巴哈马,带来了高度发达的技术技能。20 世纪 50 年代初,第二次技术浪潮以大型离岸公司的形式席卷巴哈马,这些公司是高度资本化和商业化的农业企业。

第一批大公司中包括殖民开发公司,它是英国政府的一家机构,位于安德鲁斯和伊鲁萨拉。伊鲁萨拉岛洛克湾的三湾农场是该公司所有的农场之一。然而,在 1952 年至 1953 年,殖民开发公司放弃了其农场的经营。

这时还有两家杰出企业,分别是新普罗维登斯的 21 世纪农业有限公司和伊鲁萨拉岛斧头湾的伊鲁萨拉有限公司。

1958 年,主要的大型企业有伊鲁萨拉有限公司、伊鲁萨拉岛洛克湾的巴哈马畜牧公司、阿巴克斯岛马什港的天然胶乳种植园、安德鲁斯岛马斯蒂克角的

---

① 在美国 1 蒲式耳相当于 35.238 升。——译者注

安德鲁斯岛种植公司和富兰克林农场有限公司。

天然胶乳种植园针对本地市场种植了种类繁多的水果，包括柑橘、木瓜、牛油果、杧果、香蕉和甘蔗，并出口黄瓜、番茄和甜椒到美国。安德鲁斯岛种植公司为出口种植了类似的高价作物，包括黄瓜、番茄、香瓜和甜椒。而富兰克林农场有限公司则生产草莓、番茄和木瓜，用于出口。

1960 年以后，更多企业加入了大型农业企业的行列。一些公司，如安德鲁斯（原阿巴克斯）的斯科特·马特森，为与美国进行专门的冬季贸易种植水果和蔬菜，在美国经营了一家大型生产营销机构。帕克农场也生产水果和蔬菜；伊鲁萨拉岛斧头湾的哈里斯维尔公司成立了一家高产的奶制品和禽肉企业；还有伊鲁萨拉岛洛克湾的派迪格雷·夏洛利牧场、新普罗维登斯的黄金群岛乳业、新普罗维登斯开发公司以及阿巴克斯制糖的欧文斯 - 伊利诺伊 / 巴哈马农业产业有限公司（BAIL）都属于此类公司。这一趋势贯穿于 20 世纪 70 至 90 年代。

第 2 章 »

巴哈马农业和英国殖民政策

1629 年起巴哈马受到英国统治,沦为英帝国的殖民地,一直到 1973 年才得以独立。344 年中,英国的政策决定了巴哈马经济发展的进程,影响了其经济部门在发展过程中发挥的作用。要理解巴哈马农业的发展,必须理解英国的殖民政策对巴哈马经济部门的影响。

后来,成人普选、公司投票的废除和宪法变迁等形式的政治进步,于 1964 年在联合巴哈马党政府时期带来了内部自治。1967 年,殖民地经历了另一场政治变革,进步自由党在大选中获胜。1973 年,在新首相林登•平德林先生的领导下,进步自由党政府为巴哈马人民赢得了独立。进步自由党在巴哈马连续执政 25 年,直到 1992 年 8 月休伯特•A.英格拉哈姆先生领导的自由民族运动赢得了大选。

殖民统治的特点

英帝国的基本思想基于这一信条:殖民地应与宗主国互补,促进英国贸易,其居民应遵守英国法律。

英帝国影响深远,英国殖民统治计划实现这些目标。它有官僚体制,免受政治压力,努力保持政策的连贯性。它的程序基于法律。英国殖民统治的特点是高效、公正、廉洁而不干预他国内政。

政府结构内,重点要做的事情是维护法律和秩序以及使殖民地在财政上有能力自我维持。英国经济的参与需要建设基础设施,以提高殖民地的经济和社会生活水平,使殖民地有能力支付和维持生活便利设施。英国资本家将通过开发殖民地的自然资源利用基础设施,从而促进英国财富和权力的扩张。这种统治方式的副产品是为殖民地"臣民"创造了机会。

在英属西印度殖民地的背景下审视巴哈马很重要。20世纪40年代，英国工党政府检查殖民地的基础设施建设，结果是决定通过基础设施建设优先于帝国殖民地实现自治促进社会和经济的复兴。

这促使调查委员会调查了英属西印度群岛的社会经济条件。该委员会建议工党政府对基础设施建设拨款和贷款的具体目的进行立法，比如公路、桥梁、运河、诊所、医院和学校的建设。工党政府通过了《殖民地发展法案(1940—1945)》，但鲜有迹象表明该法案在加勒比地区实现了其目标。即使实现了，巴哈马也没有获益。

一个健康的、问题最少的社会和经济环境对殖民地很重要，而大多数殖民地官员缺乏管理殖民地经济的工商业方面的培训。相反，他们依靠基本的财政措施引导自己制定与经济增长和发展相关的政策。

20世纪40年代，工党政府很关心经济发展，因为他们担心私人投资会利用殖民地的资源。因此，他们成立了殖民地发展局，以发展有利于殖民地臣民和殖民地本身的经济。

1950年至1953年，殖民地发展公司在巴哈马伊鲁萨拉岛的洛克湾和安德鲁斯的斯丹那德湾经营农场。殖民地发展公司终止其在巴哈马的业务，有可能是由于经营成本高，从而使得他们的产品不具有竞争力。来自美国的离岸种植业务填补了殖民地发展公司撤出留下的空白，并继续顺利地将大量农产品出口到美国和加拿大，这突显了殖民地发展公司的效率低下。

殖民地当局认为经济和社会发展有先决条件。在巴哈马，选择农业部门开展经济活动将促进发展。在其他殖民地，可能会选择修建铁路和港口以运输原料，或是建立电信系统以改善通讯。

可靠的供水和稳定的电力来源对区域的发展往往至关重要。同样重要的还有社会服务、教育系统的维护(至少到小学水平)和卫生保健系统，以根除地方病。这些组成了殖民时期发展计划的基本要素，同时也是农业必须与之竞争的领域。

回顾殖民政策，关于其目标有很多解释。一些政策分析家认为，帝国政策的各个方面是为了通过市场的力量促进附属国的经济发展，在"开放的经济"中，依靠资本主义制度的推动，将"落后"社会转变为"现代"社会。与此同时，人们普遍希望将殖民地经济与宗主国经济拴在一起，从而使其摆脱各自的地理环境，融合成一个帝国经济体。

殖民统治下的农业

殖民地当局认为农业是经济收益可观的生产活动,有利于英帝国。在此背景下,农业是所有热带经济的基础,也是出口贸易的主体。农业为进口买单,而进口也被征收关税,以支付宗主国政府和殖民地自身政府的运营成本。

为了保证殖民地农业的成功,英国建立了一个精心设计的科学网络,来支持他们凭借帝国影响力拥有和控制的这一全球行业。

对于派往殖民地管理农业各部门的英国顾问而言,首要培训机构是特里尼达圣奥古斯丁的帝国热带农业学院。帝国热带农业学院因重视研究热带农业而举世闻名。如果非洲和加勒比地区殖民地想继续维持世界市场上英国在热带作物方面的支配地位,这个学院将成为殖民地农业发展的关键。

在帝国热带农业学院完成培训的官员通常毕业于剑桥、雷丁和伦敦崴学院,当然还有其他大学。这些殖民地的官员最终将做巴哈马等殖民地的农民和小规模农场主的顾问。

除了帝国热带农业学院,还有英联邦农业局和其他支援机构,举几个例子来说,有英联邦生物控制研究所、英联邦昆虫研究所、英联邦真菌研究所、英联邦园艺和种植园作物局、英联邦土壤局和科学与工业研究部。在帝国衰微的日子里,海外开发部既发挥了援助机构的作用,也充当了解决前殖民地经济发展问题的外交政策手段。这些前殖民地现在已经成为经济陷入困境的第三世界国家。

进入 20 世纪,农业部门成功的因素在巴哈马仍然缺失,这受到了伦敦殖民地办公室的极大关注。这在殖民地大臣 1930 年题为《巴哈马农业》的备忘录中显而易见,备忘录指出:

> 我们(殖民局)不能无视以下事实,即殖民地的生产力已经减少到接近消失点,而巴哈马在英国殖民地中几乎是独一无二的,其生产力和对英国贸易的贡献已经变小而非变大。
>
> 近年来巴倒退很远,以至于殖民地现在连热带水果和人们很大一部分的主食都要进口。也许无人慎重考虑民众是否有其他手段维持生计,但事实上却是人们谋生的机会减少了,而不是增加了。

人们认为农业能像海绵一样吸收不断膨胀的劳动力,而巴哈马很令英国殖民局担忧,因为农业既没有生产粮食,也没有创造就业机会。

殖民地农业的土地和劳动力

殖民地政府通常面临两大劳工问题：要么有劳动力，而土地供不应求，要么有土地，但劳动力供不应求。（菲尔德豪斯，1981）这些困难出现在有以下情况的殖民地中：

（1）很多人愿意在自己的土地上从事生产劳动；

（2）有充足的未充分利用的土地，但缺乏有意愿的劳动力，比如在巴哈马；

（3）大批英国永久定居者想要经营农场，但遭遇了土地和劳动力短缺。

在巴哈马，这一情况因 19 世纪初柑橘、菠萝和番茄的出口得以解决。然而，殖民地政府认为剑麻行业是提供就业机会、促进贸易以支持政府运作和各种种植企业的主要农业机制。为了鼓励该行业，1890 年，约 10 万英亩土地被指定用于种植剑麻。

1931 年，尽管尝试了恢复，但剑麻的出口活力还是衰退了。1950 年 9 月，英国殖民局非常担忧。因此，殖民地国务大臣通过殖民地大臣办公室和农业及海产委员会主席交流了剑麻产业的状况，特别是机械清洁剑麻和出口市场剑麻的表现。同年 2 月，殖民地大臣也曾表示他对殖民地农业生产的担忧，并建立了监测体系。

1951 年的年度报告指出，剑麻种植面积没有扩大，原有植株生产了 196 吨，价值 19 422 英镑。相比之下，1950 年的产量为 252 吨，价值 16 376 英镑。

1958 年，殖民地国务大臣在总督和农业总监的陪伴下，参观了阿克林斯、崎岖岛、长礁区，视察巴哈马东南部的农业活动。

巴哈马殖民地官员认识到，农业部门无法容纳多余的劳动力。对此，他们和美国合作组织了一项农场工人移民计划。1918 年，巴哈马约有 3 000 名男性前往南卡罗来纳州查尔斯顿工作。农业及海产委员会的年度报告显示，移民对维护就业市场的平衡非常重要。

此外，20 世纪 50 年代，美国离岸跨国公司对巴哈马北部群岛的吸引力也很大。公司在安德鲁斯、阿巴克斯和大巴哈马岛（松树群岛）上提供木材产业和经济作物生产方面的就业机会。

殖民地农业生产的类型

殖民地的农业生产一般有两种类型：资本主义和非资本主义。资本主义式农业包括独立的欧式农场、种植园农业（这两者在巴哈马都没有）以及大型林业公司进行的林业开发，如巴哈马的欧文斯 - 伊利诺伊公司。

非资本主义式农业由种植经济作物的小规模农场主组成，他们为出口市场种植剑麻、柑橘、番茄和菠萝。

另一种类型的非资本主义式农业为生计农业。农业及海产委员会的年度报告将这一类型归为小规模农场主农业，指的是来自外岛各个农作社区的农民群体，他们不仅为自己生产，也为拿骚市场供应水果、蔬菜、谷物、羊肉和猪肉。

殖民政策一体化

殖民地的农业政策主要由总督通过殖民地大臣办公室实施。1930 年之前，巴哈马没有农业管理人员。20 世纪 50 年代，情况开始改变，因为一些地区的殖民政策开始一体化，特别是在作为技术人员的殖民地官员的征募方面。

1952 年 7 月，农业及海产委员会收到了发给其高级农业官员的邀请函，该官员是当时参加瓦伊学院农业主任会议的最高级的专业人员，会议定于 1953 年7 月 6 日至 9 日举行，巴哈马有代表参加。巴哈马农业及海产委员会还通过殖民地大臣办公室请求派一名观察员并申请加入英国加勒比地区农业咨询委员会。

图 2.1　世纪之交的一个外岛（家庭岛）农场。利用马拉犁进行作物栽培，用马车运送原料、产品和劳动力。

巴哈马的农业发展在很大程度上受到殖民政策的影响。出口销售的重要性在于能收入外汇，用于政府管理和提供就业机会。

热带农业生产已成为英帝国经济稳定的重要因素。产品不仅是食物来源，也是英国工业原材料的重要来源。殖民地当局利用这些机制来维持自己的影响力，控制巴哈马的农业发展。

第 3 章 ››

农业部门的管理

在巴哈马农业调整前，曾通过立法保护特定的自然产物。

1882年通过了一项法案，用以保护海绵行业。通过的法案还有1905年的《野生鸟类保护法案》、1915年的《剑麻保护法案》和1917年的《纤维植物、水果和蔬菜法案》等。1925年通过了一项整体法案，决定成立委员会，保障农业和渔业的发展。

巴哈马农业政策的制定和实施受到三类行政机构的影响：农业委员会、农业及海产委员会以及农业和渔业部。

各殖民地官员推出不同机构，巩固殖民行政机关，或保障统治巴哈马的宪政发展。农业和海洋产品都对巴哈马的经济起着重要作用，特别是在提供就业机会和出口创汇方面。

1926年之前有两个委员会，一个负责农业，另一个负责海产。现在还存有自1909年起两个委员会的报告。

农业委员会(1916—1924)

关于这一时期的委员会年度报告，一个有趣的因素是没有提到委员会成员。唯一提及的是委员会签署报告的两位主席，一位是L.G.布莱斯先生，另一位则是吉尔伯特·A.奥尔伯里先生。

报告经主席起草并签署后，会送给殖民地大臣，殖民地大臣将其转发给总督，再由总督转给由选举产生的众议院。

L.G.布莱斯先生担任主席(1916—1918)

第一次世界大战正在进行，一些年轻的巴哈马人（包括本书作者的祖父约翰·亨利·桑德斯)前往欧洲为国王和国家而战。与此同时,巴哈马的主要出口作物之一柑橘受到了白粉虱和蓝灰色蝇的破坏,殖民地因而失去了赚取外汇的能力。因此,人们为重振殖民地的粮食生产能力采取了一些行动。

为消灭新普罗维登斯和伊鲁萨拉的白粉虱和蓝灰色蝇,人们实施了喷药计划。植物站(推测为新普罗维登斯奇平汉姆的植物园,后被称为试验站)建设了育苗场。

菠萝是1855年以来的重要作物。为激发农民兴趣并鼓励菠萝生产,委员会确定了签订合同的"栽培者"或种植者,为他们提供幼苗和化肥。

剑麻生产也受到重视,其中纤维是主要的出口农产品,其生产正在扩大。然而,有人担心那种"称为填塞法的毁灭性做法,即把叶和茎从树干上挖掉,以获得尽可能多的纤维,留下裸露的树干,任凭风吹日晒"。

另一种主要出口作物为番茄。1916年番茄的价格十分可观,有可靠的运输工具将其运往纽约。但次年,出口因运输不畅和纽约的严寒而受到影响。

洋葱、红薯和玉米等作物的生产也得到了鼓励。委员会进口种子,激励在国内种植"战争菜园"(抗击因战争造成的粮食短缺),教育委员会则举行学校菜园比赛。

委员会制定方案,以分发发芽的椰子种子,鼓励椰子生产,以之作为食用油的来源。显然,进口食用油和本地食用油都非常昂贵。

委员会对羊肉和猪肉生产也投入了大量精力,引进了改良品种。他们为殖民地购买了两只公南丘羊;一只送往长岛育种,因为长岛是主要的羊肉生产地区之一;另一只留在拿骚的植物站,鼓励畜牧业主带来母羊,免费育种。

尽管1916年植物站爆发了猪瘟,委员会仍从牙买加购买了一头大黑巴克夏猪,用于育种。除了鲜猪肉,人们也食用本地的咸猪肉。

报告没有提到农业工作人员,尽管当时有人给果树喷药、检查果树。

吉尔伯特·A.奥尔伯里先生担任主席(1920—1924)

委员会为维持巴哈马番茄的出口市场而劳心尽力,这是农业计划的核心。番茄生产意味着就业机会、农民的收入和殖民地外汇的来源。

番茄生产主要在伊鲁萨拉进行,不断有新土地投入生产。1920年,新普罗维登进行了一项高调的广告计划,张贴海报,使400英亩土地投入生产。1924年,人们认为猫岛拥有种植外销品质番茄的潜力。

出口营销计划的融资通过国外采购商进行,国外采购商提供资金购买需要的材料,生产作物。种植者和"外国资本家"之间达成了协议。

1922 年,本地种植者对外国买家支付的番茄价格非常失望。1923 年和 1924 年,番茄产量很高。1924 年,佛罗里达州遭遇了严重的洪涝灾害,这抬高了巴哈马番茄的价格。

交通运输是番茄出口的一个关键因素,因为纽约是主要市场。因为伊鲁萨拉的番茄必须运到拿骚进一步转运,所以运输变得复杂起来了。

交通顺畅时,巴哈马农民的农作物一般能卖个好价钱。"枫叶号"汽船等船舶和迈阿密轮船公司是运输农产品的主力。

J.S. 约翰逊公司加工成熟的番茄,装罐后运到古巴和牙买加。

重振柑橘产业的努力从未间断。该产业最初在新普罗维登受到白粉虱和蓝灰色蝇的影响,最终虫害波及伊鲁萨拉的西班牙韦尔斯、卡瑞恩特镇和布拉夫。

1916 年,《植物保护法案》开始施行,喷药计划开始实施,被感染的树木被摧毁了,这也是迫不得已。植物站和猫岛建立了育苗场,以培育树苗。

通过引进改良的品种,委员会鼓励种植各种蔬菜,希望促进农作物销往拿骚市场。巴哈马各地举办了菜园竞赛和展览。

委员会引进家畜改良品种、提高当地牲畜品质的方针坚定不移。他们进口了 3 只南岗什罗普公羊,还购买了伯克希尔郡和德文郡的生猪,以提高生猪产量。委员会还引进了罗得岛红羽鸡,鼓励家禽生产,并从牙买加进口了 1 头公牛,以扩大牛肉生产。

蜂蜜生产是一个成功的领域。1920 年,委员会进口了 4 个意大利蜂群。到 1922 年,已经有 10 个养蜂场(新普罗维登斯 5 个,伊克祖马斯 2 个,长岛、伊鲁萨拉和西班牙韦尔斯各 1 个)。到 1924 年,当地的蜂蜜产量已供大于求。

委员会继续鼓励剑麻生产,并试图振兴崎岖岛和阿克林斯岛的苦香树树皮生产以及猫岛的棉花生产。

农业委员会的时代于 1925 年结束;1925 年的年度报告无从查询。尽管缺乏受过专业训练的人员,但 1916 年至 1924 年的报告目标全部一致。

农业及海产委员会(1925—1963)

1925 年 5 月 14 日,《农业及海产委员会法案》应运而生。该法案管理了农业部门近 40 年。巴哈马最终成为部级政府后,一个新的权威人物将引领该领域的管理进入新时代。

农业及海产委员会有一点很有趣,即总督每年会任命一个不超过五人的委员会,其中包括众议院的两名成员和一名主席。

该委员会的主要任务是"进行所有的相关调查、试验和研究,收集和发布所有相关信息,只要他们认为有助于以最赚钱的方式推动土壤培育和产品处理,有助于促进畜禽育种和养殖……"

审查该法案时,殖民地大臣在1930年的报告《巴哈马农业》中写道:

"在西印度群岛中,或者可以推测,在所有的英国殖民地中,唯独巴哈马没有农业管理人员。

"农业委员会也需要资金聘请指导员和助手这样的高效工作人员;他们应该做的是提供非常便宜的种子、植物和肥料,维护育苗场。他们应该与教育委员会密切合作,协助教育委员会管理学校菜园。目前,很多学校菜园的价值都遭到怀疑。对于宣传、广告和提供生产设施的需求,和旅游交通需要的帮助一样迫切,未来几年的需要更迫切。

"这不是在建议殖民地寻求一流的科学家的服务,或投入大量资金用于学术研究。明显需要聘请一位具有农业经营方面实践经验的农学家,农学家在实践方向开拓和提高产量方面的作用原则上则会缩水……"

殖民地大臣清楚地知道自己想要什么,毫无疑问,他决心做到这一点。这一点有一方面很有意思,即他可能会首选殖民地农业部门的英国人骨干。他可能会和委员会妥协,从西印度群岛选人,那里的人通常比英国人的薪水低。众议院可能会认为,因为是黑人,他们将会更好地整合并融入农业社区,从而达到更好的整体效果。

1928年,殖民地大臣经委员会批准,与牙买加政府商议,为巴哈马提供第一支农业技术官员队伍。

在农业委员会的协助下,招募了七名农业教师,由他们向巴哈马农民和中小学生传授和展示现代农业方法。

已故的克利夫兰·H.里夫斯先生在信中回忆道:"作为教育委员会的秘书和业务经理,我很荣幸能到码头迎接这些老师的到来,在等待其永久性任务期间让他们在拿骚暂时安顿下来。"

他们得到如下分配:哈兰·瑞安先生(特立尼达)前往伊鲁萨拉的惠姆斯海湾;J.T.温特先生到伊克祖马斯的乔治城;P.J.鲍威尔先生到长岛的克拉伦斯镇;

R.W. 布朗先生前往猫岛的阿瑟镇；I. 德维克斯先生到安德鲁斯；N.M. 利奇先生去新普罗维登斯福克斯山的桑德伦村；L.A. 杰维斯先生到新普鲁维登斯奇平汉姆的政府实验菜园。

毫无疑问，这些人在自己任教的农业社区完成了任务。有证据表明，他们代表农业委员会协助了出口农产品的分级和认证。他们在植物培育和香蕉生产方面做出了巨大贡献，特别是柑橘、牛油果和杧果的培育。

需要牢记的是，这都是巴哈马的困难时刻，因为美国经济举步维艰。这些农学家从西印度群岛刚来不久，大萧条就发生了。

由于在巴哈马没有工作，大量巴哈马人移居美国，特别是迈阿密，这引起了人们的关注。1920 年巴哈马的人口为 57 800 人；到 1928 年，人口减少至 53 000 人。农业被视为创造就业机会的领域之一，而务农就是那条通途。殖民地政府的政策是促进农业生产，因此对农业的这种态度与政策相一致。

"重振农村（外岛）曾经存在而后又消失的繁荣，而不是创造新的繁荣。"他们看到了这一政策的成绩。

聘请这些农业教师是使务农成为可行的经济活动的尝试。发展全职小规模农场主才是最终目标。

1928 年，"西印度七大农学家"来到巴哈马。此后又过了 23 年的时间，巴哈马才迎来第一位受过大学教育的农学家。

委员会行使职能

农业委员会和海产委员会于 1925 年合并，在巴哈马开创了政府新风貌。虽然巴哈马人向众议院选出了他们的代表，但这只是一种修改过的民主形式，因为投票权与土地所有权联系在一起；成人选举权不是人人都有，女性没有投票资格；企业可以投票；全国各地的选举不在同一天举行；选区并非严格基于选民人数。

殖民地总督在巴哈马不仅代表英国君主，而且在这些岛屿行使令人敬畏的行政权力。为了让当地人参与行政管理的某些决策，议会组织围绕众议院而建立，选出的代表都在众议院。而实际上，立法委员会是上议院，委员们任期为 10 年，每次连任期限为 5 年。

众议院的成员确保议院的政策得到执行。根据委员会的会议记录，番茄行业曾出现委员会的观点与众议院相冲突的情况。1950 年 5 月，委员会的会议录中这样记录：

"接下来宣读了众议院特别委员会关于番茄产业的第二次临时多数人报告,经过商议,命令委员会秘书邀请特别委员会成员与委员会会晤,以说明他们的建议,以此让委员会顺从众议院的意愿。"

1926年,农业及海产委员会主席一职继续由吉尔伯特·奥尔伯里先生担任。委员会的农业项目并没有改变方向,重点依然放在番茄出口上。剑麻被飓风摧毁了,不得不作为二级产品出口。振兴柑橘产业的努力仍在继续。委员会继续分发种子,鼓励蔬菜生产。

1926年至1949年间,委员会的年度报告无从查询。

1949年,据记载R.T.西莫内特阁下担任主席。计划没有显著的变化。然而,委员会聘请了专职兽医官,并对农业主任和高级农业官员的工资补贴进行了规定。

畜牧生产蒸蒸日上,成为重要的子行业。绵羊、山羊、带角的牛、生猪和马匹的数量大幅增长。这使得动物健康愈发重要,提高牧草质量以增加巴哈马的载畜量同样不容忽视。委员会引进优良牲畜品种的计划也卓有成效。

旅游业起初只是季节性的经济活动,后来渐渐演变成了全年性的经济活动,为巴哈马的发展壮大提供不竭的动力。在此背景下,农业及海产委员会主席罗兰·西奥多·西莫内特先生强调了殖民地政府对养殖和农业的重视度。

西莫内特先生是一位很有影响力的政治人物。他是联合巴哈马党的领袖,该政党在1964年巴哈马获得内部自治时执政。他于1959年被授予爵士称号,并且成为巴哈马第一位总理(1964—1967)。

但是西莫内特家族的政治影响力和能力并不只体现在罗兰爵士一人身上。他的儿子罗伯特(鲍勃)曾是联合巴哈马党时代的下议院议长,他的小儿子布伦特在自由民族运动政府担任两项部长职务,该政党于1992年8月19日开始执政。布伦特·西莫内特先生在1992到1994年间担任旅游部部长,1995年1月到5月担任司法部部长。

因为富可敌国,西莫内特家族一直是巴哈马强大的政治力量。像英国贵族一样,罗兰爵士也明白土地是财富和地位的关键,这构成了他们经济和政治力量的基础。因此,几十年来,甚至几代人以来,他们一直将西莫内特家族政治影响制度化。

总督主持的执行委员会是政府的行政部门,相当于今天的内阁。委员会由九人构成,包括殖民地大臣、司法部部长、收税官和财政部部长以及所有当然委员。

另外六名成员由总督推荐产生，由君主任命，他们通常为下议院中颇具权势的政治家。

在那时，总督被视为殖民地的"第一先生"和议长、"第一公民"。这就是英国殖民地政府在全盛时期形式最纯正的构成。

新成立的农业及海产委员会似乎是为精英政治人物掌握行政权力提供便利的殖民地政府机构。通过它，他们扩大自己的权力，从立法和预算审批到在重要经济领域影响和制定策略，确保能反映政策决定的计划的实施。

1950 年的年度报告无从查询，然而 1951 年的年度报告显示，除农业及海产委员会之外，这一年又成立了一个咨询委员会。它由执行委员会中的一名成员任主席，其他成员来自下议院，包括亨利·弥尔顿·泰勒先生、威廉·卡特赖特先生、农民、渔夫和商人。

黑人群体中发生过很多次政治动乱。泰勒先生、卡特赖特先生及其他几个人是进步自由党的发起人和创建者，该党在 16 年后从罗兰·西莫内特先生领导的联合巴哈马党手中赢得了政权。泰勒先生被女王授予爵士称号，成为第三位巴哈马总督。

全体委员的技术能力日趋专业化。1949 年，人员编制显示有给农业主管和高级农业官员的预算拨款，以此壮大专职兽医人群。

高级农业官员一职由奥利斯·斯坦利·拉塞尔先生担任，他在佛罗里达大学取得了理学士学位和农学硕士学位。他于 1951 年 9 月 1 日得到任命，1954 年被提升为农业主管。

在拉塞尔先生任农业主管期间，通过说服委员会雇用更多技术专员，他扩大了农业部门的工作。这让巴哈马迎来了英国殖民官时代，开启了巴哈马战后的农业调整。

包括兽医和水产业在内的多个部门雇用了专业人员，植物园还聘任了一位园林设计师担任管理者。此外，还任命了牲畜、农作物专员及一名市场专员，监管公营部门的市场运行。

这些专员中，有很多位在其他英国殖民地有过相关工作经历。拉塞尔先生被提拔为常任部长时，查尔斯·林恩先生接替他成了主管。林恩先生在热带农业方面经验丰富；他在殖民地公职机构备受尊重，在组织国土资源调查方面发挥着重要作用。

拉塞尔先生不仅仅是一位杰出的农学家，作为政府公职人员，他的能力也是世所公认的。他是第一个在公共服务领域被提拔为常任部长的巴哈马人。因为在殖民地大臣办公室的工作经验,拉塞尔在巴哈马获得独立(1973 年)之前在很多时候都担任主任秘书。独立后,他被调往外交部担任常任部长。

即使在奥利斯·拉塞尔先生还没专管这一部门时,他就对环境保护问题很感兴趣,大力支持巴哈马国家信托会的活动。

1951 年,拉塞尔先生被任命为高级农业官员,这一年发生了很多变化,这些在年度报告中都有记录。委员会的工作更加明确。咨询委员会似乎也曾帮助委员会的技术人员弄清农业社区面临的问题。

图 3.1　奥利斯·斯坦利·拉塞尔先生,理学士(农业),农学硕士,是第一位担任农业主管的巴哈马人。从 1954 年到 1965 年 10 月 5 日,拉塞尔先生担任主管,后被提升为常任部长。1982 年,被授予英帝国官佐勋章。

除分配种子、牲畜和果树新品种之外,通过对外岛进行技术咨询访问以及改良牧场以促进牧业生产,农业技术推广工作的重要性得到认可。

这是改变巴哈马农业官方看法的一大进步。1951 年年度报告的引言中写道:

"除殖民发展公司在洛克湾、伊鲁萨拉和安德鲁斯的农场及安德鲁斯－巴哈马发展有限公司、新普罗维登斯的 21 世纪农业股份有限公司之外,农业依旧按照农民产业的模式运行。"

20 世纪下半叶面临的任务是转变"农民产业",这一产业主要针对国内生产,要将其转变成由农业综合企业推动。

20 世纪 50 年代的农业

与农业及海产委员会一样,咨询委员会也成立于 1951 年。它的成员来源跟委员会一样。咨询委员会从 1951 年到 1953 年处于运行状态,但此后突然被裁撤了。

有了农业主管,农业及海产委员会的工作主要围绕着拿骚奇平汉姆的试验站,工作重点为以下几个方面:

图 3.2　中心农业站。殖民地农业专员伊恩·丁沃尔先生正在试验田里收胡萝卜。丁沃尔先生离开巴哈马去了哥斯达黎加,在那里生活到去世。

植物繁殖

优先繁殖售往农业社区和园艺场所的发芽的柑橘树、嫁接的牛油果及杧果。

巴哈马的柑橘产业持续受到白粉虱和蓝灰色蝇的困扰。他们计划延长牛油果短暂的种植期,引进新的改良的杧果品种。

除种植果树外,还引进并种植了观赏植物,以便广泛地分配。

品种试验

外岛小型农场的种子主要是由委员会分配的。引进新的种子是委员会的重任,对不同种子进行试验也是委员会工作的重要方面。

委员会不断地对洋葱、甜玉米、番茄、木瓜和香瓜的种子进行试验,所产都会在物产交易所出售。

牲畜

畜牧业地区的大部分工作都围绕着鉴别牧草品种以便利用牧草展开，这在猫岛和长岛这样的矮林岛尤为明显。人们还引进了绵羊、山羊和生猪的改良品种。另外，家禽数量也有了很明显的增长，尤其是在伊鲁萨拉和新普罗维登斯岛。在南伊鲁萨拉，伍德-普林斯养牛项目增添了300英亩牧场和300头阿伯丁-安格斯牛。

技术人员中有一位兽医，一直监控着殖民地牲畜的健康，以防牲畜疾病扩散成流行病。

屠宰场在市场后面。人们用单桅小船将牲畜从外岛运到附近的候宰圈。由于意识到了牲畜数量的增加，1955年的《公共建设工程法案》拨出了专款建设一个新的屠宰场。工程于1958年完成，此前因寻找可靠水源有所延期。相同的设施已投入使用，并不断进行改进，以与科技同步。

图3.3　乌兹罗杰尔步行街的老集市。屠宰场就在左后方，前方为典型的单桅小船，这些船将动物运到拿骚。

国际合作

1952年委员会与佛罗里达农业试验站签订协议，由试验站工作人员担任委员会顾问，并为他们支付交通费，提供生活津贴。

植物保护计划

虫灾和植物病害都受到了密切的关注。试验站作为总部，制定了喷药计划。

人们可向试验站申请喷药服务。

扩展及外岛参观

委员会技术人员有限，很难提供一个强有力的扩展计划。然而，人们已经意识到，为了向农业社区推广新作物和畜牧业技术，扩展计划是必需的。

碳化钙的推广为菠萝生产带来了重大创新，碳化钙催熟菠萝，延长了收获季节，满足了国内市场的需求。

出口作物

委员会不断地鼓励小规模农户种植出口作物，20世纪50年代主要为秋葵和番茄。

巴哈马番茄一直被运往加拿大和美国，但佛罗里达进入这一市场后成了巴哈马的主要竞争对手。关键时刻，交通的不便使得巴哈马番茄种植者颇伤脑筋。

巴哈马的番茄生产处于这样一种境地：伊鲁萨拉和新普罗维登斯的罐头厂对番茄的需求量（1955年为75 000蒲式耳，1956年为80 000蒲式耳）大于出口量。

少量的卡藜皮仍向国外出口，但巴哈马的柑橘、菠萝和剑麻出口在世界市场上已失去了竞争优势。秋葵和番茄出口竞争力的丧失也只是时间问题。

国内市场

物产交易所是外岛当地产品的主要销售渠道，交易所设在拿骚，但没有冷藏设备，保质期较短，作物的储藏空间也有限。

图3.4　市场（右前方）上驴车、货车和马车是主要的运输工具。市场的左面为冰库，右边为稻草商的区域。

1951年，物产交易所购买了30 000多英镑的农产品，包括大约50种果蔬，其中有些因当地市场需求有限，导致了季节性供应过剩问题。巴哈马群岛的主要岛屿中，有13个岛屿将农产品运至交易所。

1955年，木豆是运往交易所数量最大的作物。木豆产量如此之高，必须要用55加仑的桶来储存。

农业综合企业

除了自给农业和小型经济作物农场外，还有几个外国公司在运转。除了之前提到的，伊鲁萨拉斧头湾的伊鲁萨拉有限公司、阿巴克斯马什港的克罗克特发展公司、安德鲁斯马斯蒂克角的安德鲁斯岛种植有限公司及伊鲁萨拉洛克湾的伍德-普林斯养牛开发项目（巴哈马畜牧公司）也都在巴哈马成立了办事处。

这八家公司代表了巴哈马的大型商业性农业。他们为许多巴哈马人提供了就业机会，带来了新技术，展示了新的管理技能，为殖民地赚取了外汇，特别是那些从事出口的公司。

基础设施的完善

1953年，试验站的办公大楼毁于火灾，取而代之又建造了一幢现代化的综合办公楼。1957—1958年，试验站扩建得到了专项拨款，增加了植物园区。

图3.5　市场右后方的白色建筑为委员会、部门和部长管理时期巴哈马农业总部的驻地。

1954年12月，委员会及其员工搬进了位于贝街市场区的新办公室。那里有一间小型实验室、一间会议室，还有出售农用品的地方。办公室位于大楼的第二层，一层为现代化的鱼类市场。办公用房是委员会在 50 多年里第一个常设地址。

劳动力

整个 20 世纪 50 年代，成千上万的巴哈马男性受雇到美国农场工作。报告称"许多工人继续在美国当雇佣农工，不然他们也是在殖民地干农活"。

在这个"项目"（巴哈马人是这样说的）下工作，为许多巴哈马人提供了见识大规模农业和赚取丰厚薪水的机会，工资也都寄给了国内的家人。

第二次世界大战刚结束时，巴哈马就业机会有限，因为旅游业仅是季节性的，只是在慢慢发展成全年性的经济活动。

20 世纪 60 年代的农业

20 世纪 60 年代的巴哈马发生了翻天覆地的变化，尤其是政治事务方面。像遥远的英帝国的殖民地一样，巴哈马也追求实现制度进步以对管理自己的民族事务拥有更大的权力。

1964 年，在伦敦的宪法会议上，巴哈马被授予内部自治权，这也意味着部级政府的开始。三年后，1967 年的 1 月 10 日，在声势浩大的大选上，由少数白人控制的联合巴哈马党落选，败给了黑人占绝大多数的进步自由党。在巴哈马的政治史上，这是第一次反映了 85% 的人口构成的政党，通过政府威斯敏斯特体系下的民主程序，获得了管理巴哈马的权力。

新政府制定了新政策和计划，意味着农业部门在进步自由党的带领下，在经济中扮演的角色将与以往不同。

农业及海产委员会在 1964 年更名为农业和渔业部，它的巴哈马主管成为该部的第一位常任部长。许多殖民官员受雇担任技术职务，1968 年巴哈马农学家开始取代殖民官员，扩大了专业技术的层次与范围。

随着专业人员数量的增加，农业部门踏上了新的经济发展进程。

政策

1960 年以前，农业被认为是农民产业。20 世纪 60 年代，农业被视为经济活动。

委员会的总方针为促进殖民地农业发展及牲畜和家禽的养殖。

委员会的其他目标包括：① 保证殖民地人畜粮食尽可能自给自足；② 在条

件允许的地区鼓励种植出口经济作物；③ 进口、选择、生产、分配粮食和牲畜良种，致力于提高、鼓励粮食作物和牲畜的生产，以此增加农业社区的福利，改善人们的营养状况；④ 调查引进可行的病虫害防治措施；⑤ 在合理的范围内，保护本国农产品免受同类进口产品竞争冲击。

翻阅委员会的记录簿，毫无迹象显示该政策是由委员会提出的。那么，这一定是农业主管的决定，目的是为巴哈马农业指明新方向。

委员会的工作主要围绕以下方面展开。

作物及畜牧生产

农民种植的蔬菜、果树和饲养的牲畜种类丰富，如绵羊、山羊和猪。外岛的小规模农场主通过物产交易所，将果蔬用船运到拿骚的市场。

绵羊和山羊为外岛传统农业社区主要的牲畜品种。在新普罗维登斯，鲜肉市场周边就有屠宰设备，因此饲养猪基本属于小规模农场主活动。

家禽和牛肉面向商业企业。有个禽业协会，肉鸡和蛋鸡产量接近 1 000 吨，产蛋量为 1 200 万只。

伊鲁萨拉的巴哈马禽业公司负责牛肉生产，1963 年有 700 多头健壮的阿伯丁安格斯牛及安格斯和夏洛莱杂交牛。仅有一小部分牛肉在当地销售。

出口市场由几家美国离岸公司供应，即安德鲁斯马斯蒂克角的阿巴克斯农场有限责任公司、S & H 农场、富兰克林农场、金土地农场、大巴哈马自由港的绿湾农场。

1961 年，这些离岸企业有 3 500 英亩土地生产冬季蔬菜（如黄瓜、番茄、笋瓜、茄子、灯笼椒）和水果（如罗马甜瓜和木瓜）。

新普罗维登斯奇平汉姆试验站

试验站的重心一直放在植物繁殖、品种试验、发芽和嫁接果树及观赏植物的销售上。牲畜的改良品种向社会销售，植物园的发展工作也已开始。

建设活动

在猫岛和长岛建设牧场是委员会的主要计划。猫岛确立了 13 处地点用于发展牧场。在长岛，建设了很多支路，以便为牧羊提供更多灌木牧场。

兽医机构

由委员会兽医巡查各个养殖场是不可取代的委员会职责。动物健康事关重大，1960 年，委员会花费大力气通过了《动物传染病法案》。

部级管理：农业和渔业/海洋资源部的建立

新宪法授予巴哈马内部自治权。1964年1月7日，巴哈马内阁政府应运而生。

根据新宪法，霍恩·乔治·贝克出任农业和渔业部部长，他曾担任农业及海产委员会主席多年。他的职责范围包括渔业、农业工厂、动物健康、野生鸟类保护、委员会商人注册法案、植物保护、动物传染病法案、公共市场及屠宰场。

新的部级政府并未出台新政，但酝酿着筹划一个五年的农业发展计划，强调对技术员工的需求、外岛的示范单位以及对涉及新品种和肥料需求的主要作物的研究。

为了适应新型政府，公职进行了行政变更。农业主管奥利斯·拉塞尔先生被调到内阁办公室，几个月后，于1965年被提拔为新设的常任部长。

这次升职意味着主管、副主管和高级农业专员位置的空缺。1966—1968年，这些专业职务全部由殖民地官员担任。

这一部门1965年的主要活动为通过其子公司——巴哈马农业产业有限公司在阿巴克斯开拓了欧文斯-伊利诺伊的业务。1966年，新物产交易所和零售商店在波特礁营业，市场基础设施随之升级。

1967年1月10日，在林登·奥斯卡·平德林先生的领导下，进步自由党成立了新一届政府。

推广工作

尽管需要履行推广职责，但委员会并没有推广单位。因为接受过专业训练的人员的数量有限，只能定期巡视各个农耕地区，主要是提供咨询建议。

1963年，运转了38年的农业及海产委员会不再作为巴哈马的农业行政部门行使职责。

20世纪70、80和90年代的农业

背景

20世纪70年代之前，巴哈马的食品生产体系主要是部分时间工作，运用的基本上都是传统技术。除四个家禽业单位、两三个猪肉生产商、两个奶牛场（一个在新普罗维登斯，另一个在伊鲁萨拉的斧头湾）和两个美国离岸公司外，巴哈马食品生产体系的技术发展水平极低，产出完全是季节性的，有些方面还呈现出下滑趋势。

1973 年,发生了两件大事,一是巴哈马农业研究、培训和开发项目在北安德鲁斯成立,二是巴哈马不同地区的几百英亩土地被开垦用于农业生产(通过政府协助)。与此同时,扩大免税优惠、商业银行信贷、家庭群岛推广专员的安排及具体作物和牲畜产出计划的发展等问题出现。

巴哈马农业研究、培训和开发项目,其缩写为 BARTAD,主要处理巴哈马农业三个具体方面的事务。

研究:在巴哈马农业研究、培训和开发项目成立之前,关于巴哈马土壤农业性能的调查少之又少。巴哈马农业研究、培训和开发项目的意图就是多指明一些能给巴哈马农民机会并与进口产品以世界价格竞争的农业活动。

培训:为使巴哈马农业研究、培训和开发项目成为有效的研究机构,有必要培训不同水平的巴哈马人。这个培训项目与政府奖学金项目一起,培训出了 28 位拥有专业农业技能的巴哈马人。这些人中大部分也都已取得研究生资格和经历。这是个重大转变,因为在 1968 年,部门中仅有一位巴哈马专业官员。

开发:为提高巴哈马农民的技术能力,发展规模为 40~80 英亩的家庭农场很有必要,农场中有各种产业集合(蔬菜,牲畜,果树),拥有这么一个农场的个体收入可以与旅游业和建筑业工人的收入相提并论。

巴哈马土地调查显示,大约有 238 000 英亩土地是农业发展的理想之地。1973 年,仅有 5%或者说 12 000 英亩土地是投入生产的。有这么多可用资源,政府为巴哈马大范围的土地开垦项目提供了补助。尽管约 124 000 英亩的此类土地是在安德鲁斯(134 000)、阿巴克斯(50 000)和大巴哈马(30 000)①,但传统的农业岛伊鲁萨拉、伊克祖马斯、长岛和猫岛仍得到了大部分土地开垦补助。针对巴哈马东南部地区,特别是阿克林斯岛、玛雅古纳和崎岖岛,政府会实施一个特殊计划。

20 世纪 70 年代的部门绩效

农业基础设施完善和人力资源开发使得部门出现了影响重大的增长模式。表 7.2 为巴哈马国家食品账单(不包括活畜)。增长的进口食品账单源于旅游业的发展。

巴哈马游客人数创了新高,超过 1971 年的 150 万人次。这一时期,相较于邮轮而言,中途停留和乘飞机旅行的游客数量占大多数。游客数量的增加加速了国内粮食消费。旅游业不仅会对供游客消费的进口食品产生重大影响,对巴

---

① 原文如此。——译者注

哈马饮食也有潜移默化的影响。

一方面，旅游业促进了食品进口，但另一方面，积极的政策框架又推动了当地生产。1974年，当地食品产出总价值为1 050万美元，到1977年，产量增长，略高于1 650万美元。新政的方向就是抓住食品部门，对其产生积极影响。

以上的趋势代表着每年的复合平均增长率为16.4%。同时期每年的整体经济（GDP）增长为5.4%，总值从6.85亿美元增长至8.02亿美元。

家禽和果蔬作为子行业平稳增长，具体数据如下：

当地家禽产值	新鲜果蔬产值
1974年——7 074 200美元	1974年——1 738 200美元
1975年——8 697 600美元	1975年——2 173 400美元
1976年——9 600 000美元	1976年——3 279 000美元
1977年——11 184 000美元	1977年——4 726 738美元

毫无疑问，食品进口从1973年的44.4%降到1977年的35.4%，家禽产量的增长为这其中牲畜和家禽进口的减少做出了贡献。

当地果蔬产值从1973年的170万美元增长到1977年的470万美元。这意味着每年的复合平均增长率为39.6%。增长如此迅速，在这段时期内扣除物价因素，新鲜果蔬的进口保持平稳或下降都是不足为奇的。

农产品的出口平稳增长。1974年，农产品出口总计389 652美元，1976年为1 075 640美元。然而，1977年又出现了下降，农产品出口降至688 967美元。1973年，农产品出口低于总出口量的1%，但到1976年，增长到了6.2%。

统计预测估计，基于1973—1977年间的增长，到1985年，当地产值应会超过3 400万美元，果蔬占1 500万美元，家禽约占1 800万美元。

1977年的GDP预测已公布，各部门总值约为8.02亿美元，其中农业部门的贡献率约为2%。增长和发展会继续，到1985年，农业贡献率增长到3%～3.5%是完全有可能的。

在1970年的人口普查中，从事农业的人口为3 099人，占总劳动力（69 791人）的4.4%。1978年，农业人口普查显示农业劳动力增长至5 561人，占总劳动力（93 450人）的6%。8年内农业就业增长了82.7%，同时期内总人口增长了33.9%，所以农业就业的增长率高于总人口的增长率。因此，可以得出结论，要么农业作为一种谋生手段变得更加吸引人了，要么可供选择的工作减少了或魅力减退了。这还表明这个部门能够使家庭群岛的农业社区因可持续就业而保持稳定。

市场基础设施

当时巴哈马农业部门的发展潜力就像几乎40年后的今日一样显而易见。然而,增加的产出不能仅仅作为进口替代而分销,还要有一部分出口北美和欧洲,这是我们不可逃避的现实。不论是国内还是国外消费,高质量的产品都是必需的。为实现这一愿景,一系列措施付诸实施,完善本地种植产品的市场基础设施。一大成果就是在生产基地建立了仓库。这些理念是为了方便农民在农业社区内运送作物并及时收到报酬。八个仓库,其中北安德鲁斯岛一个,伊鲁萨拉两个,伊克祖马斯三个,猫岛和长岛两个,与大巴哈马自由港负责批发的物产交易所一同建立起来了。

农工联合企业的发展

作为农业的一方面,农工联合企业的发展并未受到足够的鼓励。在20世纪70和80年代,农工业活动仅局限于食品加工。巴哈马有三家罐头厂——两家在拿骚,在伊鲁萨拉的那一家已经停业。这些罐头厂消费了当地大量番茄和秋葵这样的原材料。罐头厂想要多样化和扩大经营,但有时当地原材料供不应求,还存在价格过高的情况。就像1996年的情况一样,农工联合企业也受到协调关税的消极影响。这一倡议导致很多商品减税,如肉鸡生产、木豆、番石榴和番茄加工及轻工业和制造业。

随着农业产业部门的扩大,其工业化也应更加明显。如果出现了工业化现象,那么新的工人诉讼委托人也会应运而出,就像其他农业产业已经出现的那样。巴哈马农业的这一方面被严重忽视了。政府食品技术部门对整个食品行业的影响并不像人们希望的那么积极。

20世纪80年代

20世纪80年代,农业部门身负厚望,要在经济中扮演更加积极的角色。积极的角色需要扩大增长和发展,这就意味着私营部门要更多地参与农业活动。在过去的20年里,小规模农场主几乎获得了所有的关注和优待。为了实现"腾飞式"增长,私营部门需要提供必要的增长催化剂。资本密集型的机械化生产技术和农业综合企业发展是发掘阿巴克斯、安德鲁斯和大巴哈马等松树群岛农业潜力的基本要素。规模经济必须要在农业部门发挥作用,以确保高效、充分地利用财力和人力资源,从本质上提高整个部门的竞争力。

农业部已确定了10%的最低年增长率。为了实现这一目标,依赖公营部门筹措资金是完全不合理的，因为这会增加巴哈马纳税人的负担。

部门鼓励私营部门更加密切地关注食品加工领域的潜力，更具体地说，指供当地消费的猪肉及其制品的加工。20 世纪 80 年代，潜在市场每年有400～500 万美元的利润等待挖掘。同样，果蔬加工也未被完全挖掘。出口和当地市场大规模的原材料生产和加工相互联系：每年 400～500 万美元利润的潜在市场唾手可得。

另外一个领域为公营／私营部门在阿巴克斯 20 000 英亩优质农业用地的开发布局，这些土地用于种植出口作物。20 世纪 80 年代巴哈马开启了发掘东南部潜力的时代。诸如玛雅古纳、阿克林斯岛、崎岖岛、猫岛这样的岛屿受到了前所未有的关注，农业成为拉动发展的火车头。保鲜期长的产品（如木豆）和卡藜皮这样的农林作物的生产将会受到更大的关注，催化了以阿克林斯岛为中心的加工业的产生。

农业衰退：20 世纪 90 年代

在 20 世纪 80 年代后期，农业产值反复无常，引起关注。1985 年，产值为3 400 万美元，1991 年，增长至 5 300 万美元，其中有约 3 500 万美元来自作物生产。急剧的增长源于离岸种植者的农业活动，其产值最高为 2 100 万美元。从总数中除去离岸作物产值，这一数字将会减少约 60%。

16 470 英亩高产土地用于种植出口作物。阿巴克斯有五家高度机械化的工农业综合企业，占地 14 670 英亩，大巴哈马为 2 400 英亩，安德鲁斯为 600 英亩。在南伊鲁萨拉，另有 1 200 英亩土地种植牛油果，产品销往美国市场。

离岸种植为北安德鲁斯和阿巴克斯的农业社区提供了大量就业机会，尤其是阿巴克斯北部。正是这种大规模的工业化农业使得海地人涌入阿巴克斯，从事农业劳动。因为农场劳动的需要，好几个海地社区建立起来了。非官方报告称海地人的数量超过了阿巴克斯当地人。海地农场工人的社会学影响为阿巴克斯的人口状况带来新的因素。这种情况与北安德鲁斯大不相同，在那里，安德鲁斯人为劳动力；与大巴哈马的状况也不一样，市中心自由港的劳动力很混杂。

1985 年的肉类产值大约 55 万美元；1991 年，这一数值为 53 万美元。这是由当地畜牧业生产下降导致的，这种下降同时也反映在政府屠宰厂屠宰牲畜的数量上。10 年前，也即在 1982 年，屠宰场屠宰牲畜数量为 6 000 头；1991 年，这一数值缩减为 2 200 头，仅比 1982 年数量的三分之一多一点。活猪生产经历了最大的下滑，1982 年为 5 112 头，1991 年为 1 850 头。肉牛、绵羊和山羊生产减少的数值与之相同。

家禽业是个例外,尽管这一行业一直被认为有潜力使巴哈马鸡蛋和肉鸡生产自给自足。1985 年的禽业产值为 2 000 万美元;1991 年为 1 740 万美元,六年内减少了 260 万美元。

新政府,新政策

新政府重组后,农业和渔业局属于贸易和工业部。1969 年以前,并没有农业和渔业部。1969 年 1 月 13 日恢复了部门称呼*(*见部门投资)。

新的委员会受命成立了,由乔治·L. 汤普森先生担任主席。汤普森先生是中伊鲁萨拉议会的议员,他在那里从事农耕,经营一家罐头厂,主营菠萝制品。

通过贸易和工业部及农业及海产委员会,新政府上台没多久就宣布了新农业政策,新政策如下:

(1) 支持和提高当地食品生产,以维护初级生产者利益,使经济多样化;

(2) 谋划农业和渔业的发展,以更好地确保国家粮食安全,尽可能降低生活支出;为与新政方向保持一致,部门重组,分为五个分部:

① 总部——负责管理、筹划、协调、直接服务和监管;

② 现场工作部——负责勘察、调研、咨询工作和植物园;

③ 动物健康部——负责疾病控制、公共屠宰场和犬类管控;

④ 渔业部——负责勘察、调研和咨询工作;

⑤ 经济和市场营销部——包括物产交易所和零售商店。

员工中有一群骨干技术官员,还有巴哈马专业官员,部门达到了为农业服务的鼎盛时期。

全新的管理和技术人员的加入使得部门工作更加明确。然而,殖民地官员发现,发展和壮大农业部门的规划缺乏基本的信息和数据。

1969 年 1 月 7 日,一份名为《进行巴哈马土地资源调查和土地产能评估以为发展战略提供依据的提案》的文件递交给了巴哈马内阁。提案获批准通过。根据提案,英国海外发展部将花费 100～130 万美元进行调查。1969 年 3 月,调查开始了。

试验站已过时,发展成了植物园。因此,农业和渔业部很想要新的现代化的调研设备。1968—1969 年,提议建立的中心农业站的地址被选定了,1970 年开工。

值得注意的是,农业部门的很多工作都围绕着现场工作部门,高级农业专员重视咨询工作,其中包括农业推广教育原则的有关方面。

巴哈马农耕以下面几点为基础进行了分类:

◆ 自给农业。

◆ 小规模耕作。

◆ 中、大规模无机械化耕作。

◆ 开垦地的中、大规模农耕（离岸种植者，松树群岛）。

◆ 新普罗维登斯的农耕和园艺。

◆ 阿巴克斯的甘蔗生产。

部门投资：

平德林政府取得的主要农业成就

年份	活动	费用
1969 年	新普罗维登斯格拉德斯通路中心农业站的建设和成立	200 万美元
1970 年	土地资源调查 全面评估巴哈马土地产能/土壤及水资源的物质资源	300 万美元
1971—1979 年	① 开荒计划 ② 米勒路农垦计划（土地分配）	48 万美元/年 数据不详
1973 年	① 巴哈马农业研究、培训和开发项目（美国国际开发署/巴哈马政府合作项目） ② 政府奖学金计划引进，培训农学家（计划 28 名）	1 000 万美元 数据不详
1973—1980 年	在北安德鲁斯、北伊鲁萨拉、中伊鲁萨拉、南伊鲁萨拉、猫岛、北长岛建设并配备了 6 家包装厂，在自由港建立并配备了批发市场	100 万美元
1974—1975 年	① 通过合作社团法开展合作运动，尤其是农业合作社 ② 购买伊鲁萨拉斧头湾的斧头湾种植园及其在新普罗维登斯的地产	数据不详
1976 年	将专业的农学家安置在家庭群岛（即伊鲁萨拉、伊克祖马斯、长岛和大巴哈马）的推广办公室	数据不详
1978 年	农业普查	数据不详
1979—1980 年	圈养羊计划，在北长岛调查灌木牧场条件下的羊肉生产（联合国粮农组织与巴哈马政府的联合计划）	数据不详
1981 年	食品技术与动物饲养部门的建设与成立（欧盟发展基金）	2 000 万美元以上

牧场开发项目衰落了，因为无法雇到有经验的牲畜专员。

在推广活动方面，农事论坛这个很受欢迎的广播节目对外岛的各个农业社区产生了影响。

农业和渔业部的营销计划饱受代表家庭群岛农业社区议会的政府成员的批评，处于风口浪尖。

一系列积极措施正在实施，以便为农业部门带来新动力。

农业人口数量（1978—2006）

年份	人口普查（1978）				人口普查（1994）				人口普查（2005）				人口普查（2006）			
	男性	女性	合计	协商英亩数	男性	女性	合计	协商英亩数	男性	女性	合计	协商英亩数	男性	女性	合计	协商英亩数
农民	2 976	1 238	4 214		1 192	535	1 727									
农场工人			1 276		2 852	766	3 618									
家庭成员	2 272	1 955	4 227		555	795	1 350									
合计			9 717	80 000			6 695	50 000			1 242				943	6 000

注：协商英亩数农业年普查（1978—1994）* 协商英亩数 来源：农业部统计单位。

结 语

巴哈马的农业部门深受政策之害，农业政策目光短浅，与当时的经济现实不符，范围和性质均很肤浅。

20 世纪 60 年代前，土著居民将农业视为农民产业。60 年代后，从贸易保护主义角度出发，国内生产得到了一定重视——离岸生产者被视为企业家和投资者，他们活动的经济重要性得到重视。

贸易保护主义态度同样也影响到了离岸生产者。委员会的会议纪要显示了离岸种植者是如何被拒绝进入国内市场的。在委员会看来，离岸种植者在巴哈马仅仅为出口市场从事生产。只有在特殊情况下，且必须得到委员会许可，他们的产品才可以流入当地市场。

在委员会运行期间，行政事项调查一直不断。委员会一直关注免税许可的授予、离岸企业申请从事农业的批准以及人事相关问题（如升职和加薪）、回复农业社区的投诉及其他信件、向执行委员会建议经常性的资本预算以及最后向议院建议。

委员会官方强化贸易保护主义观点，建议依据当地生产商给市场的供货量提高或降低进口果蔬的税率。委员会似乎从未对在巴哈马实行农业综合发展政策感兴趣过。

在 20 世纪 60 年代制定一个综合农业政策极其困难，因为巴哈马在 1964 年获得了内部自治，3 年后，又成立了新的政府。

为了实现巴哈马农业的兴旺，综合农业政策应包含以下内容：

◆ 本地食品消费。
◆ 农工联合企业所用原材料。
◆ 创收就业。
◆ 更好的收入，带动其他工业、商业和服务活动的发展。
◆ 发展出口市场以赚取外汇，增加产出。
◆ 通过进口替代品来节省外汇。
◆ 通过发展农业综合企业增加税收和扩大就业。

这七项也是今天推动农业部门蓬勃发展的要素。积极的农业社区、有竞争力的农业综合企业群及有能力的专业人士和技术人员可以推动农业的腾飞。

这七项必须齐头并进，将农业提升到新的高度，增加农业在巴哈马经济中的重要性。

1970 年农业和渔业部门报告的结论段落中说：

> "除非并且直到政府制定出具有前瞻性的政策，区分复杂现代社会中顾客需求与保留外岛定居点的社会需求及支出，这些麻烦和批评才会消除。
>
> "现代机械化农业和大多数现有生产者的社会福利是完全不同的两件事，都值得关注。"

20 世纪 70 年代，2 000～2 500 万美元的投资注入国营经济，农业部门因此有了长足的进步。这些投资用于人力培训与发展，改善市场和研究基础设施。因为佛罗里达遭遇了严重的春寒，度假地开发使得耕地紧张，美国农业综合企业将巴哈马作为生产现场，这使得农业部门的投资潜力备受关注。70 年代代表着巴哈马农业的分水岭。

1980 年当地产值为 2 000 万美元，1989 年为 3 400 万美元，80 年代其他年份的产值就介于两者之间。这一时期正值萧条，萧条不仅体现在产量上，生产土地面积及农业工人和小规模农场主的减少也体现了经济的不景气。

1994 年农业普查的数据证实农业部门已缩减到前所未有的水平。巴哈马农业困难重重。这一时期产值在 3 600 万美元和 5 500 万美元之间徘徊。随着巴哈马转变成城市社会,进口量上升。而随着全球贸易环境更加自由化,这一情况也会更加复杂。到 1995 年,除巴哈马外,该半球所有国家都已是 WTO 成员。

到 20 世纪末,全球人口会超过 60 亿,20 年前人口还不到 30 亿,但到 2050 年,人口会突破 95 亿。世界农业部门必须能够养活不断增长的世界人口,而世界人口的 90% 来自像巴哈马这样的发展中国家。到 2000 年,几乎要多种植 50% 的粮食。世纪末将需要额外的粮食供应,来克服饥荒和营养不良,来满足改善营养的需求,满足新兴经济体(印度、巴西、中国、俄罗斯和南非)增加收入的需求。

过去三四十年经济不景气,导致饥饿和营养不良的苦难笼罩着巴哈马社会,尤其是新普罗维登斯的市中心社区。

我们生产粮食的能力因农业的衰退而受到威胁。在下个十年,我们应制定开明的农业政策,不仅是为满足国内消费,也为使巴哈马农业综合企业发掘出口市场成为可能。

21 世纪的头十年,随着巴哈马及其他加勒比国家的崛起,这一地区的粮食产量严重不足,甚至成了粮食短缺地区。旅游业蓬勃发展,会增加粮食进口。

在全球范围内,粮食生产受到来自全球变暖、水资源安全、人口增长、进行第二次绿色革命及化石燃料需求量上升的挑战。国家及地区粮食生产政策必须要能成功地解决粮食安全问题。

第 4 章 »

农业部门的组织

纵观历史,农耕是巴哈马的基本活动。巴哈马人在欧洲人难以应付的、完全不同的种植环境中生产粮食。自给粮食生产是农业的第一要务。随着生产技术的提高,剩余产品可以出口。

在哥伦布发现新大陆后,又过了 300 年巴哈马才有了粮食出口的能力,尽管早在 17 世纪末和 18 世纪巴西木和棉花就已出口。

巴哈马缺少庄园主阶级,基本上是中小规模农场主户从事农业生产。他们为生计而种植几种经济作物供国内市场消费,剑麻、菠萝、番茄和柑橘供出口。

能力得到展示后,巴哈马成了吸引外国农业企业家的地方。在 20 世纪早期,农业委员会的年度报告中说:

> "农业前途一片光明。在卖完上一年的作物之前,外国资本家就按捺不住了,占用土地,与当地种植者签订合同,准备预付必要资金,确保种出殖民地产量最高的番茄。"

在整个 20 世纪,外国农业企业家一直是这样。因为靠近美国本土,又无霜冻,种植条件与佛罗里达霍姆斯特德的石质地区相近,佛罗里达的种植者将他们在巴哈马的业务视为"应对霜冻灾害导致损失的保险"。

离岸农业企业的吸引力一直是项目吸引外国投资者到巴哈马的一部分。这些外国农业综合企业带来了新的农耕技术,提供培训和工作,帮助巴哈马节省并且赚取可观的外汇。

鼓励性措施包括设备及供应的免税许可证、利润汇回本国、高产农田自由和长期租赁安排、专业人员工作许可的保障。

除了离岸企业,这一部门的剩余部分由巴哈马掌控。

农民群体

农民群体是农业发展不可分割的一部分,各种形式的农民实体在巴哈马早就建立起来了。

20世纪20年代,人们认为"西部地区的农民联盟希望能够与福克斯山的农民联盟联合。在合理组织的情况下,这些联盟可以发挥大作用"。

联盟被认为可以向农民传播农业信息、教授新农耕技术,最重要的是,可以帮助农民集体出售产品。

这些农民联盟的细节很粗略简要。在委员会20世纪40年代末和50年代的年度报告中有一段文字记载:

> "伊鲁萨拉和猫岛并没有合作社,而只有20个番茄种植者协会。农业委员会会给这些协会提供预付番茄和其他作物的种子和肥料贷款的协助。委员会会出售这些作物,并将预付的费用从每笔交易中扣出来,直到还清整个欠款。物产交易所也为殖民地65个农民协会经营、销售农产品。"(巴尼特,1984)

这些协会在国内和出口农业方面的作用不容小觑。尽管在出口方面,"外国买家"不得不与许多小规模农场主周旋,但这些协会成了将农民集合成一体的机构。协会的统一很难确定,他们对种植者的控制也很难确定。

协会运往物产交易所的产品有时会处于不成熟状态。这样会造成损失,有时损失相当大。让种植者给他们的番茄定合适的等级很困难,因为他们缺少自律,委员会只能雇用番茄检查员。

合作社运动作为农民的一种经济手段直到20世纪70年代才付诸实践。《合作社法案》于1974年通过,合作社发展部门于1975年开始运转。

在巴哈马研究、培训和开发项目支持下,北安德鲁斯农业合作社成立。自此以后,一系列农业合作社在巴哈马如雨后春笋般涌现,其中包括长岛(1978年)、伊克祖马斯(1979年)、北猫岛(1979年)、玛雅古纳岛(1984年)、大巴哈马、阿巴克斯(1990年)及新普罗维登斯(1995年)。

各个合作社的作用由农村公社或农业分组(如牲畜、农作物)的需求决定;然而,《合作社法案》赋予合作社很多优惠条件,这些优惠条件对农民成立这些实体来说是鼓励性的。最重要的鼓励性措施为免税进口物品及免除印花税。除了合作社，农民还被鼓励参加博览会。

早在20世纪20年代，就有不同岛屿上的农民相互竞争的事件。

教育委员会为政府性机构，鼓励学校间的作文竞赛，尤其是外岛上的学校。菜园展览、学校种植的果蔬竞赛也举办过。"西印度七大农学家"在增加全国对学校菜园比赛兴趣方面发挥着重要影响力。

在20世纪70年代，开始出现了英联邦博览会。展览会独一无二，来自所有岛屿的农民都被鼓励参与。单独的岛内竞赛在全国比赛前进行，最优秀的选手会被挑选出来送往拿骚参与全国比赛。

比赛内容并不局限于农业，还包括手工业、家庭作坊、制造业、艺术及制造商产品展览。

这一赛事在克劳德·史密斯先生任职期间创立，他是在英国接受过教育的农学家，曾在牙买加的甘蔗种植园从事甘蔗育种工作。史密斯先生回到家乡，为巴哈马农业产业有限公司效力。1966年，该公司在阿巴克斯岛上种植了25 000英亩甘蔗。当公司于1971年宣布破产时，史密斯先生加入农业部担任农业主管。他是担任此职务的第二个巴哈马人。

1993年，英联邦博览会由国家农业和工业博览会取代，后者旨在通过强调农业和制造业的重要性来使巴哈马经济多样化。博览会受农业部国家农业咨询委员会支持，委员会协调农业和渔业部、巴哈马农业和工业公司及巴哈马商会共同组办博览会。

从影响农业政策方面而言，巴哈马的农民群体未起到实际作用。并没有能够代表巴哈马农民群体的全国性团体。然而，农民们意识到了建立这样一个实体的必要性。

农业教育和培训

巴哈马专业的农学家在全世界接受了培训。在过去的20年里，大部分农学家在美国、英国和加勒比学习。

在20世纪70年代，大多数接受过培训的农学家在公共服务部门任职。虽然农业部门扩张，农业综合企业发展机会增多，但是开始时，鼓励巴哈马年轻人在农业科学领域找工作并非易事。就业机会有限，外岛的活动距拿骚和自由港的市中心甚远，因此很少有人响应号召。

巴哈马政府意识到需要接受过训练的农学家，支持这一行动的政府人士为霍恩·卡尔顿·E. 弗朗西斯。他是一名教育家，从政后于1967年在进步自由党政府担任财政部部长。

　　作为一名教育家，弗朗西斯先生深知布克·T. 华盛顿博士关于黑人教育的理念。弗朗西斯先生为高中毕业生在拿骚格拉德斯通路的中心农业站组织了一个农业培训项目。因为之前做过教师，弗朗西斯先生很清楚"西印度七大农学家"在各个外岛学校做过的工作。

　　他对一系列高校进行了官方访问，如佛罗里达大学、西印度大学及美国几个历史上的黑人学院。阿拉巴马的塔斯基吉大学已与得克萨斯的普雷里维尤农工大学签订了协议，为巴哈马学生保留位置，以便他们学习农业课程。许多巴哈马年轻人前去学习。

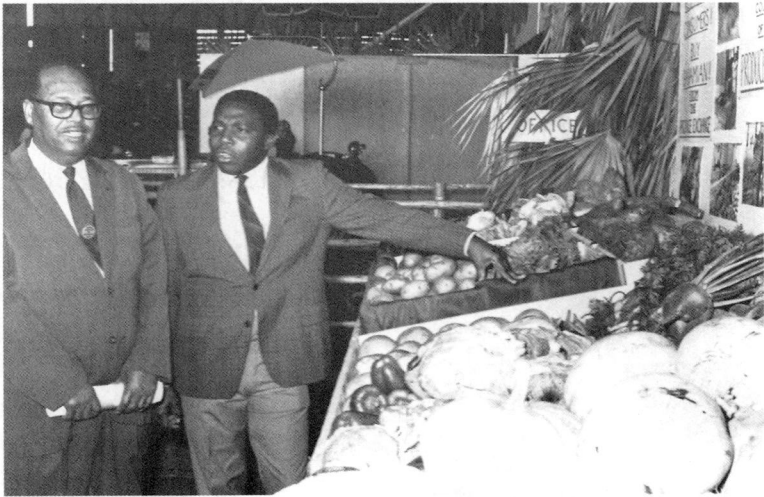

图 4.1　1970 年前后本书作者与乔治·希斯蒂先生在新普罗维登斯举办的农业展览会农业部的展台前。

图 4.2　1996 年 4 月，政府南卡罗来纳州麦克弗森中学学校菜园的围栏区。

巴哈马原来与塔斯基吉大学一直保持联系，但后来关系淡化了。1936 年，六个巴哈马教师前往塔斯基吉大学暑期班学习农业、家政学和木工活。这个项目每年都会举行，但第二次世界大战爆发后被迫中断。20 世纪 60 年代早期双方又恢复关系，有很多优秀的农业科学专业学生毕业后继续攻读了博士学位。

P. K. 比斯瓦斯博士是塔斯基吉大学食品科学专业教授，很关注这些早期学生。在过云的 40 年里，他曾教导过许多巴哈马学生。

比斯瓦斯博士早期的学生包括 P. A. 波纳米博士，他毕业于牙买加农业学校，在巴哈马担任农业主管，后又在农业和渔业部担任副部长；罗伯特·泰勒博士成为亨茨维尔阿拉巴马农工大学的一名农业专家，专于土壤科学，现任佛罗里达农工大学院长；格什温·布莱登博士在佛罗里达成为药理学家／从业医师。泰勒博士和布莱登博士曾是巴勒斯坦·迈克尔先生在奇平汉姆试验站的学生。其他巴哈马学生有塞尔玛·坎贝尔博士、汉伯和俄莱科·赫伯恩博士。

自从 20 世纪 60 年代早期，巴哈马就在私营和公共部门建立起了强大的、训练有素的兽医群体。巴哈马超过 85% 的兽医在塔斯基吉大学接受过培训。基斯·坎贝尔博士是政府首席兽医官，也是 20 世纪 70 年代中期首个从塔斯基吉大学毕业的学生。

图 4.3　1983 年 2 月，公立高中学生平整学校菜园，此为农业课的一部分。

弗朗西斯先生除安排巴哈马人到塔斯基吉大学和普雷里维尤农工大学学习外，在访问圭亚那时，他又安排巴哈马人莫兰·韦伯到圭亚那农业学校学习。

巴哈马农业研究、培训和开发项目是巴哈马人接受培训的另外一条重要途径。工作人员及受训者都到宾夕法尼亚州州立大学接受各种初级和高级课程的专业训练。

巴哈马学院于 20 世纪 70 年代中期建立,农业归属于自然科学系。许多毕业生在结束两年课程后继续攻读学士学位,很多到了塔斯基吉大学。

教育部在公立学校开设了农业科学课程,向学生介绍农业科学。"西印度七大农学家"开创的惯例至今仍在沿用。

实践课或实地实习作为推广教育计划的一部分,在提高农民和农业妇女技术技能方面有所缺失。随着部门的扩张,需要更多不同层次的农业专家,需要专业人士提供专业知识。巴哈马在开发农业人力方面取得了长足的进步,在过去的 70 年里,积累了很多专业技能。

图 4.4 洪·乔治·A. 史密斯是下议院议员及农业和渔业部部长。图中他从一组书中取出了一本由英国政府通过英国高级专员公署捐赠给巴哈马的书。洪·乔治·A. 史密斯部长左侧依次是克劳德·史密斯先生、农业部主任以及位于史密斯先生左侧的本书的作者。同时照片中还有渔业部主任罗纳德·汤普森先生以及合作社主任罗斯福·芬利森先生。本照片摄于 1975 年。

农工联合企业化

巴哈马农业部门进口诸如种子、肥料、农药、饲料、种鸡、种蛋及其他所需的生产物资。巴哈马支付数百万美元用于购买主要由美国制造商制造的生产物资。

为了保持与进口食品同等的竞争力,巴哈马应要求批准了免税豁免权且正在制定关于生产物资的相关法律。

　　根据《关税法案》，饲料拥有免税豁免权。如果一位农民需要农业工具，他需要向农业部门申请免税许可，免税许可不一定会被批准。如果得到了批准，随后则对该工具颁布免税许可。所有真正的农户及农业企业均可采用此措施。

　　为了满足小型农户，农业部经营了一个广泛销售农业生产物资的供应仓库，在这里农民购买商品享有一定的补贴。这是几十年来农业部负责的工作的一个方面。在20世纪60年代，这成为农业部的政策之一并一直延续到今天。

　　有时候，供应仓库急需投入的存货（如肥料）存储量很低，这就给农业造成了一定程度的不稳定性，原因是许多小规模农场主户完全依靠供应仓库为其提供生产物资。供应仓库不能独立运营，销售收入存储在由财政部掌管的国家综合账目中。然而，供给的补充是由财政部的要求以及给供应商的付款决定的。财政部掌控资金。没有它的购买命令，就不能进货。农业部不能命令财政部优先进什么货。从长远来看，小规模农场主会夹在中间受罪。为了使小规模农场主不再严重依赖政府的设施，他们被鼓励建立合作社。

图4.5　农业推广官员——照片中由左至右分别是伊克祖马斯岛的查理斯·劳埃德先生、本书作者、厄尔·德沃先生、伊鲁萨拉岛的塞西尔·多赛特先生以及长岛的科玛尔·史密斯先生。本照片摄于1980年9月。

　　由于巴哈马土壤的自然属性的原因,肥料是种植庄稼的主要生产物资。尽管如此,巴哈马没有商业生产或混合肥料。20世纪70年代中期,一个混合设施开始在新普罗维登斯岛运营,然而却由于质量控制措施低劣而停产。

　　像巴哈马柑橘种植有限公司这样的大型企业在农场上混合自己的肥料。该公司在其柑橘园使用液体肥料,因而建造了一个现场混合及储存肥料的设备。

　　巴哈马到了应根据部门需要进行肥料制造和混合的关头。继续进口昂贵的袋装化肥成品成本太高,这对于小规模农场主来说难以承受。肥料的制造和混合是巴哈马农工联合企业化的一个方面,对巴哈马来说是非常可行的。

　　在畜牧业生产中,60%～65%的生产成本是饲料。饲料在巴哈马每年的交易额为2 000～2 500万美元,其中家禽业是最大的进口商和消费者。

　　在过去的30年里,一些美属饲料供应商调查了在巴哈马开设饲料工厂的可能性。通常他们都会把厂址选在新普罗维登斯岛,然而在最近几年里,大巴哈马岛及阿巴克斯岛发展了现代家禽设施。虽然该产业大部分坐落在新普罗维登斯岛,但是由于受到基础设施和环境的限制,饲料粉碎设备并不适合安装在这座岛屿上。

图4.6　照片中间是P. K. 比斯瓦斯博士,右边是本书作者,左边是作者的儿子戈弗雷。本照片摄于塔斯基吉大学农业学院所在的米尔班克大厅前。

　　其中主要的限制是码头缺乏设施以适应原材料如玉米的卸载。目前,对进口量较大的家禽业散户和一两个猪肉生产商来说,饲料是免税进口项目。

小家畜农户特别是那些做猪肉生意的农户，他们购买昂贵的成袋的饲料，这造成了猪肉生产的边缘化。

斧头湾公司在其庄园中建造了一个工厂并将其饲料原料运往伊鲁萨拉岛，在那里它们被混合成为肉鸡和蛋鸡的饲料。由于与使用进口成品饲料的家禽生产者相比本地混合饲料的性能水平相当低，所以设备很快被淘汰了。

本地饲料制造的这一方面引起了一些生产商的关注。能够跟上新的行业趋势是至关重要的，特别是当生产商在与国内生产商竞争的同时还需要与进口产品竞争。有一种观点认为，本地生产的饲料在技术上是落后的。本地饲料制造业仍然认为随着畜牧业和经济规模的不断扩展，农工联合企业经营在不久的将来将会实现。

食品加工向来都是农业中的一个重要组成部分。然而，食品加工商没有收到能够促进他们扩大经营动力的水平认证，尤其是那些通过艰苦的抗争而得以生存并持续与亨氏、坎贝尔及德尔蒙特等加工巨头工厂保持竞争的工厂。

当地工厂在定期获取新鲜原材料方面存在着困难，造成的结果是依靠进口浓缩物和其他材料，这方面最好的例子是木豆和番茄。木豆生长在巴哈马，同时也是巴哈马的主要饮食组成部分之一。为了维持木豆的生产线，工厂从东非进口木豆。1960年，巴哈马出口了近1 300箱木豆，在这当中有超过4 000蒲式耳是由小规模农场主户生产的。

巴哈马的农民只为能在菜市场销售而种植番茄，而不种植用于加工的番茄。由于工厂购买番茄的价格远低于市场，故工厂并不是种植番茄的农民的主要市场。为了使果泥和果酱达到理想的浓度，与使用用于加工的番茄品种的罐头厂相比，使用新鲜番茄的罐头厂需使用两至三倍的新鲜番茄量。为了补充当地供给，番茄浓缩物在这一过程中起到了巨大作用。

巴哈马罐头厂对于水果和蔬菜的加工呈下滑趋势。在20世纪50年代和60年代，在巴哈马的主要番茄生长区之一的南伊鲁萨拉岛有一家罐头厂。在20世纪70年代早期，这家工厂倒闭了。这家洛克湾罐头厂属于贝克兄弟——约瑟夫和乔治。他们兄弟二人皆为伊鲁萨拉岛的议会代表。乔治·贝克先生是农业部第一任部长，同时也是联合巴哈马党政府的最后一任。在20世纪50年代，番茄罐头是一项非常重要的农工联合产业。1960年，巴哈马罐头加工量为84 000蒲式耳，价值41 000英镑，支付工人工资12 500英镑。

伊鲁萨拉岛的格雷戈里镇是菠萝的主要产区，汤普森兄弟在这片土地上生产菠萝酒、菠萝汁和菠萝酱。乔治·汤普森先生曾是此区域的议院代表，在其死后，工厂便破产了。

到 1995 年，巴哈马只剩下 P. W. 艾伯瑞父子和索耶食品两家罐头厂，它们都位于拿骚。它们生产诸如番茄酱、番茄、木豆和果酱等食品。

通过在中心农业站的食品工艺装置，使用当地的蔬菜和水果为原材料的家庭手工业的发展得到了鼓励。一些经营者把市场上各种各样的优质商品既销售给本国人，又作为纪念品销售给每年来巴哈马旅游的 300 万游客。巴哈马农业和工业公司建立了一个小型商业发展机构，用于帮助那些对此行业有兴趣的人。

巴哈马柑橘种植有限公司开发出了一种非常美味的鲜榨橙子和柚子汁，此产品的保质期约为 10 天，广受居民和游客的好评。随着该公司的倒闭，包括果汁、果酱、果冻和橘子酱在内的柑橘加工的进一步发展也并没有得以实现。

当地的奶制品对市场的影响不大，原因是奶制品总是一项反复无常的活动。尽管斧头湾公司在与进口牛奶和冰激凌的竞争方面做出了巨大的努力，最终结果却是它们退出了这项业务，开始用奶粉生产牛奶。

黄金岛乳品有限公司为 E.P. 泰勒先生所拥有。E. P. 泰勒先生是来佛礁的开发者，黄金岛乳品有限公司在 20 世纪 70 年代开始投入生产，最终却以失败告终。巴哈马乳品农场 1991 年建于大巴哈马岛，然而由于经营问题导致无法维持高品质新鲜牛奶的生产。

使用当地原料的乳制品业没有发展成为一个大型的农业综合产业。1995 年，乳品生产行业发生了新的转折，特别是在鲜奶的生产上。坐落于新普罗维登斯岛的假日农场引进了新鲜农场品牌。他们开始通过进口美国的鲜奶作为制造鲜奶产品的原材料。这种生牛奶将被加工成鲜奶和其他奶制品。这种经营方法新颖，但无法保持其市场地位。

工业与农业生产紧密相连的发展，无论从输入或是输出方面来说在本世纪都应该发挥重要作用。这一领域将增加就业机会，帮助农民生产出更多具有竞争力的产品，且能够促使农业经济有一个更加多元化的前景。

巴哈马农业和工业公司

1981 年，巴哈马政府决定解散巴哈马农业公司和巴哈马发展公司，成立巴哈马农业和工业公司（以下简称 BAIC），该公司于 1982 年 3 月正式建成。

作为一个法定机构，它本质上是政府一系列活动的私营机构。这一系列活动中比较重要的一点是农业、轻工业和制造业的商业公司的所有权问题，或是从事包括这些活动在内的合资企业活动。

　　成立巴哈马农业和工业公司之前，政府从利维不动产公司手中收购了斧头湾伊鲁萨拉有限公司，并将它放在巴哈马农业公司（以下简称 BAC）下进行管理。这一行为造成了很大的争议，特别是在政治圈内。

　　伊鲁萨拉有限公司是伊鲁萨拉岛上的主要雇主，同时还代理了斧头湾和拿骚的大量房地产。据政府透露，造成这种现象的主要原因是在拿骚和斧头湾（主要是斧头湾）需保留约 200 个工作岗位，这吸引了附近的格雷戈里镇、爱丽丝镇、詹姆斯水库及远到南边的帕尔梅托等地的工人。此外，该区域代表了政府成员所掌握的选区的定居点。爱丽丝镇是选举中最大的投票区和政府据点。购买设备给政府造成了极大的政治压力。

图 4.7　霍恩·保罗·L. 阿德利是前巴哈马农业公司主席和财政部前部长。阿德利先生明确阐释了政府在购买斧头湾这件事中的态度以及它将在农业部门发挥的作用。此照片为霍恩·保罗·L. 阿德利先生（中）与巴哈马信息服务部西里尔·史蒂文森先生（左）及本书作者在巴哈马农业公司新闻发布会上的合影。

　　农场和它的各个部门在本国和国外都产生了大量的债务，因此其运营的各方面受到公众的广泛监督。公库需介入并在许多方面救助其负债的经营。这变成了一种循环式操作。反对派政客通过为其贴上政府严重管理不善的标签使其成为一个问题，认为它是巴哈马纳税人的一个财政负担。他们还声称这是一个政府不应当介入的活动。

　　媒体围绕政府的参与和公司面临的问题发表了大量的文章。最拥护政府参与斧头湾事务的人是霍恩·保罗·L. 阿德利,他是负责巴哈马农业公司的外交部部长。

为巴哈马农业公司的参与辩护时,阿德利先生指出:"为了实现农业自给自足的目标,巴哈马农业公司有责任在巴哈马的粮食生产方面发挥其作用。"这是他作为巴哈马农业公司主席了解到的像斧头湾这样一个实体在农业部门发挥的作用。

斧头湾存在着问题,但大多数问题都被政府接手。它购买了一个破旧的、过时的设备,这个设备需要大量的资金进行升级操作。此外,公司还产生了人浮于事和效率低下的问题。

包括媒体在内的巴哈马商界的许多方面都怀疑政府介入私营企业。1978年 11 月,阿德利先生指出有人尝试"摧毁斧头湾的信誉、国有设施的经济可行性及大约 135 名巴哈马人在拿骚和斧头湾的工作……该公司并非国有垄断,而是与私有企业进行竞争"。阿德利先生的这番话对上述批评进行了回复。

作为农业综合企业,斧头湾从未成为一个经济上的可行实体。所有者去世后,它的继承人放弃了生意,由政府接手。它坐在那里等待着巴哈马经济重新发现它的作用。

巴哈马农业和工业公司从 1982 年开始生产以来介入了几个合作农业项目。其中最著名的是本·G. 哈蒙公司在阿巴克斯的柑橘项目。巴哈马农业和工业公司在本·G. 哈蒙公司和巴哈马柑橘种植有限公司在巴哈马农业领域滞留期间,成功地谈判了能够获取约 100 万美金的租赁方案。

当政府决定把巴哈马农业研究、培训和开发设施放手私有时,巴哈马农业和工业公司成为安德鲁斯岛农业集团(以色列)种植冬季蔬菜的合作伙伴。这个买卖遭到惨败,随后被佛罗里达的一个集团接手,在摩根农场名下经营。

巴哈马农业和工业公司在农业部门的任务主要是与私营部门进行合资经营。公司通过为中小规模农场提供管理技能来扩大其在农业部门的作用。

第 5 章 »

耕作系统

巴哈马土地资源调查将巴哈马的土地资源根据植被和性能进行了分类。有两种植被被确定并认为与岩石类型和淡水储量存在密切关系。两个主要类型的岛屿根据植被的不同分别被称作松树群岛和矮林群岛。

报告将阿巴克斯、安德鲁斯岛、大巴哈马岛和新普罗维登斯岛归为松树群岛，这些岛屿的面积占了整个巴哈马陆地面积的三分之二。（土地资源调查，1977）

松树群岛的特点是它们有庞大的淡水储备可以用来浇灌加勒比的松树（*Pinus caribea*），且薄层的棕色土壤及母体成分可以人为分解成自由土壤。

剩下的岛屿构成了矮林群岛。它们的植被特点是混合阔叶和灌木的林地。这些岛屿本身狭窄、崎岖且岛上的岩石起伏坚硬。这里的壶穴和溶洞里可以找到黑色或是红色的天然肥沃土壤。

在土地生产能力方面，岛上的土地被分为几个等次，其中 191 700 英亩土地被认定为有农业潜力。阿巴克斯（50 000 英亩）、安德鲁斯（134 000 英亩）和大巴哈马（30 000 英亩）这些松树岛上的可耕种土地是最为丰富的。

在殖民地大臣 1930 年的报告中，他对这种地形表示困惑并阐述道：

> "巴哈马的现代栽培技术的主要障碍很可能是土地无法改变的特性，乍一看，这里似乎完全不可能种植，它的自然属性决定了在这里每英亩的土地无法高产……任何在这样一片土地上发展高阶农业的尝试都会失败……甚至有人惊讶于这或多或少贫瘠的岩石上居然能生产出来东西。"（殖民地大臣，1930）

尽管殖民地大臣持有负面的观点，但他知道：

> "科学的手段从未在巴哈马的农业上得到应用，换句话说，殖民地的潜

力从未被开发。我们在农业方面的主要困难是可以被克服的,但在尝试之前,我们不能声称我们已经测试过殖民地的能力了。"

不幸的是,殖民地大臣没有土地资源研究提供的相关信息,但他知道有某种方法可以释放农业的潜力。

通过派人去或自己访问佛罗里达,殖民地大臣指出:

"描述的缺陷已经在佛罗里达得到了解决,在那里岩石地已经被铲平、被处理或转换成了肥沃的土壤,至于为什么相同的过程在巴哈马不能成功应用并没有显著的原因。"

20世纪20年代的方法包括:

"炸药瞬间就可以击碎岩石表面,而炸药已经在某些地方取代了农耕。之后,现有的土壤和粉状岩石会被打散、混合……当然这个过程是相对昂贵的,为了具有经济性它必须在大面积的土地上进行。"

在过去的70年里,与土地能力方面的土地资源调查信息相结合的开荒已发展成为高技术领域,可能技术是最影响巴哈马农业蜕变的因素。

卡特彼勒D-8型拖拉机是开荒的机械手段之一。拖拉机上附加了一块石头犁,每过一遍犁就切进岩石两英寸深。这个活动一直持续,直到深度达到8～18英寸,深度是根据作物生长需求定的。然后,把沉重的罗马圆盘耙片拖过这片土地,沿着拖拉机的轨道拖动有助于进一步粉碎土壤。土地被加工得越细,就越是肥沃。

图 5.1 在松树群岛进行开荒。一辆卡特彼勒 D-8 型拖拉机清除北安德鲁斯岛的松林以作为农业用地。照片展示了开荒过程的最后一个阶段——准备种植的状态。

　　机械开荒技术的使用意味着巴哈马的农业被彻底改变了。这项技术与殖民地大臣叙述的技术大不相同。它在殖民地大臣报告将近 20 年后才在巴哈马得以实现。它与巴哈马耕作系统成为一个不可分割的部分还要再等 25 年。

壶穴农业

　　壶穴农业可能是巴哈马最早的耕作系统。它是一种由阿拉瓦克巴哈马人创建并传承且在 20 世纪由巴哈马农民完善的耕作系统。它非常成功，在最近引入商业肥料和农药之前以所谓的"艺术农业"为基础。

　　这是一种甚至连殖民地大臣都嘲笑的耕作方式。他在 1930 年的报告中描述如下：

　　　　"巴哈马耕作的大部分土地可能会被描述为一种花盆盆栽。这些花盆因它们的宽度、深度和土壤成分不同，对相同物种的植物也不都完全合适，所以人们在同一个地方或是同一个区域可以发现多种多样的植物。

　　　　"没有整齐的栽培：在这里我们发现瓜与高粱并排种植，然后柑橘树旁边种着一些豌豆，杧果树占着一个壶穴，番茄填满了另一个壶穴。总而言之，怎么看这都是一种农业混搭。"

　　矮林群岛上的许多农民是壶穴农业成功的实践者，这是由这些岛屿上环境条件的许多独特方面造成的。

　　矮林群岛上的农民还开发了适应岛屿特点的生产实践。例如，在北伊鲁萨拉岛农民用切割和火烧的方式清除矮树丛进行开荒。一段时间之后，他们会种植诸如番茄和卷心菜等一年生的作物。这些作物用 90 天的时间生长成熟，是农民的一项收入。

　　在间作的基础上，香蕉紧随蔬菜之后，在香蕉树枯萎两到三年后其他果树紧接着种植。当果树达到它们成熟的高度时，则开始养殖绵羊。这种循环继续进行，就形成了大规模的混合农场。

　　这种体系已经从一个勉强糊口的水平发展成了中小型农场的农民为由游客和巴哈马人共同组成的高度城市化的国内市场进行生产的活动。

图 5.2 通过切割及火烧技术进行开荒,以用于壶穴农业耕作。

20 世纪 50 年代,政府开始了一项开荒补贴方案,政府和农民以 50∶50 的比例平摊开荒费用。土地使用机械进行开荒,在农业社区建立农场支线以使用轻型货车,这使得农民能够把自己的生产物资运送到田里,也方便他们将收获品运到码头或包装厂。对于拥有一定数量土地的真正的农民,这些货车通常可以免税进口。从 1971 年到 1979 年,开荒项目获得了 50 万美元。

壶穴农业耕作系统使得农民可以养活家人,建造房屋,他们的孩子也可以在拿骚或是国外受到教育。他们也因此拥有了相当高质量的生活。

大规模种植

殖民主义者们在不知情的情况下,选择了据土地资源研究显示农业生产潜力最小的矮林群岛。这些岛上高质量土地的数量低于种植棉花的土地数量。直到 19 世纪后期,土地相对更加肥沃的松树群岛才开始种植出口农作物。对于早期的定居者来说,耐火松林清理起来非常有难度,直到 20 世纪才开始使用机械进行清理。

大约在 19 世纪 80 年代,剑麻作为一种拥有出口潜力的主要作物出现了。这个行业存活了近 40 年的时间,创造了就业机会并赚取了大量的外汇。

当时官方表示新产品本身非常优良并且有着非凡的力量。然而,由于存在缺乏准备的坏习惯,且质量和等级都很低劣,产品在国际市场上名声不佳。

一位专家给出了这样的建议:"机械剥皮毫无疑问是最大的优势,使用便携式实用剥皮器需要进行测试。"但显然这并没有发生。

其他作物诸如菠萝、柑橘和番茄大量出口。竞争对手通过改进种植技术很快把巴哈马抛在了后面。菠萝与夏威夷成了同义词，柑橘则与佛罗里达成了同义词。

机械开荒使松树群岛能够大面积地投入生产。第二次世界大战之后，新一轮的农业技术潮流为巴哈马带来了农业企业家。

这些经营者中有一部分是土地投机者，其他的则是真正的农民。后者希望佛罗里达天寒地冻，这样他们便可以通过供应来自气候温暖的邻国的产品在美国市场上大赚一笔。

图 5.3　本书作者与农业部主管乔治·多赛特在北伊鲁萨拉的壶穴农业耕作区，卷心菜已可以收割。本照片摄于 1974 年 1 月。

图 5.4　壶穴农业耕作区的卷心菜地。本照片摄于 1974 年 1 月。

图 5.5 在安德鲁斯岛北部壶穴（香蕉坑）里生长的茂盛的香蕉树。

图 5.6 新开垦的松树土地最近种植了行栽作物，这展示了松树岛的大规模机械化种植。

20 世纪 50 年代，这些生意人看到了出口诸如南瓜、黄瓜、甜椒、甜瓜和番茄等高价奢侈作物的商机。来自马萨诸塞州的 J.B. 克罗克特先生在阿巴克斯的马什港创建了荷威泰克种植园。克罗克特先生最后将生意以阿巴克斯农场有限公司的名义卖给了佛罗里达皮尔斯的斯科特和马特森，后来变成了凯-沙耶农场，再后来成了巴哈马之星农场。

安德鲁斯岛的公司位于马斯蒂克角，该地区一直延伸到今天的圣安德鲁斯岛。安德鲁斯岛的种植者和富兰克林农场有限公司还生产草莓、木瓜和番茄。外国农业企业家也在伊鲁萨拉岛进行了大量投资。罗得岛州的奥斯丁·T. 莱维先生在斧头湾建立了他的农业综合企业，即斧头湾种植园伊鲁萨拉岛有限公司。此公司是一个高度多元化的公司，主要经营包括肉鸡和蛋鸡在内的家禽以及乳制品。1952年其牛奶的日产量为600加仑。

斧头湾发展成了一个公司化的小镇，附近居住区的居民或者在农场工作，或者在风景如画的游艇码头工作，或者作为海员运输成品和乘客到拿骚的市场。

图 5.7　在松树群岛机械开辟的土地上的大规模农业生产——土豆地。

莱维集团建造了一座精致的码头和分销机构。拿骚有一座储存鸡蛋、肉鸡和诸如冰激凌等其他乳产品的储存库，产品由储存库分发到坐落在拿骚各地的公司的其他仓库。在20世纪50年代，这曾经是巴哈马最复杂的农业综合企业。

到20世纪70年代，斧头湾公司无法与拿骚更专业的家禽或乳品公司及现代超级市场出售的富有竞争力的进口产品进行竞争，最后仓库倒闭了。

从技术上来看，斧头湾并非这类农业活动的最佳地点，因为该地区极度缺水。饮用水的供应是有限的，过度抽取导致了盐分侵入用于浇灌农田的淡水透镜体。

自从禽类喝了高盐度的水，家禽经营开始经历高死亡率。伊鲁萨拉岛是一个狭长的岛屿，不适宜形成如辽阔的松树群岛那样巨大深度的淡水透镜体。

到20世纪70年代中期，巴哈马政府决定从莱维房地产公司手中购买整个斧头湾的生意。这是政府首次冒险进入商业农业，但他们想让它重新盈利的努力没有成功。

一些私营公司试图从政府手中租赁设施，但没有成功。现在整个设施在伊鲁萨拉坐等坏掉。

表 5.1　1901—1995 年农产品出口表

主要出口农产品（1901—1995）

农作物		单位	1901—1910	1911—1920	1921—1930	1931—1940	1941—1950	1951—1960	1961—1965	1966—1970	1971—1975	1976—1980	1981—1985	1986—1990	1991—1995
柑橘属果树	橙子	短吨	4.97	1.21										359	4 040
	柚子		2.66	2.28									2 130	19 764	61 668
	柠檬												1 123	24 968	17 437
	酸橙												2 875	8 221	130 215
	橘柚													391	325
		打	42			2 672	6 450	20 911	14 785	653		7 976			
		箱	22.6												
	菠萝	美元					1 924	11 175	3 900	44 188					
		盒						1 050	1 050						
		美元						1 369		134 306					
水果	牛油果	个										1 208 000	357	697	1 405
	木瓜	蒲式耳							6 885	1 523			1 479	3 187	1 701
	笋瓜	美元							34 223						
		美元							38 136	66 110	351 220				450 260

续表

主要出口农产品（1901—1995）

农作物	品名	单位	1901—1910	1911—1920	1921—1930	1931—1940	1941—1950	1951—1960	1961—1965	1966—1970	1971—1975	1976—1980	1981—1985	1986—1990	1991—1995
蔬菜	洋葱	短吨						356							0.03
		磅									90 865				60
		美元						15 089							20
	番茄	（板条箱）	9 611	348											
		蒲式耳					139 158	500 337	17 431	50 384					
		美元		342 997	995 928	101 920	1 196 000	62 000	8 382	4 225 593					1 787 240
	罐装番茄	箱							6 475						
		美元							11 838						
	番茄汁	美元							10 970						
	茄子	蒲式耳							10 751						
		磅							81 800	26 623					
		美元							905 000	89 613					
	甜椒	蒲式耳							17 453	5 324					
		美元							13 398						621 480

续表

主要出口农产品(1901—1995)

农作物		单位	1901—1910	1911—1920	1921—1930	1931—1940	1941—1950	1951—1960	1961—1965	1966—1970	1971—1975	1976—1980	1981—1985	1986—1990	1991—1995
蔬菜	秋葵	磅						3 241 600							417 420
		美元						92 800							183 870
	黄瓜	蒲式耳							23 411 944						
		美元						83 271							10 481 900
		磅						37 958	1 383 993	488 725	7 294 363	120 000			31 430 560
	木豆	磅								30 834 715		30 840 938			
		箱						1 298						13 641 短吨	
		美元						1 932						18 811	90 946
	其他蔬菜和水果						7 980 (英担)				8 238 847				
		美元					19 356				775				
	小芋头	蒲式耳								5 081			6 239		
		美元								22 873		4 525		29 422	
	糖	美吨													
		美元								2 591 426					
	剑麻	吨					252	676							
		美元	365 816	764 290	197 948		16 886	26 586							61 386

伊利诺伊州芝加哥的威廉·伍德·普林斯先生在伊鲁萨拉岛的洛克湾建立了畜牧场。伍德·普林斯先生曾是联合畜牧场及运输公司的主席，在养牛方面有专业的知识。1952年，他成立了巴哈马畜牧公司，公司发展成为拥有600头亚伯丁安格斯牛、为当地市场供给牛肉的公司。

到20世纪70年代，牛肉产量下降，该公司被作为检疫站使用，因为夏路来牛从法国向美国出口时会经过巴哈马和加拿大。

美国企业能够从松树群岛的大型型材森林租到长期采伐权，其中一个企业是欧文斯·伊利诺伊。1966年，巴哈马农业产业有限公司，即欧文斯·伊利伊公司的一个实体，在阿巴克斯25 000英亩的土地上开始了甘蔗经营，并投资1 800万美元生产蔗糖，1 000万美元建造糖厂。工作人员来自整个加勒比地区，这其中包括在牙买加蔗糖企业工作过的巴哈马人克劳德·史密斯先生。1950年4月17日的《农业及海产委员会会议纪要》中指出，根据"针对结束战时服役的殖民地居民的职业培训计划"，要去英国剑桥大学求学的史密斯先生获得了一份研究奖学金。

巴哈马政府与欧文斯·伊利诺伊、它的总公司和巴哈马农业产业有限公司合作，从而能够获得美国政府的一个蔗糖配额，确保了蔗糖市场。但有几个因素对经营造成了负面的影响。糖料作物生产量低但成本高，在石灰岩的土地上生长有困难，且在生长初期实际降雨量低于所需降雨量。此外，古巴在市场上大量倾销糖导致世界市场上的糖的价格下降，扰乱了价格的走势。1971年，巴哈马农业产业有限公司停止了经营，甘蔗生产从此再未复苏。

巴哈马农业产业有限公司地产被弃置了近20年的时间，直到本·G.哈蒙集团开始从事柑橘出口生意才重新启用。

资本密集型农业

1995年，巴哈马消费了大约2 500万磅的肉鸡、6 000万个鸡蛋。当地的肉鸡产业只能满足需求总量的60%，而鸡蛋生产商则可百分之百地满足需求。目前，有400～500人受雇于肉鸡或鸡蛋生产行业，且家禽的投资额已接近5 000万美元。

巴哈马的家禽业是农业综合企业中重要的一项，同时也是巴哈马农业部门中资本最密集的农业企业。该行业限制在巴哈马的三个地点：拿骚与自由港这两个主要的市中心以及人口密度排第三的阿巴克斯岛。

20世纪50年代，家禽生产商有斧头湾的伊鲁萨拉有限公司、阳光农场、格拉德斯通农场、戈代家禽农场以及新普罗维登斯岛的士兵路农场。在这十年里，巴哈马家禽联盟充满活力，他们每月开一次会讨论新兴产业所面临的问题。之后在新普罗维登斯岛出现了洛奇农场、彩虹农场和黄松农场，格雷家禽、阳光农场以及巴哈马家禽股份有限公司也在 60 年代后开始在大巴哈马岛进行经营。

1995 年，这些生产商中有许多都垮台了。新普罗维登斯岛只有两个蛋鸡农场（阳光农场和彩虹农场）以及肉鸡农场（格拉德斯通农场）幸免于难。生产鸡蛋的阳光农场以及生产肉鸡的巴哈马家禽股份有限公司在大巴哈马岛一直都有市场。

人均肉鸡消费量非常高，每年约 85 磅，这使得肉鸡行业在过去的 40 年里大幅度扩大。

格拉德斯通农场从 1959 年的每周生产 300 只肉鸡增长到 20 世纪 90 年代的每周生产 60 000 只。1988 年 11 月，它开始使用自己的孵化器，不再从美国进口活鸡苗。

大巴哈马岛的肉鸡和蛋鸡生产企业都是巴哈马人经营和所有的，比如新普罗维登斯岛就是这种情况。阳光农场从事鸡蛋生意已有 40 年的时间，它的竞争者彩虹农场也在蛋鸡生产方面经营了长达 25 年的时间。阿巴克斯肉鸡生意在 1995 年开始运营，其目的是为了迎合岛上不断扩大的市场的需求。

为了促使巴哈马能够在鸡肉方面更加自给自足，格拉德斯通农场开始着手进行饲养者联络项目，其目的在于扩大家禽业的所有权和参与度。

图 5.8 1981 年斧头湾的肉鸡。

1994 年，加拿大农业综合集团公司 O.T. 国际成为格拉德斯通农场的共有者和经营者。新的管理能够有效地提高农场的水平和禽类质量，得到了当地消费者和食品进口商的广泛认可。

家禽养殖的消亡

猪肉生产仍然是一个小规模农场主的活动。与家禽行业相比，这个行业的资本投入非常小。拿骚、自由港和北伊鲁萨拉最大的猪肉生产商都是100头母猪的规模。

巴哈马猪肉生产面临几种限制条件。这些限制条件包括高昂的饲养费用、加工设备的缺乏、高成本的土地（尤其是新普罗维登斯岛）以及对环境存在威胁的废料的处理。

然而，新鲜猪肉和加工猪肉市场很大且在增长。猪肉加工的技术水平因为巴哈马政府和中国台湾省的一个合资猪肉加工项目而得到提高。

苗圃产业也取得了进展。几个高度资本化的企业生产高质量的观赏植物景观和家庭室内及室外季节性盆栽。现今巴哈马的猩猩木可以自给自足，且其他类型的植物群范围也在不断扩大。

巴哈马的资本密集型农业在北安德鲁斯岛、阿巴克斯、大巴哈马岛将会有光明的未来。这种类型的生产在土地资源、水资源有限且环境问题严重的新普罗维登斯岛受到限制。在未来的几年里，整个家禽行业将从新普罗维登斯岛搬迁到北安德鲁斯岛。在北安德鲁斯岛整体环境条件更加有利，城市扩展的威胁性小。这样的情况同样适用于猪肉生产。

表 5.2　1979—1996 年家禽产量和价格

家禽行业统计数据				
年份	肉鸡		鸡蛋	
	价格（美元）	数量	价格（美元）	数量（磅）
2010	11 858 276	9 656 961	10 744 461	6 036 214
2009	10 191 043	8 415 298	9 629 633	6 017 010
2008	10 515 012	9 111 192	7 450 512	5 476 200
2007	11 473 012	9 877 692	7 250 765	5 329 680
2006	7 298 580	6 239 897	7 250 765	6 437 370
2005	7 298 580	6 239 897	7 765 469	6 437 370
2004	7 298 580	6 239 897	7 765 469	6 437 370
2003	8 615 181	7 356 141	7 764 906	6 438 330
2002	17 065 290	15 191 057	7 397 796	6 130 470
2001	17 148 067	15 282 021	7 094 549	6 012 330

续表

家禽行业统计数据				
年份	肉鸡		鸡蛋	
	价格(美元)	数量	价格(美元)	数量(磅)
2000	17 834 318	16 589 504	6 478 801	5 490 510
1999	16 191 901	14 406 242	6 186 683	5 242 950
1998	21 039 840	18 986 273	5 232 580	4 434 390
1997	22 403 774	21 323 401	4 986 869	4 226 160
1996	20 990 000	19 440 000	5 260 000	4 460 000
1995	18 150 000	16 350 000	5 200 000	4 350 000
1994	15 180 509	14 457 708	5 084 457	4 345 690
1993	15 510 483	14 038 033	4 853 174	4 148 012
1992	10 700 000	9 150 000	4 350 000	4 070 000
1991	12 711 160	10 860 000	4 616 982	4 200 000
1990	11 230 000	9 590 000	4 470 000	4 060 000
1989	14 405 747	13 195 264	3 989 138	3 499 244
1988	17 440 000	16 000 000	4 000 000	3 600 000
1987	18 200 000	16 900 000	5 000 000	4 900 000
1986	16 200 000	14 800 000	5 000 000	4 200 000
1985	15 500 000	14 200 000	5 000 000	4 200 000
1984	16 700 000	1 500 000	5 000 000	4 100 000
1983	14 500 000	13 300 000	5 000 000	4 100 000
1982	12 500 000	11 500 000	4 000 000	4 000 000
1981	16 800 000	15 400 000	5 000 000	4 200 000
1980	14 800 000	13 600 000	5 000 000	4 500 000
1979	14 100 000	12 900 000	4 000 000	3 900 000

来源:农业部计划和统计部门。

表 5.3 1970—2010 年绵羊和山羊屠宰量

政府屠宰场屠宰的绵羊和山羊			
年份	绵羊	山羊	总量
1970	2 160	1 414	3 574
1971	1 765	3 285	5 050

政府屠宰场屠宰的绵羊和山羊			
年份	绵羊	山羊	总量
1972	981	971	1 952
1973	959	712	1 671
1974	873	544	1 417
1975	110	737	1 840
1976	668	670	1 338
1977	886	566	1 452
1978	808	615	1 420
1979	692	539	1 231
1980	590	502	1 092
1981	568	321	889
1982	480	304	784
1983	357	262	619
1984	195	216	411
1985	133	122	255
1986	118	188	306
1987	107	202	309
1988	127	165	292
1989	133	206	339
1990	151	178	329
1991	172	186	358
1992	177	176	353
1993	109	255	364
1994	155	193	348
1995	172	237	409
1996	159	188	347
1997	169	103	272
1998	199	146	345
1999	199	130	329

政府屠宰场屠宰的绵羊和山羊			
年份	绵羊	山羊	总量
2000	195	111	306
2001	208	120	328
2002	72	106	178
2003	69	96	165
2004	86	92	178
2005	172	155	327
2006	0	0	0
2007	88	124	212
2008	210	120	330
2009	133	73	206
2010	169	55	224

表 5.4　1958 年、1974 年及 2010 年绵羊和山羊数

年份	绵羊	山羊	总量
1958	22 300	14 300	36 600
1974	10 945	13 244	24 189
1994	6 292	13 580	19 872
2006	1 497	812	2 309
2010	4 901	6 290	11 191

广泛的畜牧生产

传统情况下，绵羊和山羊的饲养会在有灌木牧场的伊克祖马斯岛、伊鲁萨拉岛、长岛和猫岛进行。灌木牧草是包括加姆贝和天竺草在内的阔叶植物。

1958 年，牲畜的统计数据显示有绵羊 22 300 只，山羊 14 300 只。农业部启动了一项计划，在主要牲畜生产社区建立改良牧场以作为商业用途。经过在奇平汉姆试验站对不同类型的草地的广泛试验，该部门建立了有盘固草和滨海百慕大草的公共牧场。基于可用的统计信息，这可能是在传统饲养模式下饲养绵羊和山羊的顶点。

传统生产模式下的小规模农场主绵羊产量在 40 年里大幅下降，山羊产量则

相对停滞。

为提高生产，新的牲畜生产措施被定期引入。在 20 世纪 50 年代，建立了有改良品种牧草的公用牧场以扩大生产，但缺乏维护程序导致猫岛和长岛的牧场恶化。

绵羊圈养项目旨在重振全国羊肉生产，但在这里此项目没有真正开展，这导致了牲畜数量的下降。

图 5.9　20 世纪 70 年代巴哈马农业研究、培训和开发项目时期的北安德鲁斯岛农场里的山羊。

生物技术和本土农业知识

当巴哈马在 1973 年通过多数裁定原则获得其政治权利进而获得独立时，科学家们努力克服人类粮食生产所面临的挑战。他们的努力产生了绿色革命。

在 20 世纪 60 年代到 70 年代间，为增加农业产出，技术被引入绿色革命，特别是在发展中国家。巴哈马受益于越来越多的改良种子、新款化肥以及农药。这些昂贵的生产物资在波特礁由农业部的鱼类和农产品供应商店在补贴的基础上提供给农民，在这里进口品通常以成本价或是略低的价格销售。

在 20 世纪 80 年代期间，科学家评估了由绿色革命引发的技术趋势。专业人士的注意力由投入导向向调查耕作方式转变，特别是在资源匮乏的农民当中。

20 世纪 90 年代，科学方法方面发生了重大转变。其方向开始向耕作方式以及本土和西方科学技术知识应用方面转移。

图 5.10　在巴哈马东南方的矮林地壶穴里种植的番茄。

表 5.5　1989—2010 年巴哈马牛羊肉类生产的数量和产值

年份	羊肉	山羊肉	猪肉	牛肉	总量	单位
1989	85 197	71 083	240 763	17 096		磅
	187	155	321	36	690	1 000 美元
1990	106 416	64 844	209 520	38 464		磅
	233	139	274	82	728	1 000 美元
1991	117 673	63 783	184 281	53 377		磅
	258	139	241	110	748	1 000 美元
1992	121 364	61 034	190 552	38 505		磅
	264	131	240	78	714	1 000 美元
1993	76 800	92 923	276 686	63 105		磅
	175	209	420	127	931	1 000 美元
1994	107 703	67 139	330 296	26 519		磅
	244	151	510	57	962	1 000 美元

年份	羊肉	山羊肉	猪肉	牛肉	总量	单位
1995	119 442	81 917	311 712	41 254		磅
	265	181	482	92	1 020	1 000 美元
1996	110 044	65 558	310 141	30 627		磅
	245	144	479	69	937	1 000 美元
1997	5 549	2 762	318 518	17 389		磅
	259	79	580	78	996	1 000 美元
1998	7 048	3 795	353 517	13 634		磅
	230	91	894	62	1 277	1 000 美元
1999	103 464	41 407	397 557	28 064		磅
	226	63	864	73	1 226	1 000 美元
2000	96 162	33 822	418 647	37 494		磅
	211	73	956	76	1 316	1 000 美元
2001	115 908	31 440	405 278	31 844		磅
	230	68	912	66	1 301	1 000 美元
2002	35 642	23 923	393 087	23 087		磅
	78	52	884	46	1 060	1 000 美元
2003	36 233	22 231	311 896	24 102		磅
	59	36	704	40	839	1 000 美元
2004	50 516	19 497	34 114	22 082		磅
	76	29	767	35	907	1 000 美元
2005	91 329	32 891	313 819	22 513		磅
	137	49	706	36	928	1 000 美元
2006	91 329	32 891	313 819	22 513		磅
	137	49	706	36	928	1 000 美元
2007	69 161	32 770	360 220	11 197		磅
	233	107	1 068	33	1 441	1 000 美元
2008	110 959	26 179	331 973	16 877		磅
	193	45	747	32	1 017	1 000 美元
2009	244 409	233 813	4 876 985	209 535		磅
	489	468	11 063	471	12 491	1 000 美元

年份	羊肉	山羊肉	猪肉	牛肉	总量	单位
2010	268 680	277 485	5 034 549	211 150		磅
	537	555	11 418	475	12 985	1 000 美元

在广泛的生物技术领域看到新技术被开发以用于识别本土作物和畜牧业生产这件事很有趣。

有殖民背景的国家已经历过利用标准的研究技术对出口作物展开农业研究。发达国家或者工业化国家,其中包括一些殖民强国,控制了世界上的农业科研机构。这些机构位于英国、加拿大、美国、欧洲、澳大利亚和新西兰的国家资助的农业大学,包括诸如英国洛桑和荷兰瓦赫宁恩的殖民研究设施、诸如特立尼达圣奥古斯汀的前帝国热带农业学院这样的国际半球研究中心、诸如殖民发展公司这样的私有企业以及联合国粮食及农业组织这样的全球机构。

当地农民成功使用的农作物和牲畜生产方式被忽略,被认为没有什么科学价值,因此不适合进行详细的科学调查。

这些农民通常使用刀耕火种的传统农业技术。农民通过燃烧杂物对小范围植被进行开荒,他们将植物种进充满灰烬的土地。当燃烧杂物产生的灰烬中的肥料被消耗光,为了生存,自耕农将移到另一块区域再进行开荒。废弃的土地过几年后将会恢复它的自然植被。

在农业学者和专业人士中,"土著知识"是一个术语,没有公认的定义,但有许多描述,也就是"地方性知识""特定地理位置和文化的知识"以及"特定的社会或民族所独有的本土化的知识体系",上面这些描述正在被使用。

"实际上,那些土著科技语通过区域群落得到发展,以用来解决考虑到当地所有的相关因素的特殊问题。在农业领域,这些解决方案是由农民提出的。

"这些技术和知识是针对农场的环境条件和农民的需求的,帮助他们生产足够的养活家庭的产品,很多情况下还可以有所盈余提供给当地市场。"

在巴哈马,行政及调查机构在殖民时代和现在的独立时期都没有对哥伦布1492年到来之前的耕作方式进行过研究。

壶穴农业可能是巴哈马最古老的耕作方式。它是一个非常成功的系统,而且是巴哈马农业的基础,直到最近商业肥料被引进到土著自给农业才式微。农耕方式由父亲传给儿子，一代接一代地传承。

在我担任农业部主任期间，年轻的毕业生作为推广员被安置在岛上的农业社区并根据指令研究和鉴别农业技术。农业方面的科学知识与农业技术相结合，会产生一种联系，以创建一种改进后的农业体系。从长远来看，这能够使传统农民接受新的农耕方式。

科学界用了太长的时间才认识到这些信息的科学价值。直到现在，研究人员得出结论认为，高外部输入的农业（以下简称 HEIA）没有像设想的那样对农业有强烈的影响，特别是对发展中国家而言。向低外部输入的农业（以下简称 LEIA）的转变的重要性正日益在科学界得到认可，原因是高成本的商业输入将小规模农场主放在了缺乏竞争力的位置上。

图 5.11　巴哈马本·G. 哈蒙有限公司（最终演变成巴哈马柑橘种植有限公司）与巴哈马农业和工业公司签署租约。

图 5.12　巴哈马柑橘种植有限公司在为成熟的柑橘林喷雾。

表 5.6 1990—1999 年的本·G. 哈蒙柑橘产量

巴哈马柑橘种植有限公司的预计生产量（以果园采摘箱为单位）		
时期	红葡萄柚	瓦伦西亚橙
1990—1991	11 400	0
1991—1992	58 590	2 500
1992—1993	154 500	9 000
1993—1994	263 000	20 000
1994—1995	510 000	35 000
1995—1996	750 000	55 000
1996—1997	1 200 000	72 000
1997—1998	1 470 000	85 000
1998—1999	1 850 000	105 000

在巴哈马的这个情况中，由于存在独特的地形和生长环境，壶穴农业的发展是一个合理的农业体系。如想完善这一体系，需要进行认真的调查。

巴哈马并不是个例。还有其他国家的本土耕作方式已被发展但由于与壶穴农业同样的原因被忽视。在科学界的眼中，正如人种学认为自身是合理的一样，像壶穴农业这样的系统也将会获得科学凭证。

图 5.13 已故的财政部前部长卡尔顿·弗朗西斯与已故的莱昂内尔·戴维斯先生及本书作者会见佛罗里达州农业部部长霍恩·道尔·康纳。

图 5.14　站在圭亚那亚瑟·钟主席右侧的是已故的财政部前部长卡尔顿·弗朗西斯，站在他左侧的是已故的国会议员、政务次官莱昂内尔·戴维斯先生及圭亚那驻巴哈马的名誉领事奥斯卡·菲利普先生。本书作者在弗朗西斯先生的右侧。本照片摄于 1974 年 4 月。

　　在许多第三世界国家，如果能够认真尝试通过国际机构资助的研究项目研究本土农耕方式，农业发展的步伐会更快且更容易持久。20 世纪在这一领域的错误应该在 21 世纪得到纠正。

重大农业项目（1965—2001）

历届巴拿马政府已经认识到巴哈马的经济极易受到外界因素的影响的原因是由于巴哈马严重依赖旅游业和银行业。尽管巴哈马的经济规划人员认为旅游业依然是巴哈马经济的引擎，但农业部等多个部门却把经济多元化作为其目标。

农业被视为一个提供就业机会和赚取并节约外汇的手段。它有能力阻止人口从外岛向自由港和拿骚的市中心流动，并可以通过提高农业社区的收入水平加快外岛的基础设施建设。

巴哈马农业面临的困境是各届政府都没有阐明农业部门应对整个经济如何做出贡献。在过去的 30 年中，公共部门通过各种政府活动影响了农业经济增长和发展的速度。然而，私营部门在开发的过程中只扮演了一个次要的角色，这可能是这个部门的增长和发展速度不一致的主要原因。

为了使巴哈马的农业实现其全部潜力，私营部门应该成为发起者，公共部门应该成为促进者。在过去，大量公共资金被用于投资部门的资本发展项目。公共部门的项目价值约 2 000 万美元，私营部门投资了约 4 000 万美元。

为了理解巴哈马的农业发展模式，本章按时间顺序对公共和私营部门的活动进行了叙述，并对项目和政策进行了描述。

巴哈马柑橘种植有限公司

1983 年的圣诞节是佛罗里达历史上最冷的。价值数百万美元的柑橘和蔬菜被冻坏，这给佛罗里达农民造成了巨大损失。

当种植柑橘的农民正要走出 1981 年 1 月和 1982 年冻害的阴影之时，长时间的低温灾害严重破坏了北佛罗里达的柑橘和柚子等作物。

来自佛罗里达清水镇的本·G.哈蒙受够了这里的严寒天气，所以决定寻找一个天气暖和的地区。经过慎重考虑之后，他最终从加勒比地区多米尼加共和国和中美洲的哥斯达黎加等国家中选择了巴哈马。

哈蒙先生的选择源于以下几个原因，比如靠近美国的地理位置、政治稳定、国际金融中心、良好的生长条件以及会说英文而且受过良好教育的劳动力资源。

最初，该项目考虑落户于北安德鲁斯岛，因为这里有相当大面积的土地，有利于大规模机械化种植，例如阿巴克斯地区的甘蔗种植。而且，北安德鲁斯岛也是地方政府花费大笔资金扩展井场来增加新普罗维登斯的供水的地区。

政府认为这是一个重要的项目，阿巴克斯是一个理想之地，因为不需要花大费用进行开荒了。已倒闭的巴哈马农业和工业公司的甘蔗田还在那里，此前已存在了将近15年。

在本·G.哈蒙集团参观了阿巴克斯之后，他们深信自己与巴哈马政府做出了很好的安排。

在佛罗里达遭受冻害两年后的1985年11月7日，本·G.哈蒙集团通过巴哈马农业和工业公司与巴哈马政府签署了一项协议。协议规定投资5 000万美元将20 000英亩土地发展成综合的柑橘农业综合企业用地。

从1986年的首次种植一直到1992年1月，共计种植1 870英亩柑橘，包括1 710英亩红柚和160英亩瓦伦西亚橙子，代表着巴哈马地区最大的柑橘单一种植面积。1990年前后，本·G.哈蒙集团（巴哈马）的所有权发生了变更，并将公司名称更改为巴哈马柑橘种植有限公司。

尽管这个项目具有潜力，但在1994年，由于财政困难所有者放弃了该公司。租赁费用和免税进口生产物资的印花税增加，伴随着出口税的强制执行，营业费用上涨。当红柚在美国佛罗里达和得克萨斯以及南美洲巴西大规模种植，美国和世界其他地方的红柚价格下降时，最严重的财政负担到来了。

像欧文斯-伊利诺伊20年前试图建立的制糖业一样，一个崭露头角的行业虽然致力于农业部门的经济多样化，但8年后也一样屈服于命运安排。

巴哈马土地资源研究

政治变革摧毁了在印度、非洲和加勒比地区建立的英帝国。20世纪60年代末，巴哈马群岛是殖民主义的最后堡垒之一。职业殖民官员曾在许多非洲早期独立的国家中任职，他们是巴哈马群岛上层社会公共部门的重要组成部分。

1968—1969 年间，农业和渔业部门的高级官员都是由具有广泛的农业经验，特别是那些致力于提高英国利益和促进技术推广的官员组成。

这些有见识的殖民官员劝诫由几乎没有执政经验的男性构成的新政府，指出在巴哈马发展农业项目优先考虑的是土地资源调查。这项调查几乎花费了巴哈马纳税人 150 万美元。

团队的管理和调查都是由英国人来完成的。他们的巴哈马同行都是没有经验的应届毕业生。

宣传声明"为了巴哈马政府，调查项目由英国政府与巴哈马政府机构和西印度群岛大学研究人员合作完成"。

巴哈马政府同意进行调查，因为它呼吁"通过调查和描述巴哈马的自然土地资源来评估国家土地生产能力，为巴哈马政府发展规划提供依据"。

图 6.1　高级农业讲师巴勒斯坦·迈克尔先生与学员，包括罗伯特·泰勒博士、格什温·布莱登博士和本书作者（蹲坐者）一起在奇平汉姆的试验站。

对于像巴哈马这种自然资源不仅脆弱而且极其有限的国家而言，土地资源调查对于规划来说是一项非常有用的工具。调查展示客观存在的资源（包括地下水）、构成土地表面的土壤与岩石、松林及其他有用且重要的植被（例如，阔叶植被和西印度苦香树）。农业活动的记录、气象数据的收集、根据产能制图和进行土地分类等都已开展。

调查于 20 世纪 70 年代早期结束。那些年中，尽管忽略了茵那瓜岛、圣萨尔瓦多岛、玛雅古纳岛和新普罗维登斯岛，但作为水资源参考，调查产生了极大的影响。

试验和研究设施

巴哈马在农业研究方面没有任何传统，可能因为这里没有重要的出口作物，不需要不断监测新品种、害虫和疾病的控制措施，不需要提高产量，不需要完善肥料条件或对石灰土在热带农业生产中的作用进行评估。今天，研究活动通常局限于应用工作、实地试验和牲畜饲养。

殖民地大臣在 1930 年的报告《巴哈马农业》中表达了自己对于缺乏科学研究能力的担忧。他说：

"我坚信成功的必要条件是更多专家的意见。没有证据能表明，在所有农业国家中，唯独巴哈马不需要科学知识和方向。

"做任何农业项目之前，我倾向于由称职的农学家和经济学家做一个全面的调查，来确定农业前景和哪种生产重点可以获得最大盈利。"

殖民地大臣的意见首次被位于伦敦白厅的殖民局接受，然后由巴哈马的立法机构通过。为了改变这种情况，殖民地采取了措施，对巴哈马农业的科学调查开始了。

新普罗维登斯岛奇平汉姆政府试验站

政府的试验站坐落在现在的植物园内。它本质上是作物繁殖的地方，也是养殖牲畜（猪和羊）以便卖给家庭群岛和新普罗维登斯岛的农民的地方。

农作物种植包含观赏园艺和经济园艺。常见的出芽生殖、嫁接、插条和高枝压条技术被用来繁殖巴哈马各种类型的植物。20 世纪 50 年代，人们对饲料草（主要是盘固草和百慕大草）做了大量研究来改善牧场。

伴随着植物园的各种试验，植物园里种植了一片小型柑橘林和其他果园作物林，如牛油果。

除了作物繁殖与牲畜销售工作，民众可以购买新的和改进的果树品种。喷洒项目由试验站开展，也可以承包给私人。这个项目在处理 20 世纪 30 年代的果蝇危害柑橘产业的问题时发挥了重要作用。

设施在 20 世纪 20 年代晚期开始建立。农业试验站的研究技术的水平代表了巴哈马群岛殖民地农业的尊严。

L.A. 杰维斯先生于 1927 年来到巴哈马，是"西印度七大农学家"之一，也是发展试验站的主建筑师。他在试验站待了 19 年的时间，由他发起的工作项目在农作物培植和观赏园艺领域是非常成功的。作为高级农业讲师,他于1951年退休,受到了国王的尊敬,荣获英帝国勋章奖(BEM),其职位由巴勒斯坦·迈克尔先生继任。

格拉德斯通路中心农业站

试验站在20世纪60年代被认为设施陈旧。必须通过开发一个现代的研究设施帮助巴哈马农业迈入20世纪。

在试验站成立40周年之后的1969年,200万美元被分配来以便构建中心农业站。在新普罗维登斯西部地区的格拉德斯通路的南端200英亩原始松林成为农业站地址。

试验站在建成早期进行了大量的试验活动。然而,在20世纪80年代后期至20世纪90年代的大部分时间里,试验站里的工作极大恶化。

格拉德斯通路农业中心(GRAC)

20世纪90年代,中心农业站的名字改为格拉德斯通路农业中心(简称GRAC)。除了中心农业站设施,还建立了渔业诊断实验室。

食品技术实验室被转换为渔业实验室。这项决定符合欧盟要求。该要求呼吁所有向欧盟国家出口食品的国家的食品安全实验室设施必须到位。政府非但不扩展整个国家的农业基础设施,却决定缩减它,手段是通过砍掉有能力辨别和创造增值商品的机构以减少作物种植者的利益。巴哈马大鳌虾或龙虾是一个1亿美元的产业,其主要市场是欧盟地区。

图6.2 北安德鲁斯岛巴哈马农业研究、培训和开发项目的圣达格鲁迪斯牛。

北安德鲁斯岛巴哈马农业研究、培训和开发项目

中心农业站由巴哈马政府全额出资。位于北安德鲁斯岛的巴哈马农业研究、培训和开发项目成立于 1973 年,但因其是由美国政府出资 1 000 万美元建立的,因此略有不同。

这个项目由两位参议员负责组织,是庆祝巴哈马独立日(7 月 10 日)的一份礼物。美国国际开发署代表美国政府,项目于独立后不久开始运行。

巴哈马农业研究、培训和开发项目集多种功能于一体,包括三个部分:研究、培训和发展。

研究

一项精心设计的实验项目由宾夕法尼亚大学的科学家与农业部和巴哈马项目人员共同组织。

研究纲领包含 5 个学科,发展了 50 个研究项目。

学科包括:

◆ 农业经济学和农村社会学——成本分析、农作物和牲畜的企业分析。

◆ 农学——重要的热带草本植物和豆类。

◆ 动物科学——主要是肉牛、绵羊和山羊。

◆ 农业工程——对开荒、监测淡水透镜体的地下水水文和准确记录温度、降水、风速和每小时的阳光给予特别关注。

◆ 园艺——特别是热带果树、冬季蔬菜、灌溉技术和害虫预防管理。

培训

巴哈马的各级专业和学术人员都有获得培训奖的资格。有 12 人在宾夕法尼亚州立大学学习理科学士或理科硕士学位课程。另有 23 人被派往得克萨斯州技术学院,有 8 人被派到美国其他机构学习。

开发

位于得克萨斯州韦科的西方科学和技术研究所负责提供后勤保障,负责采购机械和供应并且监督建设项目工地的工作。

研究所建立了一个 500 英亩的研究站,在 900 英亩的未开发土地上建立了 16 个试点试验农场,把 260 英亩区外土地分发给安德鲁斯岛农业合作社的成员(这是一个加强制度的新元素)。它还改善土地保有权和信贷设施以帮助农民进行融资。信贷方面发展成为一个国家针对农民的信贷计划,被称为农业信用保证基金。

图 6.3 北安德鲁斯岛巴哈马农业研究、培训和开发项目正在屠宰牛。

试点试验农场展示带有混合企业的家庭类型农场的经济可行性，包括畜牧业生产。大约 45 位农民在完成 3 个月的培训课程后被分配到了农场。

为使试点试验农场成功，人们做了很多努力。在试用第一年，农民获得了投资及来自驻扎在项目地的技术人员的技术援助。他们获得了足够的收入来维持他们的家庭。在试用期后，他们会签订农场长期租赁合同。融资来自担保信贷，也是项目资金的一部分，通过商业银行办理。通过成为当地合作社的成员，农民得以维修机械，购买生产物资并且通过政府的食品加工厂销售产品。

建成的培训中心配有员工宿舍、住房和公寓，还有办公楼和机械设施、设备存储大楼。

该项目期限为 5 年，由美国国际开发署员工弗兰克·马登博士负责，他在第三世界国家中实施这些类型的项目具有丰富的经验和知识。巴哈马方面的负责人是厄尔·德沃先生，他在 1993 年到 1995 年期间担任农业局局长。

除了德沃先生，还有其他专业的农业先驱连同家人在北安德鲁斯岛定居，参与创建新农业。这些先驱包括奥德利·格里斯夫、阿诺德·多赛特、瓦莱丽·凯里-奥屯女士、西弥斯·凯索彭利斯、约翰·海顿和西米恩·平德。

他们与美国技术官员一起工作一段时间之后被派到宾夕法尼亚大学攻读他们从事的特定学科的研究生学位。

除了凯索彭利斯和海顿先生进入私营部门之外，其余人员被提拔到农业部门的高级技术和行政职位。

该项目引起了人们对巴哈马农业的关注。这是农业第一次处于科学的前沿。它终于接近殖民地大臣于 1930 年曾希望在巴哈马看到的水平。有史以来第一次有两个研究机构在巴哈马运营，20 世纪 70 年代农业的未来看起来是光明的。

1983 年巴哈马政府接手管理之后，尽管发展顺利，但也遇到了严重的管理问题。设施研究失去了方向，卫星农场计划土崩瓦解。农民培训项目不复存在，最终整个发展状况让政府难堪。1991 至 1992 年，政府决定将试验站租给私人经营。20 年中，由于糟糕的管理和领导无能，一个前景光明的价值 1 000 万美元的项目陨落了。

像米勒路的农业开发项目一样，该项目本来有崇高的目标，即

◆ 继续农民培训项目，联系巴哈马学院为农学专业的学生提供实践的机会。

◆ 清理其他的 200 英亩土地，增加农场工作，可以为大约两人提供多年工作机会。

◆ 创建更多的试点试验农场。

◆ 协助合作社发展更多农场。

◆ 为国内外市场生产更多农产品。

◆ 为当地市场生产更多当地牛羊肉。

以上目标均没有实现。

长岛北部绵羊圈养项目

多年来，巴哈马培育出了品种良好的无绒毛羊。来自联合国粮农组织的专家确定，巴哈马羊与热带地区著名的巴巴多斯黑腹无绒毛羊具有可比性。

1976—1977 年，因该项认定，巴哈马政府与联合国粮农组织签署了一项联合项目。其主要目的在于通过改善羊群来获得可持续的羊肉产量。北长岛地区因羊肉生产在巴哈马东南地区（尤其是长岛）具有悠久的传统从而被选为项目所在地。

项目的关键在于呼吁灌木牧场的发展计划，引进改善羊身体健康和畜牧业的技术，从全国范围内选择最适合繁殖的品种。

该项目在当地刺激了产量，但并没有产生全国范围内的影响。

食品技术和动物饲料单位

农业部门已开始扩大生产，新需求得到了满足。巴哈马政府于 1981 年与欧洲经济共同体（简称 EEC）签订协议发展食品技术和动物饲料单位。该单位位

于中心农业站。欧洲经济共同体将为这个项目融资 100 万美元。该单位的两项作用分别是：

（1）食品技术——将本地水果和蔬菜加工成新食品；

（2）动物饲料——加工当地原材料，如木薯、高粱、玉米和家禽内脏，为动物提供饲料。

几年来，此项目培养了一批具有丰富的专业知识的专业人员，有能力为农业部门做出重要贡献。该项目的鼓动者是微生物学家西德尼·罗素先生，他在 1982 年成为农业主管。

在过去的 70 年里，巴哈马在提高自身在农业科学领域的科研能力上已经走了很长的路。保守估计已经有 1 500 万美元投资用于为巴哈马农业提供试验和研究设施。项目的短板不再是设施方面，而是缺乏专业人士完成研究任务。在培养专家之前，在当地科研的必要性及其对国家建设的贡献得到认可之前，巴哈马的研究能力从来没有得到发展。

公共部门的农业营销

在拿骚市场销售当地产品的问题几十年来一直没有得到解决。殖民地大臣 1930 年的备忘录《巴哈马农业》中这样阐述：

“它指出，大部分的外岛委员强烈批评拿骚买家给出的价格。当然对合理价格的看法也不尽相同，但委员们批评的价格似乎对我来说并不是低得不合理。在某些情况下，它们与进口产品的价格相同，农民要求价格超过进口产品，外岛上的价格超过拿骚的价格。

“总体的印象是外岛生产商对他们的产品价值产生膨胀性的想法。农民甚至还有繁荣的想法，他们没有意识到他们必须与进口商品竞争，否则零售商将继续进口——如果他不购买岛上产品，那么他将有更多便利。

“岛民将因此而处于不利地位，这是真正的问题所在。生产点零星分散在许多岛屿上，这些岛屿彼此之间及与拿骚之间相隔辽阔的海域。产品被零星收集，随机发货，委托船长代表业主销售。作为报酬，船长收取运费或者收取运费和佣金。

“在这种情况下，外岛的农民发现很难销售他们的产品，他们也处在一个恶性循环中：农民因为没有销路而减少生产，买家因为利润太少而减少购买。

　　"人们建议的补救措施是成立一个方便的物产交易所，议院的一个委员会很多年前就建议成立这样一个物产交易所。也请记住，这个物产交易所无论是政府运营还是私人运营，都会在生产者与消费者之间引入一个中间人。"

图 6.4　物产交易所大量的洋葱。本书作者与克莱姆·平德先生（巴哈马畜牧业和农业农民协会会员）、弗雷德·朗利先生（城市市场连锁超市的买家）、已故的塞德里克·史密斯先生（负责波特礁地区产品交易所的经理）合影。

　　基于该报告，很明显殖民局已经意识到了问题所在，当时的政客们认识到他们必须找到一个切实的方案来解决这个问题。

　　几年后，议院通过立法允许农业委员会建立物产交易所。由于议院主要是由资本主义商人组成，所以这一定是一个艰难的决定。对他们来说，允许巴哈马政府参与私人部门活动严重偏离了他们的商业和政治哲学。

物产交易所

物产交易所设在市场房屋中，以便协助家庭岛生产商在新普罗维登斯为他们的产品找到出路。它为生产者和消费者提供服务，但是没有储存设施，这意味着存货必须立即出售。物产交易所起初是一个批发实体，后来发展成零售业务。物产交易所原先的位置在20世纪70年代后期被大火吞噬，如今成了稻草市场。

第二次世界大战之后，巴哈马作为旅游目的地赢得了国际声誉。到20世纪60年代，巴哈马不仅成为该地区旅游目的地的领头羊，也成为该半球主要的金融中心之一。联合巴哈马党因此开始用资本发展计划来改善港口设施和改造位于拿骚市中心的海湾街。

邮船和小型船舶被从乔治王子码头和伍德·罗杰斯区域移走了，人们在波特礁为岛际船只建造了一个新的对接设施。与这一举措同步，一个新的物产交易所萌生了。

图 6.5 拿骚老市场一角。

1967 年，新的物产交易所在波特礁开门纳客。市场回归零售业务。另一个零售商店毗邻波特礁批发设施，也建立起来了，还有一个零售商店在罗宾逊路上成立了，以取代毁于大火中的那个商店。

家庭群岛的发展是政府一项重要的议程。随着更多资金对开荒和农场支线公路建设的支持，更多的新土地被用于生产，这意味着更多的农业产品被生产出来，运往物产交易所的产品也增多了。

几种类型产品的季节性生产导致供大于求。这导致了拿骚市场遭受生产充足但是无法出售的压力。供应过剩不是唯一的原因；质量差和不成熟也是主要原因。物产交易所作为一个公共机构不执行严格的分级标准。

家庭岛的农业社区对于该体系非常失望。为了控制购买，物产交易所采纳农业部门建议，通过广播告诉农民交易所购买哪种类型的产品。无法直接将产品卖给超市、酒店或产品供应商的农民正在遭受巨大损失，因为他们无法将广播前就已经收获的产品销售出去。

政府追切寻找解决方案的政治压力将农民的失望变成了绝望。

有关方面决定通过在家庭群岛主要农民社区建立和运行包装工厂来扩大物产交易所的职能，深化公共部门的参与度。

农民现在可以努力生产，因为包装工厂负责收购、分级、存储和运输购买的产品。

包装工厂的规划和房屋建设始于 1973 年，第一批设施于 1976 年完成。设施建在北安德鲁斯岛，伊鲁萨拉岛的北部、中部和南部，长岛北部和中部，猫岛和伊克祖马斯。零售设施建在大巴哈马岛自由港。有关方面投资了 100 万美元用于市场基础设施建设。

除基础设施之外，每个包装工厂招聘大约 12 名本地员工。

人们也曾考虑建设冷藏设施和某些农业社区的特殊性。例如，因为伊克祖马斯是巴哈马主要的洋葱生产地，所以工厂配备有干燥洋葱的设施。

物产交易所与包装工厂建立的目的是缓解家庭群岛小规模农场主所面临的问题。随着许多农民掌握了新农业技术，特别是作物产量更高、土地面积更大的松树群岛（安德鲁斯岛、阿巴克斯岛和大巴哈马岛）上的农民，一些农民开始将大量不符合标准的产品交给物产交易所和包装工厂。

这给公共财政部门造成了严重的财政负担，因此农民们不得不等待更长时间才能获得卖到包装工厂的产品补偿。

政客吓到了当地员工，这也导致了系统内的职权滥用。由于系统需要现代化，因此早就该对物产交易所和包装工厂的操作程序进行大幅修改了。

政府认识到其深度参与市场营销给某些行业的私营部门带来了很多问题。1975 年 8 月 15 日，农业部通知议院，政府部门通过关闭其在波特礁和罗宾逊锚地的零售商店退出零售业务。

随着零售商店的关闭，新农贸市场将在北大西洋辖区的加姆贝村开工建设。预计这些设施将提供给产品供应商，为农民提供一个销售他们产品的区域。

可以确定的是，在 20 世纪 70 年代，巴哈马 30% 的产品都通过物产交易所和包装工厂进行交易。通过该系统购买的产品的年度价值曾经一度达到约 500 万美元。

物产交易所和包装工厂在巴哈马成为促进农业发展的独特工具，但如今作用尽失。未来的任何成功都依赖于农民和他们的组织在经营部门的参与度。

农民的产品以何种方式在哪里销售对农民有直接影响。他们再也不会坐视不管并允许政府机构为他们承担所有的责任。巴哈马产品必须在国内和国外市场采取一种新的营销方式，包括参与营销链的相关各方。

市场

殖民主义的行政特征之一是市场。无论是在非洲、加勒比地区、印度，还是在亚洲其他地区，所有的殖民列强（英国、荷兰、法国、比利时）都利用市场作为社会经济工具直接控制其海外附属地的商业活动。

在巴哈马，像在英帝国的其他地区一样，市场的主要作用是满足非常基本的商业需求，本地区的民众在市场上获得基本食品和其他消费品。

市场的位置加快实现了这一目标。市场位于拿骚的市区，靠近主要的航运和航海港口。市场让殖民地的商业生活变成了现实。

从市场功能上看，市场提供了一个非正式的环境和地方，人们在这里交换观点，互相寒暄。因为在这个时代，需用一定的货币购买日常生活用品，在很多情况下货币数量代表着每小时、每天或者每件工作的收入。

此外，某些冰箱制冷有限，因此食品保存与新鲜度和盐分有关。电冰箱是富人和小康家庭的选择——这些人是控制着殖民地的商业和政治生活的殖民阶级和商人。

市场的标准样式是仓库类型的结构，建立它们是为了保护供应商和其易损物品免受灰尘、雨水、阳光和夜间偷盗的影响。主要的目标是建成功能性基础设施来满足卫生的基本条件，并减少街头小贩在不卫生的条件下出售他们的产品的现象。摊位每天支付费用，获得牌照，公共卫生检查员确保清理垃圾，并将环境卫生保持在一个可接受的水平内。

英国依靠政治权力实现了对殖民地和殖民地人民的管理。殖民总体设计旨在改变巴哈马"原住民"的精神面貌。这些"原住民"是奴隶的后代。因为英国海军将奴隶船封锁在公海上，他们跟他们忠诚的主人来到这里或者被运到这些海岸。

这种改变当地人的精神面貌的概念并不局限于剥削他们的劳动，当地人还必须在社会、政治和殖民地商业生活中遵守英国的民事行为模式。

卖方市场主要由黑人（包括水果和蔬菜的摊主，通常是女性）、鱼贩子、廉价产品的供应商和农民构成。他们来自家庭群岛、福克斯山等新普罗维登斯的偏远地区及松林地区（烧炭地）与家庭群岛附近的农业社区，例如西班牙韦尔斯和北伊鲁萨拉卡罗斯。

殖民商业行为被本地城市社区采用，他们通过扮演中间商和"小商店"运营者的角色，带着启发他们参与市场经济的目标，直接参与了殖民地的经济活动。

在文化上，市场对于本地居民来说具有重大意义。几十年来，这里是一年两次佳卡努庆祝活动的举办地区。对于巴哈马人民的精神灵魂来说，市场是一个文化偶像，其遗产作为文化机构在巴哈马民俗文化中根深蒂固。

产品供应商

很大一部分拥有摊位的供应商组成了产品供应商，他们在市场和市场的周边地区出售新鲜的农产品，通常是在今天叫伍德罗杰斯锚地的码头附近。

除产品供应商之外，还有鱼贩子、廉价产品供应商和其他供应本地生产的手工艺品的商贩。

在市场链中，产品供应商是重要的中间人。他们直接从农民手中购买产品，由农民将产品送到停靠在新普罗维登斯和各个家庭岛的邮船或其他船只上。

产品供应商也是物产交易所主要的买家，负责运输拿骚家庭和餐厅乡土菜所需的大量水果和蔬菜。零售商直接影响了拿骚消费者的生活成本，他们设计了特殊的定价方法。

从社会学角度来看，供应商，包括廉价产品的供应商和生产商，都是女性，她们在新普罗维斯登的商业中扮演了企业家的角色。她们当中的许多人都是家庭的经济支柱，负责资助孩子的教育、房屋建设、车辆的购买和多元化投资其他企业。

产品供应商继续在农业部门这个主要的渠道上发挥着战略性作用。通过这一渠道，巴哈马人民种植的农产品已被市场化。

西非的"市场女性"这一传统通过生产和廉价产品供应商这一角色仍保持在流散的巴哈马人民中。

米勒路农业发展项目

政府在 1969—1970 年面临的棘手问题之一就是土地问题。巴哈马人感觉到他们很多代以来已经被剥夺了获得公有土地的权利。

多年来，土地和调查部门负责公有土地，该部门由来自南部加勒比的合格的非巴哈马调查员领导。在这段时间内，巴哈马人通过将这些人称为西印第安人从而把自己与南部加勒比人区分开来。

对于巴哈马人来说，加勒比一体化是一个遥远的梦想。除了作为英国殖民地的共性以及英语这一共同语言之外，巴哈马人倾向于北美地区。

具有非洲血统的巴哈马后裔感觉自己被遗忘了，大块的公有土地分给了现在已经不存在的联合巴哈马党的追随者。还有一种更深层的感觉，土地和调查部门的西印第安人更加同情与他们类似的其他人而非土著巴哈马黑人。

进步自由党政府基本上没有办法解决数百人申请公有土地这一难题。

1971 年 4 月 30 日，发展部部长杰弗里·汤普森阁下在公有土地形势不乐观的情况下与农业和渔业部部长米勒·B. 巴特勒共同主持召开了会议，旨在找到解决这一政治问题的办法。

新普罗维登斯的米勒路和考本路上大约 500 英亩的公有土地已经被确定为可能实施农业发展项目的地区。农业部坚持真正的农民应该优先获得拨款，其次是潜在的、有所需的金融资源的农民。有政治关系的投机者，连同那些渴望有机会拥有更多的公有土地而寻求土地的个人，也都出现在排行榜上。

农业部的专业人员通过设置给予土地的标准建立了完善的甄选程序。项目分为两个阶段。第一阶段有 70 块土地，总计 293.6 英亩。另外的 200 英亩预留给第二阶段以满足需求。

土地最终被用于畜牧业生产，特别是涉及小规模农场主的猪肉生产。猪肉生产在巴哈马主要是一个自家后院的活动。通过鼓励米勒路上的活动，可以将技术升级到资本密集型商业水平从而减少猪肉进口，而在当时每年进口猪肉花费超过 100 万美元。

到 1971 年 6 月，超过 300 位申请者申请 120 块土地，几乎是三位申请者竞争一块土地。对于公共官员来说，兼顾政治考虑平衡农业能力是一个困难的工作。在最后的分析中，政治考虑超过农业能力。这在很大程度上影响了规划项目满足规划者生产预期的能力。

一份关于项目潜力的报告阐述如下：

> "这个提议的发展可能是对巴哈马近几年新兴农业经济最重要的贡献之一。单就畜牧生产而言，订单的预计产出是 500 英亩每年产出 500 万美元……但即使有一个初始 500 万美元的产出目标，这也预示着每英亩年收入约 1 万美元。"

畜牧业生产的目标从来没有实现，因为：
◆ 没有能力改变农业实践。
◆ 缺乏有能力的推广人员。
◆ 农民选拔糟糕。
◆ 缺乏正确的指导方针来合理管理项目区域。
◆ 缺乏建设基础设施的资金。
◆ 农民缺乏资金来发展分得的土地。

1998 年，米勒路的农业开发项目仍未得到发展。项目开始约 25 年后，开发面积不到 10%。目前正在酝酿从延期交付租金和放弃土地的个人手中收回分配的土地，其中一些土地已被别人擅自占用。

尽管目标美好，1971 年时看起来也容易实现，但是米勒路的农业开发项目宣告失败了。

技术援助

巴哈马很少有技术援助项目。工业化国家将巴哈马视为人均收入高的国家，认为巴哈马无资格获得国外援助。然而，许多政府官员认为这是一个肤浅的判断，是一种阻止巴哈马进步的方法。

这里缺乏许多专业技术，还有些领域内的专业知识需要更新。农业是一个学科，技术援助将有助于提高该行业在人力资源开发和应用技术方面的整体能力。

在 20 世纪 90 年代，两个著名的技术援助项目由以色列和中国台湾省支持。

以色列技术援助

1991年8月，以色列国际农业合作中心为农业部门的推广人员召开了关于农业推广方法和工作规划的研讨会，历时三周。

研讨会被认为是提高松树群岛和矮林群岛上推广人员知识的重要工具。

"推广工作的原则和方法"课程由以色列两位专家主讲。该课程将有助于在不同岛屿上工作而且没有接受过推广工作正式培训的年轻的专业人士与农民沟通解决问题，并且将农民的问题传达给那些做研究和实施政策的人。

这时，农业部门缺乏对农民和农民家庭扩展信息的小册子，缺乏有组织的广播和电视节目，缺乏野外时间解决特定的农业问题。

在研讨会的开幕式上，佩里·克里斯蒂阁下说："最大限度地增加外国专家的人数、技术、资源来帮助只需要一个机会的巴拿马人，这是我们的责任……而且为了使这一切变得合理有效，推广领导必须时刻在岗，必须保证巴哈马人的利益。"

以色列在世界各地开展了这些类型的课程，巴哈马有幸在这个时候受益。除此之外，巴哈马农业专家在以色列学习短期课程。旅游业的犹太游说团说服了以色列政府在巴哈马举行研讨会。

中国台湾省的技术援助

除了在农业和渔业方面的专家组之外，台湾省还为体育馆的建设提供资金支持并派出了来自不同政府部门的专家来举办培训课程。

台湾省认为他们的经济发展模式适合于类似于巴哈马这样的第三世界国家。台湾省的经济是由农业转向工业的，他们相信他们可以将这项"秘诀"传给发展中国家。

1990年5月，宋熙赛作为台湾省技术专家组的负责人开始扩大和丰富其在农业部门的工作。包括：

（1）研究和示范工作——政府和农业研究中心的前身为格拉德斯通路上的中心农业站，人们在这里对果树的繁殖、蔬菜产量和猪肉生产进行试验。经过改良的猪在新建造的猪舍内进行繁殖。为了在整个巴哈马扩大猪肉生产，该中心还把改良的猪分发给农民。

（2）植物园——观赏园艺方面的工作有利于扩大农业部的工作来协助开发、扩大和使花卉栽培产业变得多样化。近年来，一些资本密集型的苗圃开始出现，植物景观和苗圃植物的进口受到限制。

（3）植物育种和遗传学——台湾省的专家帮助巴哈马专业人员获得在组织培养方面的专业技能。

（4）培训——巴哈马农学家被派送到台湾省，在农业的各个方面进行专业训练。

（5）女王陛下监狱——专家组为这个机构提供了特别的援助，尤其是在提高监狱农场的管理、提高作物产量以满足监狱在一些作物上实现自给自足以及教授囚犯一些实用的农业技术以便出狱后有作物种植和畜牧业的技术可以顺利就业等方面给予了特别的援助。

台湾省还捐赠了一间长 15 英尺、宽 60 英尺的温室，配有一个低成本的喷射灌溉系统，并协助监狱开发了更多的粮食生产土地。他们还帮助改善了观赏植物的繁殖。

台湾省的技术援助倾向于建立伙伴关系。台湾省的专家与巴哈马工作人员并肩工作，像合伙人一样共同作出决定，双方的领导基于共同关心的问题一对一地讨论。他们的援助基于一句中国流传数百年的谚语："授人以鱼不如授人以渔。"

1997 年，巴哈马政府断绝了与台湾省的官方关系。政府像其主要贸易伙伴美国一样承认一个中国政策，认可中华人民共和国。

中华人民共和国

中华人民共和国自 1997 年以来在巴哈马一直是引人注目的存在。在大巴哈马岛，中国人是自由港主要的参与者。哈钦森 - 哈姆珀，这家总部位于香港的公司，拥有并经营自由港集装箱港口、国际机场和大卢卡亚酒店。在新普罗维登斯，中国为凯布尔沙滩上的巴哈马酒店 / 度假村项目投资 20 亿美元，并投资从林登·平德林国际机场到达拿骚的高速公路通道。

与作为其不可分割的一部分的台湾省不同，中华人民共和国对农业的主要贡献在于为农业和海洋科学的各个方面设置奖学金，帮助更大。

农业部(合并)法案(1993)

从 1969 年到 1970 年，米勒路农业开发项目反映出对土地的需求。25 年中，新普罗维登斯岛上的可用公有土地已耗尽。巴哈马人，特别是居住在安德鲁斯岛、阿巴克斯岛和大巴哈马岛上的居民，继续申请农业公用土地。土地调查部门充斥着官僚主义，让流程变得烦琐和耗时，这导致大量未处理的申请堆积。

　　土地是一种生产要素，也是农业发展的一个重要工具。每年都有新土地投入生产也是很有必要的。这对于扩大面对国内外市场的产品生产非常重要。

　　当松树群岛上的土地可以用于生产时，这些岛屿上的居民开始利用农业提供的机会。

　　为了保障具有全球竞争力的食品生产系统在巴哈马得到成功发展，必须在松树群岛考虑以下方面：

　　（1）自然资源的有效利用。

　　（2）最有效地挖掘与利润丰厚的北美大市场离得近的距离优势。

　　（3）在土地有高产潜力的地区有选择性地促进基础设施建设。

　　（4）科研保障农业稳定前进。

　　从20世纪50年代开始，松树群岛开始展示它们大规模机械化耕作的潜力。岩石土壤技术在南佛罗里达的胡姆斯泰德地区得到完善，并由美国离岸种植者传播到巴哈马地区。40多年中，巴哈马政府看到了一个又一个离岸种植者在农场工作一两个季节之后离开。

　　在这种情况下，需要新的土地分配政策来解决这个问题。1993年7月30日，自由民族运动政府议会通过《农业部（合并）法案1993》。该法案将"授予负责农业的部长法人地位，使之有权获取、持有、租赁和处理农业土地，执行合同，起诉和被起诉"。

　　这是历史上第一次由农业部与农业部门一起掌握大量的高产土地。

　　在米勒路的项目中，农业部负责挑选合适的农民，土地调查部门负责土地分配。在新法案的指导下，上面所有的事务都由农业部管辖。

　　《土地资源研究》已经确定了阿巴克斯的50 000英亩（20 250公顷）、安德鲁斯的104 000英亩（41 600公顷）和大巴哈马的30 000英亩（12 150公顷）土地为高产土地。

　　每个松树岛地图都显示着在《农业部（合并）法案》管理下的高产土地的面积和位置以及在巴哈马和国外离岸种植者管理下的种植企业。

　　1996年，巴哈马的人口略超过272 000人，其中大部分人口居住在新普罗维登斯。其他城市中心是大巴哈马岛上的自由港，约有55 000人居住。松树群岛的总人口大约有75 000人。阿巴克斯是第三大人口稠密的岛屿，马什港是最大的居住区。除了拥有庞大的人口数量，自由港优良的基础设施促进了旅游、工业和现代集装箱转运码头的发展。

松树群岛上的人口对新鲜水果、蔬菜、猪肉、羊肉、家禽和观赏植物有极大的需求。

新普罗维登斯城市化进程加快，高成本的住宅开发使农业用地成本变得更加昂贵。

严重的环境问题和对水资源的竞争进一步阻碍了新普罗维登斯的农业发展。在未来，更多的农业和农工联合企业的活动将在不发达的大岛屿上开展，尤其是大巴哈马岛，那里人口增长迅速、基础设施完善。

卢卡亚热带农产品公司和温室技术

20世纪的最后十年，加勒比地区巴哈马等岛屿小国将在农业方面迎来巨大的变化。这些变化是日益全球化的结果。全球化已经成为现实，巴哈马不能忽视或将其漠视为另一个时尚趋势。在这十年里，一个新的实体——世界贸易组织（WTO）将取代关税和贸易总协定（GATT）。WTO将成为主要负责推动全球化进程和创建环境自由化贸易体制的机构。

1995年，除了巴哈马，该半球的所有国家都成了WTO的成员。加入WTO意味着市场的开放，遵守《世界贸易组织农业协议》（AOA）规定的农业贸易法规，丧失欧盟国家给加勒比共同体国家的优惠市场。虽然不是WTO成员国，但这些因素会影响巴哈马的粮食生产和市场。

如果小规模农场主和当地农业综合企业想在一个贸易自由的世界上生存，那么巴哈马不得不像其他加勒比国家一样解决这个问题，即使其农业更具有竞争力。为了在新的全球化环境中竞争，巴哈马农业必须以技术为驱动，以研究为基础并且做到环境友好。为了实现这个目标，私营和公共部门就必须分别增加对农业的投资。

2001年8月，作为水培温室业务，卢卡亚热带农产品（LTP）公司由一群巴哈马投资者建立。这个耗资500万美元的项目目标是提供有竞争力的商品，包括一系列的蔬菜、盆栽植物、蔬菜幼苗和本地植物。

卢卡亚热带农产品公司已经引入了创新的方式来营销他们的产品，这正在对当地的市场产生影响。消费者可以通过网站下订单。此外，卢卡亚热带农产品公司在新普罗维登斯建立了几个农场市场那样的批发商店。

温室是由来自荷兰的戴尔森·BV设计的；它是具有威尼奥风格的温室。面对巴哈马的热带条件，挑战随之而来。为了更好地控制温度，人们不得不采用屋顶洒水装置和冷却灌溉用水等新举措来应对高温环境和高压成雾等问题。为了控制害虫和疾病，人们采用了生物防治策略。

与温室业务一起，在赛琳娜·坎贝尔-豪伯博士的领导下，巴哈马植物药材公司与卢卡亚热带农产品公司组建了巴哈马的第一个组织培养单位。坎贝尔-豪伯博士这样描述了她的操作和技术使用：

> "尽管实验失败，但是植物组织培养技术，也被称为离体繁殖或快速繁殖，在20世纪初首次尝试。这意味着在无菌等控制环境下，繁衍植物是当今农业生物技术领域一个必不可少的工具。从改善食品、纺织品和观赏作物到药品生产，植物组织培养在无数科学进步中继续发挥着重要作用。在巴哈马地区，通过给现有的和潜在的生产者提供在原始条件下及有可核查的遗传完整性的数百万繁殖体，植物快速繁殖可以在农业的发展中起到关键作用。经过巴哈马几代农民的努力，国家农作物库的发展已经适应了我们的气候和土地。当土地发展和飓风等自然灾害威胁森林的长期存在的时候，这个好处进一步扩展到保护原生植物上。巴哈马的未来农业产业和环境保护将因这项技术极大地受益。"

图 6.6　为后花园建成的隧道温室（30′×16′/480平方英尺）。

图 6.7　新普罗维登斯在建的温室：支撑框架由环形木材、竹、塑料软管或聚氯乙烯管建成。塑料薄膜覆盖设计（聚酯或聚氯乙烯）。尺寸有所不同。在建隧道类型，即后花园温室或者商用温室。

图 6.8　用于商业生产的标准单脊温室（120′×36′/4 320 平方英尺）。

在我的书《新加勒比：转型之地》中第 47、48 页阐述了以下观点：

"粮农组织说，如果要提高生产力和竞争力，温室技术是加勒比地区农民要走的一条路。

　　"这种说法来自粮食及农业组织（简称粮农组织）次区域的代表——芭芭拉·格雷厄姆博士。她指出,在过去的三年里,考虑到飓风和其他自然灾害所造成的脆弱性 [①],

　　"我们在粮农组织认为,如果要实现该地区生产力和在地区内外市场上的竞争力,该地区需要期待温室技术这种生产系统。"

　　在 2008、2009 年,温室建设在巴哈马如火如荼地进行着。牙买加农业技术专家勒罗伊·圣地亚哥开始在新普罗维登斯和阿巴克斯建立一系列温室。在北安德鲁斯岛,巴哈马农业和工业公司也建造了几个示范温室。技术正在发展和影响粮食生产,特别是蔬菜生产。

　　利用水培法的温室技术在巴哈马地区有一个美好的未来,特别是在有电力等基础设施的地方。为了准备植物营养液和维持酸度水平,系统必须技术化和程序化。温室产量很高,正如报告显示,1 英亩(0.4 公顷)营养液温室可以产出相当于 10 英亩大田的量(4 公顷)。在像巴哈马这样的高价劳动力市场,对除草、种植、收获整地及灌溉等方面劳动的需求被减到最低。水资源在巴哈马南部属于稀缺资源。

　　近年来,巴哈马农业并没有吸引到当地或者外国的直接投资,而温室技术可以改变这一状况。无土农业对于投资者们来说是理想的操作。这一技术的可贵之处在于它提高了小规模农场主的技术能力,使他们成为更具竞争力的农业综合企业人员。现在,巴哈马农民可以全年提供各类高质量蔬菜。这也提高了巴哈马的粮食安全水平。

---

① 原书即如此分段。——译者注

第 7 章 »

旅游业对农业的影响

第二次世界大战后，巴哈马进入了一段深刻而时有矛盾的变革时期。自奴隶制废除之后的第一次重大经济转变即将来临。

巴哈马人开始由家庭群岛迁向拿骚、自由港这些城镇化地区（详见表 7.1）。来自家庭群岛的大部分人口于 1943—1953 年间在美国落户做合同农场工人的工作。当地进行了招工，正如当地人们所说的那样，男男女女们都愿意获得这种工作的机会。然而在美国，数以百计的巴哈马人却违反合同，再也不回巴哈马了。

表 7.1　1931—2010 年岛屿人口分布情况

岛屿	1931 年	1953 年	1970 年	1990 年	2000 年	2010 年
巴哈马整个地区	59 828	84 841	169 534	255 049	303 541	351 461
新普罗维登斯岛	19 756	46 125	102 005	172 196	210 832	246 329
大巴哈马岛	2 241	4 095	25 943	40 898	46 994	51 368
阿巴克斯岛	4 233	3 407	6 507	10 003	13 170	17 224
阿克林斯岛	1 765	1 273	936	405	428	565
安德鲁斯岛	7 071	7 136	8 889	8 177	7 686	7 490
浆果群岛	222	327	443	628	709	807
毕米尼群岛	756	1 330	1 533	1 639	1 717	1 988
猫岛	3 959	3 201	2 658	1 698	1 647	1 522
崎岖岛	1 329	836	689	412	350	304
伊鲁萨拉岛	7 527	7 596	9 501	10 584	7 999	8 202

续表

岛屿	1931 年	1953 年	1970 年	1990 年	2000 年	2010 年
海港岛 / 西班牙韦尔斯					3 166	3 313
伊克祖马斯岛	3 774	2 919	3 777	3 556	3 571	6 928
茵那瓜岛	667	999	1 109	985	969	913
长礁	144	80	26	0		26
长岛	4 515	3 755	3 869	2 949	2 922	3 094
玛雅古纳岛	518	615	584	312	259	277
拉吉德岛	424	320	208	89	72	72
圣萨尔瓦多 / 拉姆礁	927	827	857	518	1 050	1 039

　　农业作为巴哈马经济的重要部分,在经济重要性方面地位正在下降。随着新普罗维登斯酒店的建设,巴哈马迎来了旅游业的新时代,同时也引发了战后重建的热潮。

　　大多数巴哈马人的工作地点从家庭岛转移到酒店,同时也将住处迁往城市。巴哈马人抓住了酒店服务兴起这一契机,从事新型岗位。这一新型行业也给巴哈马人的生活方式带来了巨大的影响和转变。

　　工作的性质发生了变化,无数家庭的父亲、母亲开始进入夜班、周末班、轮班模式,在酒店从事女佣和服务员的工作。到田地劳作的传统工作方式几乎消失。

　　随着这一系列的变化,社区开始变化。由于这一新兴的繁荣,巴哈马正在迎来新面貌。巴哈马人开始渴望更优质的教育,获得更好的工作,同时开始怀疑统治他们的政府体制。

　　尽管巴哈马由殖民主义者们紧紧掌控,巴哈马政治领导机构开始谋求打造新型经济,以使巴哈马在 20 世纪正常运行。

新发展模式

　　20 世纪 50 年代,随着旅游业成为一年四季性的活动,巴哈马重塑了经济发展模式。设计者是斯塔福·L. 桑兹爵士,他实际上掌控着巴哈马发展委员会。该委员会具有强大的政治影响力,也是巴哈马现在旅游部的前身。

　　在发展全年旅游业的同时,巴哈马政府鼓励土地开发,并邀请欧洲人和北美人开发群岛。其中最引人注目的是大巴哈马岛自由港的设立,美国公民华莱士·格罗夫斯在那里开发了一片 200 平方英里的自由贸易区。在此之前，加拿大人哈里·奥克斯爵士同泰勒先生在新普罗维登斯岛西部地区开发了大片的房地产。

1955 年，巴哈马政府通过了《毫克斯比尔小湾协定》，赋予了大巴哈马港口当局管理自由贸易区的特权，特权持续到 2054 年 8 月 3 日。自由港被提升到独一无二的位置。

《毫克斯比尔小湾协定》规定，自由贸易区企业享受免利润税、资本收益税、财产继承税、所得税、收益税、财产分配及进出口货物税等优惠政策。

斯塔褔德爵士对经济增长的研究并未局限于旅游业与房地产业。他的研究方法涵盖离岸银行业务，因为他试图让巴哈马成为加勒比地区的瑞士，打造由金融服务业部门、英国法律体系支持的税收减免环境。这促使巴哈马将自己打造成为著名的国际金融中心。

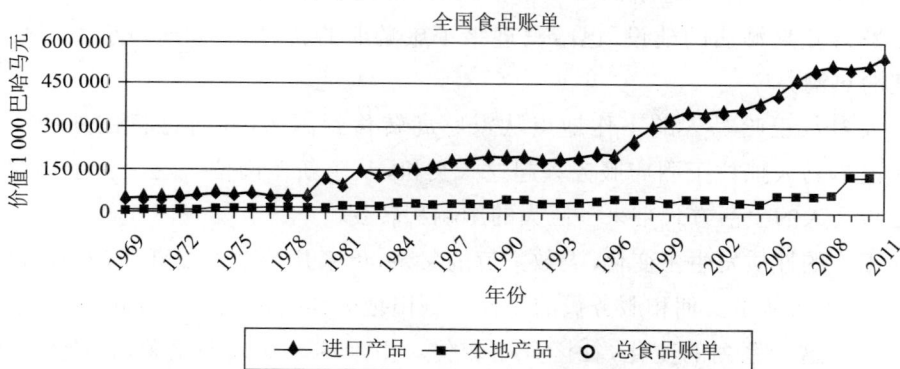

表 7.1　1969—2011 年全国食品账单

凭借稳定的政治环境、受过良好教育和训练有素的人力资源，巴哈马正走向持续的经济增长和发展之路，其中旅游业是其经济增长的引擎和外汇的主要来源。

农产品出口

正如我们所看到的，巴哈马出口农产品的历史反复多变。与其加勒比邻国始终以糖为主导不同，巴哈马出口型农业以水果（柑橘和菠萝）和针对美国东海岸地区冬季市场的蔬菜为中心。

该地区农业的不稳定特性主要源于虫害、作物生长环境的恶化、缺乏科学调查设备以及农业劳动力供给不足。农业并没有表明它可以维持人口持续增长，也不能保证能够提供巴哈马人渴望的生活水准。

大型离岸公司在松树群岛将现代农业技术付诸实践，而生计型农业则主要位于巴哈马东南部的矮林群岛。科技转化应用很难进行，当地农民墨守成规而且落后。

20世纪50年代以后，政策鼓励季节性生产，对高关税进行保护，农业政策转向进口替代。与此同时，政府允许农业生产物资免税进口。

为了促进农业发展，农业部门通过农业生产物资进口免税在生产方面接受补贴，在出口方面通过产品交易所、包装工厂接受补贴，这些交易所与工厂从农户手中收购大量农产品。

20世纪80年代后期，针对产品交易所和包装工厂的补贴维持在每年400万美元。1993年以后，政府提高了这些实体操作的现代化水平，大幅度降低了市场补贴，目标是最终停止补贴。

食品进口

到了20世纪90年代，旅游业迅速发展成为一个产值达10亿美元的产业，每年吸引游客近350万人次。巴哈马本身已发展成为一个城市化国家，拿骚和自由港人口所占比例超过全国的80%。

巴哈马人通过统计计算出的人均收入约1万美元，旅游市场不断扩大，国家收入基础依赖于关税。20世纪90年代，每年进口食品已经超过2亿美元（见图7.1）。

巴哈马已经到了无法为自己生产食品的地步。巴哈马人的饮食和消费习惯基本上是北美化的，这正好与绝大多数游客的饮食需要相吻合，因为绝大多数游客来自北美。

1995年，中途停留在拿骚和天堂岛的游客76%来自美国。这是美国市场影响巴哈马这一最大目的地的最好的例子。

从旅游业获得的所有外汇当中，大约有20%用于食品进口。农业也许一直是巴哈马经济中最为脆弱的部分，由进口食品导致的贸易赤字已经达到无法逆转的地步。

表 7.2 1969—2011 年国家食品账单 [①]

年份	进口食品价值 （百万美元）	本地产品价值 （百万美元）	总计 （百万美元）
1969	48 169	6 141	54 310
1970	47 682	6 823	54 505
1971	49 629	7 582	57 211
1972	51 458	8 424	59 882
1973	59 540	9 360	68 900
1974	65 618	10 400	76 018
1975	59 661	12 300	71 961
1976	69 765	14 400	84 165
1977	54 333	18 800	73 133
1978	53 993	18 400	72 393
1979	58 139	17 500	75 639
1980	126 244	20 200	146 444
1981	94 426	26 320	120 746
1982	147 836	22 860	170 696
1983	131 246	26 760	158 006
1984	148 597	33 630	182 227
1985	154 187	34 010	188 197
1986	163 887	28 830	192 717
1987	186 159	32 840	218 999
1988	184 230	30 270	214 500
1989	201 991	34 380	236 371
1990	195 610	48 540	244 150
1991	202 836	53 790	256 626
1992	184 285	37 150	221 435
1993	189 995	35 540	225 535
1994	196 844	42 280	239 124
1995	208 972	43 930	252 902
1996	200 000	55 070	255 070

① 原书中数据即如此。——译者注

续表

年份	进口食品价值 （百万美元）	本地产品价值 （百万美元）	总计 （百万美元）
1997	250 000	50 007	300 007
1998	300 000	47 953	347 953
1999	326 360	39 515	365 875
2000	358 530	46 933	405 463
2001	346 200	54 803	401 003
2002	360 750	50 844	411 594
2003	361 980	39 695	401 675
2004	381 480	29 596	411 076
2005	415 940	63 233	479 173
2006	466 630	61 941	528 571
2007	502 920	61 839	564 759
2008	521 560	67 830	589 390
2009	509 660	130 483	640 143
2010	520 330	137 074	657 404
2011	553 040	资料暂缺	资料暂缺

巴哈马经济的开放性让食品批发商、零售商受益,巴哈马对食品进口依赖性很强,这就使得他们有很大的盈利空间,从而导致巴哈马生活成本很高。

巴哈马农业部在开发旅游资源方面并不成功,这些资源生产者通过直接或间接方式都可以获得。高质量的农产品供应尚未实现,许多旅馆经营者、零售商不愿割裂与海外供应商的联系。家禽养殖业已经善于利用旅游资源,而其他装配、生产及手工制品等轻工业还在适应这一挑战。

总体而言,旅游业、境外金融、土地开发及建筑行业产生了巨大的利润,巴哈马因此得以从国外购买大量的食品原材料。食品安全问题还没有突出到政府将其列为重要议题的程度。

随着美洲自由贸易区协定成为西半球最为重要的行为准则,巴哈马农业部门也将承担新型责任。

挑 战

下一个千年,像巴哈马这样的小型经济体所面临的挑战主要根源于这些经济体的组织结构及其重要部门在社会发展中发挥的历史作用。

巴哈马的经验证明，一个小型经济体可以和相邻的世界上最大和最富有的经济体共同存在、共同繁荣。尽管一些与它类似的本地区以及西半球地区的经济体经济不稳且政治动荡，巴哈马却保持了其自身的身份。

巴哈马的发展道路一直是政治稳定条件下成功转型的一个案例。1950年前，巴哈马一直依靠农业来赚取外汇，为一群从奴隶制解放出来仅仅百年的人提供了大量就业机会。

20世纪50年代，巴哈马已经具备了将经济转变为第二次世界大战后富有竞争力的类型的基础。巴哈马并没有像欧洲那样得到有大量资金注入的美国马歇尔计划等援助以实现经济现代化。

只经过很少的调整，巴哈马经济在过去约半个世纪的时间里走向了成熟。巴哈马模式已渐趋成功，同类型的加勒比国家尤其是加勒比共同体国家开始采用它的模式。

据加勒比发展银行报告，除了圭亚那、特立尼达和多巴哥，加勒比英语为母语的国家的主要外汇来源是旅游业，金融服务业的重要性也日益增长。

独立后阶段，大部分加勒比国家试图实行传统的经济多样化战略，目的是将农业部门的人力转移到轻工业生产等行业中，或者扩大牙买加、圭亚那的铝土矿及特立尼达和多巴哥的石油等行业。那些没有工业基础的国家不得不选择走旅游路线。多米尼加和圣卢西亚的香蕉经济仍然处于边缘地位。

1983年，巴哈马加入了加勒比共同体，却未加入共同体的共同市场和其他贸易有关的方面。十多年来，巴哈马提高了在加勒比共同体的影响力。

由于《欧盟洛美公约》和《美国加勒比倡议》以及美国支持的《美洲自由贸易区》(FTAA)的实施，加勒比共同体的各政府首脑达成了一致的谈判政策。

巴哈马和其他加勒比共同体国家这样的小型经济体面临这样的问题：这些经济体能够在以贸易集团为准则及WTO规则被接受的全球环境中运行吗？而WTO是由富裕的发达国家创建的组织，关切的利益要比这些小型经济体重要得多。

全球化世界新秩序条件下，巴哈马面临的挑战是构建经济的战略部门以应对目前的信息时代。

45年前，巴哈马经济帮助巴哈马人民战胜殖民主义，准备争取独立，在20世纪的剩余时间里维持几代人的生活。这种新的世界秩序蕴含着未知的挑战。

巴哈马同大多数加勒比国家（加勒比共同体和法国、荷兰、英国和美国的附属国）一样，面临着巨额的食品进口的账单。这根源于该地区旅游业的发展。此外，加勒比地区像多米诺骨牌般纷纷引进美国快餐连锁店，如麦当劳、温迪、汉堡王和比萨饼店，饮食美国化，这也构成了一项因素。此外，还有观点认为进口食品比种植粮食作物更合算。这些因素导致整个农业的下滑。

　　该地区现已成为一个食品短缺的区域。政府在国际组织（如联合国粮农组织和美洲农业合作研究所）、集团（如欧盟的非洲、加勒比与太平洋国家）及金融机构（如世界银行、基金会与美洲开发银行）的帮助下，一直在制定食品安全方案，号召将更多投资用于食品生产。

　　2007年，食品进口的账单超过5亿美元。以目前的趋势继续下去，到2013年或者2014年，凯布尔海滩巴哈马项目完成后，食品进口的账单将飙升到10亿美元。这种情况并不符合巴哈马的最佳利益。食品进口将消耗巴哈马的外汇储备，成千上万的农业岗位将被外包，经济将因此面临损失。

　　旅游业加速了食品进口，饮食变化也使整个格局恶化。

第 8 章 »

农业之未来

巴哈马农业部门现在重新界定其成长和发展,同时在努力确定一项农耕技术,该技术将有效地激发该部门粮食生产的全部潜力。政策制定者和农民必须认识到的是,可耕作技术应用不当将损害构成巴哈马的脆弱的自然资源。

巴哈马的经济经历了高峰和低谷,一方面,它曾经遭受到破坏,曾经经历海盗行为、封锁和朗姆酒、毒品走私活动,另一方面,它也受益于旅游业、银行业和建筑业。但农业一直是政府政策回归的领域。

为了建成经济必不可少而又可靠的部门,农业必须充分商业化,获得科学界的支撑,并由能力突出、坚定的企业家管理。

为此,必须解决巴哈马农民、农场劳动力及环境三方面的问题。

巴哈马农民

巴哈马农民是巴哈马最具适应能力的商业人群之一。他们的工作环境每年都要受到飓风的威胁。在地方市场中,进口食品比国产食品更受欢迎。一些细化的部门处于价格监管之下。保险要么费用太高,要么不存在。他们面临高昂的移民农场工人工作许可费以及高昂的投入成本。他们的产品的价格也跟不上通货膨胀的水平。然而他们继续在土地上劳作,饲养牲畜,供养家庭。

巴哈马各地都能看到依靠土地设法谋生的个体农户。他们大多依靠着祖辈传下来的劳作技术,有些人通过采用新型农牧技术改进了这些技术,还有些人则运用了基于对其他地方的科学调查产生的新科技。

虽说过去矮林群岛在农业方面更有发展前景,然而松树群岛如今则具备形成农业体系的能力,这让巴哈马在世界市场上具有竞争力。

移民是导致农业模式变化的另一因素。在具有陆地的国家，人群从农村地区迁往城市。在巴哈马，人们已从家庭群岛迁往自由港、拿骚的城市中心地带。

这一迁移造成了农业人口的下降，农业人口从 1978 年的 4 246 人下降到 1994 年的 1 780 人，下降了 58%。（1978/1994 年数据由统计部提供）

图 8.1 从事农业劳作的妇女：农业推广员奥德利·库珀女士与农妇在北安德鲁斯农场的情景。

巴哈马农民也在老龄化。1976 年平均年龄为 55 岁，到 1994 年，上升到 59 岁。1990 年的全国人口普查显示平均年龄为 23.6 岁，而家庭群岛年龄为 34.5 岁。巴哈马的农业人口主力军为高龄人口。

教育方面，小学阶段教育普及率最高。1994 年 1 780 名农民中受过小学教育，比例达到了 74%。

农民数量下降了（1978—1994 年下降了 58%），农民平均年龄为 59 岁，农民只接受过初等教育，这些背景让巴哈马农业的前途显得暗淡。

20 世纪 90 年代余下阶段和 21 世纪巴哈马农业面临的主要问题在于，农业是否能够吸引新的、年轻的、文化程度高的男女人才进入农业综合企业。这方面的成功需要公共、私立部门的全力支持与合作。

巴哈马全国年度食品账单约 3 亿美元，当地农民还满足不了这一需求的 20%。由于气候条件的原因，加上同美国和加拿大大市场相近，水果、蔬菜的可持续出口营销计划发展前景广阔。

通过针对这些机遇对巴哈马农业进行调整，农业作为一种职业对于知识青年的吸引力将会提升。

表 8.1　农业劳动力

年份	农业劳动力	占总劳动力的百分比
1970	3 099	4.4
1973	3 320	4.2
1975	3 797	4.5
1978	5 561	6.0
1994	6 435	5.0
1996	6 445	5
1998	5 075	4
2000	统计年份资料缺	
2005	5 590	4
2010	统计年份资料缺	
2011	6 040	4

农场劳动力

巴哈马农业的一个突出特点在于巴哈马没有经历过种植园制。

种植园农业不得不依靠奴隶、契约工人或其他廉价的人力完成。回顾北部邻国（美国南部）、南部邻国（海地、古巴）以及牙买加、巴巴多斯、特立尼达和多巴哥等加勒比国家种植园农业的社会经济意义时，会发现作为非洲人后裔的巴哈马人的经历与他们的邻居有所不同。

奴隶劳动力对种植业的财政生存至关重要。1838年随着奴隶制的废除，原来的奴隶变成了自给农民、雇农或佃农，他们在北伊鲁萨拉公有土地上、在伊克祖马斯和巴哈马其他地方工作。

根据贝西·戴维森（1992）的描述，摆脱奴隶身份的非洲人和"二度被俘虏者"被作为俘虏装船运往美国或加勒比地区当奴隶。他们被英国海军抓获，之后被英国海军释放，这些人当然也不想当农场工人。其中一些可能成了拿骚格朗特镇和福克斯山的农民，不过干的却绝非苦力工作。

这些人被吸引到了贸易行业中，他们的后代最终成了各行各业的专业人士——教师、牧师、医生、律师和部长。他们住在南部地区新普罗维登斯的格朗特镇和贝恩镇，也有一些住在东部的福克斯山和自由镇。值得注意的是，20世纪五六十年代，大批巴哈马男子作为农场工人被招募到美国，即使一些美国的离岸农业公司也开始在松树群岛上大面积种植蔬菜。

农业劳动力的数量问题一直是巴哈马农业的一个限制性因素,尤其在大规模机械化农业方面。由于不能吸引巴哈马劳动力从事农业工作,如需要弯腰劳动的收割工、采集工,20世纪50年代后期到60年代,海地人大规模非法移民到巴哈马。大批的人在阿巴克斯和伊鲁萨拉北部地区定居,从事农场劳动。据估计,20世纪80年代这些移民多达4万人,实际上真实数字约为2.5万人。

农民和大型离岸公司发现海地的劳动者可靠、勤劳,工作效率高。为了证明他们的生产能力,巴哈马柑橘种植者进行了一项实验,将四名巴哈马柚子采摘工放在四个不同的地点,并将一名海地工人放在另一个地点。一天工作结束以后,发现海地的那名采摘工采摘的量比四名巴哈马工人的总量还要多。

巴哈马历届政府都意识到对非巴哈马籍农业劳动力的需求,并与农业部门合作,以较低的速率颁发工作许可证。

一些人认为商品化农业不能完全依赖于用外来的人力填补农业劳动力需求。尽管如此,不论这些工人合法不合法,大型小型农业生产都予以雇佣。新普罗维登斯、大巴哈马、阿巴克斯以及北伊鲁萨拉都有这样的情形。巴哈马东南部的农民却并不极度依赖这些外来农工。长岛的农民也以不雇佣海地劳工著称。

有人认为,巴哈马劳动力成本昂贵,供不应求,效率低下,北安德鲁斯、阿巴克斯和大巴哈马大型农业企业因此无法有效运作或参与全球市场竞争。这些岛屿上的大部分农场劳动力往往是女性,因为男性倾向于在机械领域工作。

人力资源短缺源于劳动力从本地而非全国征募这一事实。维护巴哈马劳工的人声称由于农业不发达这一事实,巴哈马劳工并不如外籍劳工效率高,而这就导致了从其他地方招工的情况。

住房

在过去,大型外国农业实体已明白农业劳动者住房问题必须解决。出现的问题不是提供住房方面的问题,而是政府能够接受的住房成本和类型问题。

过去有过这样的例子,为外国劳工提供的房屋被认为不合标准。为劳工们提供达标的经济适用房这件事是能够做到的。一般情况下,由于全国范围内劳动力充足,国外公司不会反对这个提议。如果农业部门想要吸收国内的一些失业者,提供住房至关重要。而事实上,大多数家庭岛社区的住房供应短缺,这就给这方面问题的解决蒙上了一层阴影。

培训

人力的培训至关重要,尤其是农业劳动力将不得不从拿骚和自由港的市中心地区获得。

在许多情况下，外国企业会将在巴哈马工作的工作经验不足的巴哈马工人同外国工人进行比较，尤其是美国的农场工人。这显然有失公平，因为外国合同农场工人与巴哈马本国工人的动机是不同的，同时这也忽略了支撑美国生产的优越的基础建设。

如果住房以及培训项目合适，巴哈马将能够满足农业方面的劳动力需求。外国公司可通过投资巴哈马人力资源提供这方面的协助，并在家庭岛住房以及社会服务设施方面提供资金援助。

农业生产车间的生产力问题极具重要性。养殖业，尤其是当地鸡肉的加工生产，在与美国同行业加工生产的对比方面做得非常出色。

美国家禽加工专家指出，要提高生产力，员工必须首先树立自豪、自尊与专注的职业道德。一旦具备这些前提条件，工作方面的知识、具体工作的培训及工厂组织方面就会发挥作用。之后公司就能够培养工作出色的职员，其工作表现也将易于衡量。

衡量生产线生产效率的方式之一是计算每人每小时所加工的家禽磅数。通过这种方式，格拉德斯通农场提高了生产力，节约了资金，在同等关税条件下，与美国同行业相比，成本更具优势。

最大的不足是旷工问题。美国行业标准为8%，格拉德斯通年均为13%。报酬支付日之后数据上升到20%，阴雨天气则上升到40%。

然而，巴哈马劳动力可以做到工作更有成效，做到在生产率水平方面与任何发达国家相比也毫不逊色，但培训及动力方面必须达到一定条件。

巴哈马农业有望提高就业率。当前，劳动力主要集中在生产领域。食品加工、出口营销、农业设备维护以及禽类生产方面仍有待发展。有了培训、住房以及新就业机会，失业将极大减少。

环　境

农民处于环境和发展问题的前沿。由于农民每天不断跟环境打交道，为了对农民有帮助，必须将庄稼、牲畜、家禽养殖各方面对环境有影响的问题纳入环境保护的范畴。

虽然巴哈马还不是世界粮食的主要供应商，但多年来，它已经具备了特定的食品生产、畜牧养殖方面的能力。巴哈马的农民，同世界各地的农民一样，有责任维持农业的可持续发展。

促进农业可持续发展的关键因素在于稳定的土地使用权、农业原料的安全使用以及新型农业技术的持续研究,这些都要依靠生物控制以及更好的农场实地管理。

环境方面的担忧早在1671年就已提出,当时巴西木被认为受到了过度砍伐的威胁。此后担忧非但没有减少,反而加重了。巴哈马国家信托组织是国家环境问题方面的主要领导部门,在提醒公众与政府关注环境问题及探索解决环境措施方面富有经验。

阿拉瓦克人居住的环境在欧洲人看来相当不错,哥伦布对种类丰富的本土鸟类及陆地哺乳动物物种印象深刻。令人惋惜的是,两类物种都濒临灭绝的境地。

几类仓鸮已经灭绝,包括大仓鸮、大食草龟及岩鬣蜥。阻止诸如此类物种的灭绝是巴哈马面临的任务之一。

多年来巴哈马议会通过了这方面的法案。鸟类及动植物保护方面的法案(成文法)包括:

(1)第19条惩罚法令(第229章),为防止动物受暴力恶劣对待提供保护。

(2)野生鸟类保护法案。

(3)野生动物保护法案。

(4)植物保护法案。

(5)渔业资源法案(司法与保护)。

(6)巴哈马国家信托法案。

除巴哈马国家信托法案外,巴哈马政府与巴哈马信托组织有长期租约,而这对国家公园、伊克祖马斯珊瑚礁与海洋公园、茵那瓜国家公园(保护火烈鸟)及阿巴科国家公园(保护巴哈马鹦鹉)的设立产生了影响。

巴哈马农业部的农业专家也对环境问题提出了忧虑,并列举了一些农业问题,例如:

稳定土地使用权限

农民在巴哈马处于弱势地位,他们无法获得经营农业的土地所有权。农用土地通常分为三大类:公用土地、世袭地产及公有土地。

公用土地和世袭地产起源于封建奴隶制。利用分配的公用土地,农民可以获得金融部门并不视为抵押担保品的租约。

为保证农民正常从事农业生产，需要明确法律权利。在巴哈马，这已经被农业社区提出来了，且已影响了对农业的投资。稳定的土地使用权可以为巴哈马农业实现高产、自然资源的可持续利用及可独立发展的农业社区的维持与发展提供保障。

最近已经推出一项为因建设防风林而让出自己在森林中部分土地的农民提供低利息租约的举措，他们保护了靠近森林保护区、湿地的无农药缓冲地带。

像松树群岛、矮林群岛地区大面积不加区分的土地清理将不会再被容忍。问题在于这方面的计划能否实施。

生物科技与巴哈马农业

生物科技加速了遗传学过程，而这一过程早在固定农业开始时期就已经开始了。农民自那时起就在选择和培育农作物和牲畜产效方面有所实践。

巴哈马农作物科学家认为"由于种植广泛，诸如木薯、玉米、豌豆、甘薯和豆类等口粮作物存在着基因多样性"。因此，必须努力去调查和保护本国的粮食作物，避免仅关注进口粮食作物。

土壤

巴哈马《土地资源研究》将本国土地资源定性为"年轻、贫瘠、水分流失与养分缺乏"。土壤中养分的耗尽是巴哈马停止棉花种植的主要原因。大多土壤源自鲕状石灰岩，碱性大。然而，也有些岛屿土壤含有红土黑土。近岸地区还含有白土（沙土）等土质。

水资源

有些情况下，淡水层处在离地表几英尺以下的位置，含水层可能会受到农事肥料滤除物、杀虫剂及动物排泄物的污染。

环境与自然资源管理

从可持续的角度看，环境与自然资源管理是巴哈马未来发展、农业发展方面的首要任务，也是政府、农民组织和农业综合企业方面政策制定者们规划与决策过程的重要组成部分。

公共管理

巴哈马的公共管理根植于英国殖民体系。该体系以中央集权为特征，权力通过伦敦白厅的官僚政治传播。它最初存在于殖民局,最终并入外事与联邦办公厅。

政策、法规和条例被系统地制定出来,以规范非洲、亚洲和加勒比的殖民地的管理体系。殖民地官员可以从一个殖民地调动至另一殖民地,在履行行政职责时没有困难。

在巴哈马,这一点非常明显。殖民地获得独立后,许多高级殖民地行政人员在巴哈马完成了作为常任部长和董事会成员的职业生涯。

巴哈马设计出了一套复杂的通讯存档系统。其中典型的有会议纪要、备忘录、议会文件、绿白皮书,并用不同印章对殖民服务部的等级进行登记区分。这类存档与法律体系需要文化程度高、受到严格管制的官员体系。

这套公共管理的设计旨在为帝国服务,在帝国内最初通过海路由海军、商船管理其全球各地的领土。随着交通手段的发展,其他机制也开始实行。然而,纸张的使用在殖民体系的行政管理当中起着根本性的作用。

1973 年巴哈马获得独立后,巴哈马政府处于这一状况中。政府高度中央集权化,导致大量汇编的文件收入存档系统中。

随着现代化信息科技的来临,靠纸张进行通信的高度集权化的公共管理已经过时。伴随着电脑、传真机、电子邮件、卫星传播及网络等方式,1973 年 7 月 10 日巴哈马获得独立后,新型通信手段产生了。

这些新型通信工具需要不同于殖民时期的公共管理部门以及新型行政人员、管理人员或专家以使体系正常运转。

巴哈马在 21 世纪应避免以拿骚为中心的公共管理方式。巴哈马作为群岛国家,应当采取使分权更为有效的手段,以使国家最大化地利用人力、有形资源发展经济。这对巴哈马至关重要。这不仅能使巴哈马利用临近北美市场的优势,而且能发挥作为来往欧洲、非洲、远东、中南美及加勒比的全球跨地域航运的重要中转站方面的作用。

由于拥有高度发达的道路基础设施,家族岛以及城市电气化,数字通讯与公立以及私立中等、高等教育机构方面的基础,加上文化程度高、训练有素的人力资源,巴哈马已经做好在 21 世纪经济可持续发展的准备。

在像巴哈马这样的国家,政府与经济关联很深,公共管理方面的结构与复杂性将在决定经济发展速率、步伐方面发挥决定性作用。因此,为使国家在当前全球环境快速变化的条件下展现竞争力,公共管理方面必须进行改革。

自由贸易区的益处

自由贸易区的创建是基于这样一个假设，即通过取消贸易畸形发展、关税和其他贸易壁垒，使市场有效配置资源。该地区及半球政府一直在制造壁垒，旨在为本国生产者与其他国外竞争者竞争提供不公平的优势。例如，这样的壁垒将通过对进口货物施加关税，使它们与本国产品比较时价格更为昂贵。其他贸易畸形发展的例子包括使用不必要的许可证和注册要求，以给货物进口制造障碍。支持自由贸易的观点认为，通过消除贸易壁垒，社会将受益，因为消费者能够以更低的价格选择更广泛的产品。这样政府也将受益，因为它可以从效率低及靠奖励和补助金支撑的企业中撤出补贴，并在经济领域的其他部门分配这些资源。

虽然从理论上看，每个人都希望在自由贸易条件下有更好的发展，但仍有国家因为其规模、发展水平及制度所限，不能享受自由贸易区的益处。从现实角度讲，不能期望像海地或圭亚那这种该半球最为穷困的国家能够在美洲自由贸易区条件下做出像加拿大或美国等发达国家同等水平的承诺。难道我们能期待一个像圭亚那那样每一美元中有 75 美分用于偿债的国家立即减少或消除关税吗？来自关税的收入不只是偿还债务等的关键，而且在提供必要的社会服务方面同样重要。这些都是在自由贸易区的背景下必须解决的问题。

考虑到巴哈马地区以及所在半球多元化的规模、发展以及体制能力方面的问题，为解决小型以及欠发达国家的问题，美洲自由贸易区小型经济体工作组成立了。

除了经济结构不利于这些小型、欠发达经济体利用协议所带来的优势外，同样还有体制方面的不足。自由贸易协定对知识产权进行保护，并立法防止反竞争行为的出现。所有这一切都需要政府进行立法方面的改革。

建立自由贸易区的根本初衷是为了通过取消关税和其他贸易壁垒提高总体效率水平。然而，鉴于多样性、规模和发展水平，有些国家不可能在同一时间作出同样水平的承诺。

21 世纪的农业

像巴哈马这样的小经济体，将不得不与工业化国家一起在一个以法律规则为基础并具有强制性的体系中发挥作用。实现这一目的的手段将是 WTO，其独特的功能将使经济发展更具预测性。巴哈马最终会加入其中的美洲自由贸易区，遵守 WTO 规则。

这就是巴哈马农业部门将被迫面对的竞争经济环境。生产、土地、劳动力和资本这些因素是传统经济的特征,将不得不包含机械化、生物技术、交通运输和信息技术等方面的转变。这些都是将决定农业体系竞争力的因素。

全球化带来了不受地域限制的知识型世界经济。信息技术不受任何地区或国家的约束,是可以移动的,在任何地方都可以创造出来。另一方面,农业只有将转型的因素与技术、教育和知识(生产的新手段)结合起来方能取得成功,而这些正是发达的、信息驱动的全球经济所必需的。

这将使小规模农场主处于极大的劣势中。在巴哈马,农业社区由只受过最基本的教育的男女组成。由于全球范围内都在发生转型,巴哈马普通农民将很难适应正在发生的技术进步。从本质上讲,技术正在改变生产的方式。

另一方面,巴哈马农业综合企业如果在各方面转型则可以生存下来。运营将极具竞争性,如果从整个行业而非个别企业的角度来解决问题则可以实现共存。在这个框架内可以避免不必要的重复工作、人力和设备,尤其是运输,它对群岛国家极为重要。

在西半球,美洲自由贸易区是推动农业综合企业的重要手段,而 WTO 已成为全球的管理者。在美洲自由贸易区建设过程中,农业受到格外重视,这既是有优先性的,也是与众不同的。

这一地位源于几个因素:农业的本质特征,农业涉及的风险,农业对于小型经济体国家的重要性以及农业的战略重要性,即食品安全。在此背景条件下,农业特别受到重视。传统农业创新推动了农业技术现代化及口粮农业向市场农业的转变。即将出现的问题是这一特殊待遇的停止期限。

这些制约因素将决定 21 世纪美洲自由贸易区/WTO 框架下的农业发展导向:

(1)关税将取代配额及其他市场准入障碍。

(2)国内支持将定量化并逐步减少。

(3)出口补贴将减少。

(4)限制贸易的卫生、安全监管将得到控制。

(5)依赖于廉价补贴食品的发展中国家将继续得到援助。

美洲国家贸易组织的一份文件曾对上述新举措进行综述:

> "这个问题的绝对答案在于,所有国家,不论大小,受益于贸易自由化,而小国受益较之于大国要多,原因可从国际贸易理论与比较优势论中找到。

　　　"小国通过指标和开放加强了生产集中度和贸易专业化。贸易的开放使小型经济体可以在一些生产、服务领域从事专业化运作，通过克服由于小型经济体国内市场较小而造成的规模经济的局限性，从而获得更大裨益。专业化生产扩大化将会从贸易中受益，而小国受益程度将比大国更大。"

结　语

　　巴哈马的农业系统得到了技术推广、项目的支持，实现了增长和发展，成为成功的商业部门，推动了国民经济的发展。农业的最新发展，使当地的粮食生产商得以推动当地一些季节性农事生产种植的农产品的自给自足。

　　推动农业发展的政策包括主要农业区的农业部派出机构的设立，以及构成新鲜水果蔬菜市场销售基础设施的重要元素的包装车间的建立。

　　土地清理计划的扩展使新的土地投入生产，尤其是在东南岛屿，那里鼓励生产不易腐烂农作物，如木豆和辣椒。松树群岛的出口销售项目也得到了发展。

　　北安德鲁斯岛巴哈马农业研究、培训和开发项目与新普罗维登斯的中心农业站的研究工作提供了这方面的信息，这些信息通过家庭群岛的推广官员传递到农民那里。同时，作物和牲畜生产、动物卫生、市场营销和植物保护专家组的建立提供了重要的技术支持。此外，各级技术人员收到了短期和中期培训班在职奖。

　　农民的技能也通过社区的户外实习日和推广会议得到升级。那个概述了当地 1974—1996 年农产品价值的表格显示了当地农场生产长达 21 年的产值。

　　巴哈马有可能成为加勒比地区的新鲜水果和蔬菜的主要生产国，并可能成为面向美国、欧洲和远东地区的主要出口国。随着北美自由贸易协定（NAFTA）在西半球即将实施，农业部门将能够帮助巴哈马成为自由贸易舞台上一个重要的成员。

第 9 章 »

展望：全球、国家与地区问题交织

2003 年，我被任命为巴哈马驻位于意大利罗马的粮农组织大使。作为粮农组织大使，我得以从全球视野看待农业。作为联合国的一个专门机构，粮农组织涉及世界粮食生产的方方面面。

除粮农组织外，联合国还有另外两家粮食组织：国际农业发展基金会和世界粮食计划署。国际农业发展基金会为发展中国家农业发展项目提供资金。世界粮食计划署则专向由于各种原因陷入危机的国家提供人道主义援助，如遭受饥荒、干旱、内乱、自然灾害的国家。巴哈马已成为国际农业发展基金会的会员国。在罗马，人们可以从多层面看到全球范围内粮食的落实情况。

2004 年及 2005 年，加勒比农业部部长论坛及美洲农业合作研究所（即促进全美农业发展及农业福利的专门机构）认为热带农业研究与高等教育中心董事会应该有加勒比的代表。我在该中心董事会任主任三年就是这项政策实施的体现。

热带农业研究与高等教育中心是一家重要的农业研究生学校和研究中心。它位于哥斯达黎加的图里阿尔瓦，为所有中美及拉丁美洲国家开展研究项目。中心由中美洲成员国、美洲农业合作研究所及全球捐赠团体提供资金支持。作为董事会成员，我有幸到成员国家参观持续进行的研究项目，对拉丁美洲粮食生产情况有了清晰的了解。此外，我还能够与资金捐助者就资助问题进行交流，尤其在全球粮食生产计划方面。

尽管热带农业研究与高等教育中心的职权范围包括加勒比，然而多米尼加是与之关系紧密的唯一加勒比国家。我任职期间，为推动机构间合作，曾采取增加加勒比农业研究发展中心参与度的举措。

图 9.1　特立尼达和多巴哥农贸部 1995 年 7 月 5 日在西班牙港的展览。
文森·穆尔博士（该部兽医）同阿灵顿·切尼博士（现任加勒比农业研
究发展机构执行主任）、本书作者一起。

　　1995 年，WTO 成立。该半球国家除巴哈马外，均加入了该组织。在我看来，
这是一个错误，原因在于非成员身份将阻碍国家关键部门的经济增长，即粮食
生产、轻工业及制造业。WTO 的重要组成部分是《农业协定》，为全球粮食贸易
设定了规则条例。

　　在推动粮食生产更具竞争力、创新性以及农业科技化方面巴哈马农业综合
企业以及小规模农场主已经在发展进程中处于落后位置。

　　贸易自由化正推动 WTO 前行，《农业协定》是实现这一目标的手段。在该
半球，贸易自由化已经通过提出的美洲自由贸易区显示出来。从地方角度说，按
照欧盟的划分，巴哈马与其他加勒比共同体国家被划分为非洲、加勒比及太平
洋（ACP）国家。欧盟正寻求让 ACP 国家开放市场，ACP 国家与欧盟签订的一系
列协议、举行的多次会议（雅温得协议、洛美会议以及科托努协定）就是这方面
的表现。

　　就像由美国赞助的美洲自由贸易区一样，欧盟发起《经济伙伴协议》，旨在
在欧盟与 ACP 国家之间创造自由贸易区。

　　早在 1957 年，欧盟就开始了一项经济发展政策，旨在通过欧洲发展基金组
织援助约 31 个先前的殖民地。通过欧洲发展基金组织的努力，过去 50 年里发
展基金已进入 ACP 国家。就巴哈马而言，欧洲发展基金组织为其家庭群岛地区
大量的基础设施建设提供了资金。

　　这项欧盟与 ACP 国家之间的协定已成为一个贸易集团化组织，其中 ACP

国家国获得特殊商品的特惠待遇，例如出口至欧盟的香蕉。由于特惠待遇导致不公平竞争，拉美国家向 WTO 提出上诉。WTO 为维护拉美国家利益宣布特惠待遇不合法，这导致许多 ACP 国家农业出现严重经济问题与混乱。在加勒比共同体，加勒比东部向风群岛香蕉业受到毁灭性打击。圣卢西亚成千上万的小农场主找不到香蕉出口市场的门路。

巴哈马必须认识到这一现实，即贸易自由化必须进行，而粮食生产只能通过提高竞争力实现。全球贸易议程由 WTO 的《农业协定》、美洲自由贸易区及《经济伙伴协议》规定。贸易在维持国家粮食生产经济可行性方面起到了推动作用。

全球粮食计划与贸易受到粮农组织以及世界银行、国际农业发展基金会及国际农业研究磋商组织等其他几个机构很大影响。

全球粮食生产计划影响了地区、国家政策。世界银行、国际农业发展基金会、欧洲发展基金会及资助方等为 ACP 这样的组织在发展中国家实施这些政策提供了资金。如果一个国家想要从该计划中受益，就必须成为机制的一部分。由于并未完全融入这些地区性集团，巴哈马并未从中受益。

国际农业发展基金会、欧洲发展基金会提供给 ACP 国家的资金将通过加勒比共同体调拨。国际农业研究磋商组织通过加勒比农业研究发展中心普及研究成果、确定研究项目。粮农组织与美洲农业合作研究所将加勒比认定为次级区域。从国家层面上，他们分别派出了国家代表。

在 21 世纪的关键时期，巴哈马必须更多地参与到全球议程当中。本章将讨论四个主题方面的问题。

粮食中的地缘政治

我们生活在全球化的时代，也许这个时代最突出的特点就是贸易。国际贸易是重要的因素。全球市场交易量最大的五项商品当中就有两项为粮食产品。在此背景下，粮食也应纳入地缘政治的框架之中。

作为人类，我们认为粮食供应是理所当然的。我们不了解饥荒，对粮食配给也没有概念。我们主要的食品来源是超市、快餐店。我们关心的主要问题不是供应。我们大多数人关心的是价格，以及能否通过从迈阿密进口节约费用。

然而，我们所面临的困境在于很少有人懂得或关注实现保证食品供应所需要的工作。此外，关于国家粮食战略、视野是否与粮食地缘政治接轨的问题几乎无人考虑。

地缘政治问题影响粮食

世界正在经历巨大变化，这些变化影响着粮食及其生产、供应及出口。此外，当新的因素产生影响时，这些变化是变革性的。因素包括我们地区及巴哈马气候变化、能源成本、人口增长、性别与青年发展、土地、移民（合法或非法）、都市主义、缺水、生物能源、生物多样性、农业衰退以及服务业增长等。

此外，随着巴西、印度、中国发展成为经济原动力，世界经济重新排序，这三个国家的中产阶级逐步扩大并与美国人、欧洲人、加拿大人及日本人在多种粮食产品方面开展竞争。实际上，中国与印度正越来越接近消费型国家，每年使数以百万计的人脱贫。

除上述因素外，还有实力关系方面的考量，正是这一因素奠定了全球粮食计划，推动着政策的制定。

地缘政治机构

三大实力派全球机构分别为粮农组织、WTO及世界银行。这三家机构决定了全球粮食计划。

粮农组织被定义为联合国专门监管世界农业与粮食的机构，主要目标是消除全球饥荒。与总部位于罗马的粮农组织密切合作的还有另外两家机构，一家是世界粮食计划署，主管粮食短缺、自然灾害情况下的粮食分配并提供人道主义援助。另一家为国际农业开发基金会，主要为粮食生产及农业扶贫项目提供资金援助。

WTO为国际粮食贸易制定规则条例。该组织成立于1994年，就在这一年，其前身关贸总协定解体。

1986年9月在乌拉圭举行的关税协定会议上，里根政府时期的农业部部长约翰·布洛克做了如下陈述：

> "发展中国家应该自给自足的观念是不合潮流的旧时代思想。他们最好通过依靠美国农产品确保粮食安全，这不仅可取，而且大多情况下成本也更低。"

布洛克的发言正式宣告了粮食自给自足的观念已不合时宜，因为它带来了"廉价粮食"时代。许多国家都支持这种观点。巴哈马就是其中之一。而正是这种"廉价粮食"观念阻碍了巴哈马、海地、大多数加勒比国家以及撒哈拉以南的非洲国家的粮食生产。我们的政府跟很多其他国家一样，持进口粮食要比自己种植更经济的态度。

这一理念为国际货币基金组织和世界银行所推行。在巴哈马，国际货币基金组织在 90 年代早期就建议巴哈马政府优化关税结构。在此次调整当中，关税被削减，对格拉德斯通农场、索耶粮产、埃玻利父子尤其是小型农场等农业综合企业产生了不利影响。

2010 年 3 月，克林顿总统因布洛克 24 年前倡导的"廉价粮食"政策向海地道歉。他明确提到数十年来从美国进口的"廉价粮食"，尤其是大米，破坏了当地农业，致使海地、巴哈马以及加勒比其他地区的粮食动荡，丧失自给自足的能力。20 世纪 90 年代中期，克林顿政府支持海地等国家大幅降低关税，导致这些国家易于接受美国的粮食进口。在巴哈马，关税减低到了 32% 以下。欧洲农业进口关税达到了 30%，日本则达到 59%。

1994 年 WTO 成立之时，巴哈马是它所在的半球中唯一一个没有选择申请加入的国家。去年，也即 15 年后，巴哈马政府决定加入，它也比该地区其他国家加入的时间要晚 15 年。

准备加入 WTO 对于我们而言是严峻的任务。粮食贸易方面由 WTO《农业协定》管制，主要由三方面构成：市场准入、国内支持以及出口补贴。《农业协定》被发展中国家视为偏向美国、欧盟、日本等发达国家，因此遭到发展中国家的反对。《农业协定》一个重要的方面在于卫生与植物检疫方面的措施，涉及粮食安全、动物以及植物健康。

加入 WTO 不是一件容易的事情，因为巴哈马在应用《农业协定》的专门知识及能力方面尚有欠缺。贸易专家在哪里？巴哈马的小规模农场主以及农业综合企业将面临严峻任务，不得不努力遵循《农业协定》。目前，在这个过渡阶段并没有援助粮食领域的举措。我们的粮食要达到标准，必须具备监管种植或加工的产品的基础设施，而制定标准的机构在哪里呢？

世界银行是拥有最终决定权的机构。作为全球性金融机构，它为发展中国家各类资本项目提供借款。世界银行与粮农组织赞助并领导了国际农业研究磋商组织，该组织对 15 家国际中心涉及的 100 个国家实行监管。国际农业研究磋商组织在为第三世界国家发展实用新型生产技术方面发挥了重要作用。例如，国际水稻研究所特意为发展中国家研发各类水稻就是这方面的体现。

粮食安全是现在的口号。操纵粮食地缘政治的人们已经背离了"廉价粮食"政策，开始实行粮食安全政策。

巴哈马缘何处于现在境地？

有效可行的国家粮食计划必须反映全球计划的重要组成部分。为了在贸易自由化的时代取得成功、发挥价值，像巴哈马这样的发展中国家不能在粮食生产这样的地缘政治上采取孤立主义政策。政府必须有大局观念，在可行的条件下，需要考量 WTO、粮农组织以及世界银行等主要全球组织所提出的全球日程，并将这些纳入国家地区计划之中。

巴哈马与多数加勒比国家一样，是粮食逆差或者说净进口国家，这就意味着巴哈马进口的粮食要多于国内生产的量。这就导致我们的群岛陷入了依赖于国际商品市场这一境地，因为它与稻米、玉米、肉类及咖啡等重要商品的供求息息相关。从这个角度说，巴哈马极易受到国际商品市场价格波动的影响。

2010 年，像巴哈马这样的粮食逆差国家粮食采购的支出为一万亿美元。粮食蕴藏着巨大的国际商机，能否取得粮食可以使一个国家繁荣，也可以摧毁一个国家。

世界可能正催生另一场粮食危机。1973 到 1974 年间，尤其是最近的 2007 到 2008 年间，国际商品市场价格骤涨。总体来讲，粮食价格受到恶劣天气、坏收成及减少了的粮食储备量的影响。2007 到 2008 年间正如 1973 到 1974 年间，原油价格是主要原因。

我们生活在工业化农业的时代，粮食生产主要依靠化石燃料。当原油价格上涨到每桶 140 美元时，粮食价格急剧上升导致附近的海地以及撒哈拉以南非洲等粮食缺乏地区发生了暴乱。

美洲农业合作研究所总干事办公室在 2011 年 2 月 3 日提交给拉丁美洲、加勒比农业部部长们的一项报告中指出：

> "拉丁美洲以及加勒比的粮食净进口的国家必须努力提高生产率……目前，世界市场不稳，谷类价格波动。对于目前情形对社会的影响，越来越多的人表示担忧。关于是否会出现新的单独发展或者重现 2007—2008 年危机，分析师莫衷一是。咖啡、可可、蔗糖等热带产品以及奶制品、肉类产品等的价格越来越高，这是那些粮食净进口国家面临的最严峻的挑战，而这些产品的价格在 2007—2008 年经济危机期间并未受到影响。"

粮食地缘政治问题是我们不能忽略的问题。从国家层面讲，进口主导的国家粮食计划将加深对外依赖，消耗外汇，我们必须决定是否继续推行这一政策。

当前,国家粮食消费账单超过了 5 亿美元,而且正在建设的巴哈马项目完工后开销总额可能增加到 7.5 亿美元。

另一条选择则是实行进口替代的政策,利用气候、创新科技以及高价值国内农产品市场,从 5 亿美元的国家粮食消费账单中创造成千上万的就业岗位,通过增加国内产量节省数百万美元的开支。这一政策将对国内粮食安全起到强化的作用。

饮食

严重依赖进口粮食已改变了巴哈马人的饮食结构。食品,尤其便利和快餐食品,使巴哈马的饮食结构倾向于美国化。这种转变始于 20 世纪的下半叶,大量妇女作为酒店工作人员加入劳动者队伍,母亲们走出家门走上工作岗位。与此同时,美式快餐连锁公司进入巴哈马。

如今,巴哈马成为欺骗性销售的受害者,我们饮食中含糖量及含盐量过高,生产时添加转化脂肪、过多的防腐剂及人工色素,人们健康出现危机,肥胖病、高血压、癌症等非传染性、代谢相关的疾病病例增加。每年心脏疾病导致几乎500 人死亡,致命癌症导致 300 人死亡,糖尿病并发症导致 200 人死亡。非传染性和代谢相关疾病现在每年导致约 1 000 人死亡。巴哈马饮食不周导致国内出现饮食健康问题。

有几个问题亟待解决。从整个国民角度讲,巴哈马人是决定维持完全依赖于粮食进口的现状还是寄希望于投资技术来增强我们的竞争力进而推进粮食生产呢？我们要鼓励新一代巴哈马人对快捷、方便、精加工和人工食品满意,而不是生产安全、营养、新鲜的本地食品吗？脱离现状需要新的政治思维,21 世纪巴哈马的粮食与生产需要采取新的举措。

当前,巴哈马粮食政治以满足粮食进口者、快餐以及酒店行业要求为根本。消费者不论男女,不论巴哈马人还是游客,都掌控在粮食进口者手中。

粮食地缘政治与新现实情况

粮食地缘政治为粮食创造了新的环境,尤其在粮食加工、销售及分配方面。

20 世纪见证了美国粮食工业对粮食的革新：超级快餐、高能量快餐、定制型方便食品以及甜性果汁饮料。快餐在巴哈马市场出现的态势迅猛,导致巴哈马出现灾难性健康危机,因为它带来肥胖病的流行。巴哈马以及该地区其他国家的政府并没有找到摆脱困境的方法。

旅游业主导经济的巴哈马以及加勒比其他国家的新型生活方式导致政府

转变了粮食政治的政策，从关注小规模农场主、当地生产转向满足粮食进口者、旅游业。巴哈马食品供应日益强调便利。因此，这些产品加工者控制了主要由这些新型美国食品品种构成的市场，原因在于巴哈马人已对新型美国食品品种产生依赖性。对便利食品需求的增加与已生育女性占劳动力多数这一事实有直接关系。有工作的女性在做饭方面花的时间越来越少，因为她们需要平衡家庭与工作单位的关系。最终结果是超过半数的日餐在外面制作，从快餐连锁店购买。不计其数的家庭对小吃、垃圾食品的消耗量很大。

巴哈马粮食政治不得不对巴哈马人饮食做出调整，对进口粮食类型实行引导。这个责任之前被忽略了，变成了由粮食进口者及快餐经营者自己看着办。这是 21 世纪的一个挑战。

日益上涨的粮食价格

粮价上涨成为人类共同面临的重大问题，引起了世界所有主要农业职能机构的注意。

粮农组织在一份报告中指出，到 2010 年 2 月份世界粮食价格已连续 8 个月上涨；根据联合国部门所设计的指数标准，除蔗糖外，所有被关注的商品价格也都上涨。联合国粮农组织警告说，2010—2011 年谷物类供求关系可能紧张。

联合国粮农组织在不同地区（6 月 14、15 日在加勒比的巴巴多斯）召开研讨会的目的就是对 2007—2008 年对食品价格危机的处理方式进行交流，并对粮农组织针对各国应对上涨的食品价格的指导性政策和项目性干预中所列出的应对行动的优劣之处加深了解。

联合国粮农组织副总干事何昌垂警告说："粮农组织认为国家审查其政策选择和避免做出恶化局势的决定至关重要。"在他看来，近期的粮食危机恶化了一些国家的国情，因为他们决定实行出口限制或制造"恐慌性抢购"。

粮农组织总干事强调，各国政府应关注或减轻粮食价格上涨对贫困人口的影响，并采取措施加大对农业的投资。

不仅如此，除了全球和地区的问题外，在半球范围内也有重要的关切。2011 年 10 月，美洲农业合作研究所将与哥斯达黎加政府一起召开一个半球范围内的会议以应对粮食价格上涨。该半球内所有农业部部长被敦促参加此次会议。

粮农组织指出多种因素共同导致了粮食价格上涨。其中有些因素是"气候变化导致的粮食减产，谷物等粮食储备史无前例的低水平状态，新兴国家（印度、俄罗斯、中国和巴西）对肉类和奶制品的高消耗，生物燃料生产需求的增加，更高的能源和运输成本，所有这些都导致了粮食价格的激涨"。

这种情况每天都出现，这源自对被做成玉米粉或玉米片供人类食用的玉米的竞争，以及对作为动物饲料或作为生物燃料乙醇以替代化石燃料的玉米的竞争。上述情况再加上燃料成本的不断上涨助推了巴哈马的运价（2011 年 6 月），例如每个集装箱每次出货每吨运费达 100 美元，上述因素已经影响到了粮食价格。加勒比已成为粮食匮乏区，需要依赖粮食进口维持生存。

巴哈马和该地区都处于这种状态中，因为政府被一种误导性观点所欺骗。该观点称有一种商品叫"廉价粮食"，可从很多大量补贴本国农业部门的国家获得。那些大量补贴本国农业部门的国家能够使本国农民和农业企业在世界市场上以很低的价格售卖粮食，价格是加勒比小规模农场主和刚起步的农业企业难以竞争的。这一直充当打开该区域市场的催化剂，最终导致该区域的农业不稳定和不具竞争力。

加勒比农业已成为"廉价粮食"政策的受害者。粮农组织一直在兜售粮食安全的理念，美洲农业合作研究所大力宣传"新农业"。但有些地方政府对这些呼吁充耳不闻。在他们看来，旅游与金融服务才能挽救经济，粮食生产对经济来说是次要的。

这种想法已经反过来"咬"了政府一口。2008 年海地普雷瓦尔政府就是一个典型的例子，该国首相因为在应对高粮价问题时表现欠佳被迫辞职。在出口方面，加勒比国家不得不对糖和香蕉在欧盟市场上优惠政策的丧失而进行调整。在出口方面加勒比是 WTO 所创建的全球化贸易环境的受害者。

加勒比农业在国内市场上因"廉价粮食"政策受到损害，在出口市场上因 WTO 受到损害，丧失了欧盟这个优惠市场。贸易自由化支持者的这两个正面进攻削弱了几乎每一个加勒比共同体国家的粮食生产系统。该地区的粮食价格目前正面临前所未有的水平。当地人进一步恶化了这种情况。因为城市化、收入的增加、女性就业和旅游业的影响，他们的饮食习惯已经发生变化。旅游业已增加了粮食的进口，加勒比各国人民都迷上了快捷和方便食品。粮农组织指出，加工食品和饮料占食品和饮料总销售量的 80%。

旅游业也刺激了对粮食的需求，这些粮食大部分都不由该地区生产。即使该地区有些地方生产粮食，也会受到季节性和竞争力问题的限制。

探究食品困局

高粮价不仅严重影响了巴哈马人及该地区其他民众的生活质量，而且也对该地区的经济引擎——旅游业的竞争力造成了负面影响。该地区吸引了数以百万计的游客，他们发现在某些情况下食品价格高得离谱。食品作为旅游的一项开支，因为价高已和机票、住宿相提并论了。

在拥有发达的农业的加勒比国家，如多米尼加共和国、古巴和牙买加，在食品方面的竞争力有助于他们的旅游业发展。也就是说，一方面，他们的食品生产能力使他们能节约外汇直接助力他们的旅游业和经济，另一方面，他们可以使用当地产品。

对于国内消费者来说存在市场操控，因为巴哈马生产者和农业企业不得不在扭曲的市场条件下运作。这源于在统一关税结构时没有咨询那些原本会受到职责调整影响的人或取得其反馈。粮食进口者存在这些情况，他们以便宜的价格购买产品（即禽肉），从低税收中获益，以低于当地生产者一两分钱的价格在当地销售，欺骗顾客，因为他们没有将从低税中所获得的收益转给顾客。

当地生产如果能得到政府或消费者团体的合理监督，市场的控制权便不可能落在食品进口商手中。凡有本地生产的产品的领域，消费者可更实惠地进行交易，粮食进口商在操纵粮食供应和价格时产生的影响也会更小。

前进的道路

解决食品价格高困局的真正方法是让巴哈马农民和农业企业生产更多粮食。这是让种植者利用市场粮食需求的绝佳机会。前几年农民生产的粮食只能以低价卖出，当今情况正好相反。

当今的巴哈马已然不同于以往。我们生活在一个信息科技的时代，这使得农民和农业企业能够接触到生产物资供应商，进入国内和国外市场。他们加入农民和商品团体，这样便可不再依赖政府。

与平常的供/求相比，国际市场的情况大不相同。高粮价与高能源价格紧密相关，资本密集型的机械化农业也和其他工业或制造业活动一样依赖燃料。人们需要燃料（天然气或柴油）来操作农业机械，需要燃料将农产品从农场输送到产品加工的各个阶段，最终送到消费者手中。粮食生产依赖基于石油的农药和化肥。粮食短缺国家不得不依赖进口，使得运价也飙升。

种种迹象表明，粮食价格不太可能在短时间内回落；许多因素交互作用，能源只是其中一个。我们必须面对这样的事实，即巴哈马不能继续指望别人为我们提供粮食。我们可以生产更多粮食，也有很多选择摆在我们面前。

减税政策

从一个国家的预算可窥探到该国政府的很多方面。它勾勒出了政府在经济上的政治哲学及其管理经济的方式。自由民族运动政府15个预算已向我透露了政府对巴哈马粮食生产的态度及其如何看待农业在经济中发挥的角色。

在近期"爱1997年：今日问题"的讨论中，一名内阁部长说，减税是政府降低消费者开支的一个工具。这可能就是政府的目标。现在的问题是：是否会真的这样呢？

在同一个预算中政府下调了肾透析设备的税收。这是否意味着透析治疗的费用将会减少呢？要知道这在巴哈马的医疗行业是极不可能的。

如果部长认为减税可降低消费者的开支，他是否应当提供真实数据来证明自己的观点呢？中央银行的科研部门（统计局）与金融部的经济学家可以做一些统计工作，以弄清减税省的钱是让消费者得到了还是让粮食进口商或进行透析的医生得到了。实际上，这些工作应该纳入生活水平成本的调查之中，而且每年定期举行——如果这要成为公共政策的话。

对食品减税的战略开始于1996年7月1日，同一时间政府还颁布了《税收法》。该法的一项重要内容是实行统一关税制度。《税收法》的颁布使得家禽的税率一夜之间便从70%降到35%，没有任何协商或提示。2002年，格拉德斯通农场停业，这使得约300名巴哈马人失去工作。当时格拉德斯通农场、大巴哈马的家禽公司和阿巴科大鸟公司总产值加上蛋鸡产值在1 700～1 800万美元之间。家禽业是一个产值为2 400万美元的农业综合企业。与此同时，进口禽肉的价值为1 100万美元。家禽行业的就业总数维持在1 000～1 200名工人之间。

减税损失

当格拉德斯通在2002年停业时，家禽业的产值已降至1 600万美元，鸡肉产值占总产值的将近50%。家禽业再也没恢复到2002年前的产出水平。粮食进口商控制了市场。随着2011年和2012年预算中税率进一步降低，即将到来的可能便是农业综合企业肉鸡的停产。

加勒比家禽协会

与此形成鲜明对比的是加勒比的其他国家。在加勒比共同体，农业部部长们将家禽变成一个"敏感"的产物，通过限制倾销等营销策略将其保护起来。家禽产业已成为加勒比共同体最大的农业综合企业。加勒比家禽协会被加勒比共同体贸易和经济发展理事会视为该区域农业的代言机构。巴哈马是加勒比家禽协会的创始成员，格拉德斯通农场的布鲁斯·汉森是其第一任主席兼执行董事。加勒比家禽协会诞生于 1999 年，并于 2000 年注册。

加勒比共同体中家禽的产值为 5 亿美元，近 10 万人从事家禽业，为加勒比人提供了所需的近 80% 的蛋白质，可在任何时间为加勒比共同体国家的国民经济的安全提供至少 3 个月的粮食保障。

加勒比共同体的家禽业之所以能达到当前状态是因为这里的家禽业以私营为主，并能将小规模农场主整合到生产系统中。加勒比共同体各国政府都支持可以降低成本的技术，因为这些技术增强了家禽业的竞争力。整合小规模农场主和降低成本的技术有助于家禽业的发展，同时也提高了加勒比共同体国家的粮食安全水平。

小规模农场主和农作物生产

对当地粮食生产的减税范围已扩展到水果、蔬菜或农作物。基于 2011 年和 2012 年的预算，农作物已不会再征税。

根据农业部数据，2010 年整个巴哈马共有 1 968 名小规模农场主。1 482 家农户中大部分都在伊鲁萨拉（334 家）、猫岛（279 家）、安德鲁斯（289 家）、新普罗维登斯（169 家）种植农作物，其余的分散在整个群岛，生产 124 种不同的水果和蔬菜。

主要农作物有香蕉、柚子、卷心菜、杧果、柠檬、橘子、洋葱、番茄和西瓜。相比之下，进口最多的十大作物有莴苣、番茄、卷心菜、甜椒、西兰花、洋葱、哈密瓜、橘子和香蕉。虽有重叠，但进口的前十名农作物都可以在这里生长。主要问题是巴哈马的农业不以研究为基础，不以技术为驱动，因此粮食生产技术落后，一直缺乏对畜牧业生产实践的研究。

过去的两三年间，巴哈马一直投资温室技术。温室现位于新普罗维登斯、安德鲁斯和阿巴克斯，莴苣是指定要生产的农作物之一。规模最大、最复杂的是卢卡亚热带农产品公司，坐落在新普罗维登斯西南部。它是一个价值数百万美元的高科技公司，使用了温室领域内的最新技术。很多新鲜蔬菜在这里都有种植，且价格很有竞争力。

当一个人审视该政策对小规模农场主的影响时，他或她便已面临危险并可能走向灭绝。例如，在伊鲁萨拉，根据农业部统计部门的数据，334 家农户耕种了 2 620 英亩的土地，生产重达 5 000 万磅的农产品，价值约为 3 200 万美元（价值在我看来有些高）。

有三个食品加工厂——北伊鲁萨拉、斧头湾、绿色城堡，每位农户最高要支付 9 000 美元的费用。政府支付了 300 万美元，剩余的产品要在拿骚市场上出售。家庭群岛上的小规模农场主实际上又回到 30 多年前食品加工厂还未引入的时期。投资缺乏对升级农业基础设施的限制也阻碍了行业的发展。

超市、批发商、专营运营商、酒店、美食餐厅因为各种原因都不愿意与这些小规模农场主做生意。小规模农场主的主要销路是波特礁或某个破旧的街角的农产品贩子。

出口农业

20 世纪下半叶，断断续续，巴哈马是美国东海岸很多州水果（柑橘和牛油果）和冬季蔬菜（黄瓜、番茄、秋葵甚至草莓）的主要供应商。离岸种植者如庞大的海湾 - 西方食品公司将巴哈马作为佛罗里达寒冬时粮食安全的预备队。有些时候巴哈马是北美唯一可以种植秋葵的地方。此时种植者便会赚得丰厚的利润，因为他们控制着食品的供应。全球变暖导致气候变化，巴哈马有可能在这一食品供应链上重新赢得属于自己的位置。

就柑橘类水果（橙子、柚子、青柠、柠檬、柑橘、酸橙）而言，巴哈马在阿巴克斯溃疡病暴发之前是加勒比共同体国家中种植柑橘类水果面积最大的国家，只有伯利兹和牙买加超过它。

柑橘因其出口潜力、当地市场的需求并且是很多私房业主和小规模农场主维持生计的农作物而成为一种多用途的农作物。在大多数巴哈马人成长的过程中，家里的后院都种有某种柑橘，这使得北部的阿巴克斯到巴哈马东南部崎岖岛的兰德瑞尔角一直都有柑橘种植。此外，在巴哈马的松树群岛上生产的柑橘具有比较优势，因为其无须灌溉便可商业化种植。这是巴哈马的重要农作物，不应该因为减税政策而从外面进口。

出口农业为松树群岛就业岗位的增加发挥了巨大作用。1990 年，国外种植者对海岛经济投入 2 100 万美元，当时成百上千的巴哈马人和农业季节工人（主要是海地人）在这里种植、采收水果和蔬菜，并分级和装箱，以便出口到美国。巴哈马有源源不断的宝贵的外汇资源，因为其有潜力种植农作物，扩大种植面积，增加作物种类。出口农业原本应该有助于改善国际收支状况，因为其有创汇能力。政策制定者和行政人员又错失良机了。

联合巴哈马党政府实行政策性限制，禁止离岸种植者在国内市场上销售他们的产品。本地市场留给小规模农场主。本地农业被视为个体经营，尽管其技术水平因袭已久。更进一步说，小规模农场主对国家安全至关重要，因为只有他们居住在这些偏远的岛屿。在那里，几十年来唯一的交通手段就是帆船。

罐头工厂

在巴哈马这种生产为季节性并受制于供过于求和供不应求的国家，要提高粮食生产必须有某种形式的农业产业化。一般来说，在发展中国家，农业产业化集中在食品加工领域，如罐装和装瓶。在 20 世纪 60 年代，巴哈马有三个罐头食品厂，一个在伊鲁萨拉的洛克湾，另外两个在拿骚。在伊鲁萨拉的格雷戈里镇，汤普森兄弟有菠萝加工设备。

到 70 年代末，只剩下了拿骚的两个罐头食品厂。伊鲁萨拉的洛克湾罐头食品厂主要生产番茄产品，它是巴哈马最大的番茄加工厂。该厂由已故的乔治·贝克和其弟弟所有并经营。其优势是位于生产地点，因为拿骚的罐头工厂虽然依靠新普罗维登斯的农户，但主要依靠的是农产品交易所。

1996 年、1997 年食品生产企业和家禽产品生产企业面临着相同的状况。番茄酱和木豆的关税减少，很多罐头工厂为了能够继续运营，不再加工新鲜的原材料，转而开始经营进口浓缩原料。小规模农场主已失掉这一市场。

番茄加工业务的停止给农产品交易所及其食品加工厂网络带来了很大压力，这是由于它成了番茄的主要购买者。番茄供过于求，已变成噩梦，造成了番茄的浪费、倾倒以及巨大的财产损失。

玛雅古纳岛的小规模农场主是罐头食品厂主要的木豆供应商。税一旦降低，工厂便开始从非洲和拉丁美洲进口木豆，很多农户因此失掉了这一市场。

食品安全与竞争力

农业生产部门的三个次级部门出现了，即鸡肉业（家禽业）、农作物和小规模农场主及食品加工领域。巴哈马的农业好像正在系统地被摧毁。我们身处这样一个时代，很多国际化的机构像联合国粮农组织、美洲农业合作研究所、泛美发展银行及世界银行都在督促各国努力提高粮食安全，而巴哈马却反其道而行之。

通过减税难以提高小规模农场主和农业企业的食品生产竞争力，如果目标是建立子行业、产业或农业企业的话。在这个贸易自由化的时代，成本竞争力主要依赖于自然资源（种植环境）、技术应用及发展、农业企业环境质量。需要建立新的政策框架以在这个全球化的竞争环境下生存。

联合国经济合作与发展组织将竞争定义为：在自由公平竞争的环境下，一个国家生产产品和提供服务以最大限度地满足国际市场需求，同时长期维持并提高民众的实际收入的程度。为了成功加入 WTO，巴哈马需要谋划新的机制来支持其农业，与此同时也要使农业更具竞争力。由于政府对粮食生产的态度在变，农业领域存在很大的不确定性。如此一来，吸引投资将变得非常困难。

粮食生产现状

农业一直深受口惠之害：废话很多，毫无实质性意义。最终结果是我们深受其害，因为我们迫切需要他人满足我们对粮食的需求。这使得我国粮食短缺，即粮食进口多于生产。在全球性政策面前情况更为严重，全球性政策敦促各国增加粮食生产以使粮食更加安全。我前面也已提到过巴哈马的粮食生产反其道而行。

自从近期的预算讨论开始以来，一直有对下列产品减税的讨论：很多水果、蔬菜、好几种家用商品，尤其是本地种植或生产的产品。我对当前政治领袖和政策决策者们持有的解释感到不满。在我看来，农业部编纂并出版的统计数据向我们描述的是另一画面。

小规模农场主

1978 年，也即在巴哈马独立 5 年之后，巴哈马政府明白为了规划产业，数据为必需品。在此 10 年前（1968 年），第一次农业综合调查开始了，当时的土地资源调查是由英国海外土地资源调查部开展的。作为联合国粮农组织的一员，巴哈马要求粮农组织实行农业评估。

1978 年可以看作是巴哈马农业数据的起始年。调查结果在公共政策制定者看来是难以想象的。同大多数加勒比国家一样，小规模农场主控制着巴哈马的农业部门，小规模农场主数量约为 4 246 名。安德鲁斯岛的小规模农场主最多，数量达到 771 名。调查结果让人吃惊，因为人们一直认为巴哈马东南部是主要的农业区，伊鲁萨拉（有 687 名小规模农场主）几十年来一直被视为群岛产粮区，长岛（有 607 名小规模农场主）紧随其后。

截止到 1994 年，即在 1978 年调查 16 年之后，数据令人吃惊。小规模农场主的数量减少了 69%，总数从 4 246 降到 1 760。整个群岛小规模农场主变成了一个濒危群体，原因是人口老龄化和缺乏巴哈马年轻人的补充，在年轻人看来这种工作没有吸引力。

减少最显著的是在阿巴克斯，跌幅为 77%，安德鲁斯跌幅为 71%。它们都是松树岛，占地 16.4 万英亩，适合机械耕作。到 2006 年，该行业在 30 多年间已经有超过 3 303 名农民离开。2006 年，小规模农场主的数量降到最低点 943 名。然而到 2010 年，小规模农场主的数量攀升至 1 968 名。随着全球经济崩溃，种植业成了万不得已时去从事的行业，并且是家庭群岛失业者的安全保障。

投入生产的英亩数量

1978 年农业普查报告显示，89 500 英亩的土地都在生产粮食，其中猫岛面积最大（29 919 英亩），其次是阿巴克斯（20 788 英亩）。

猫岛位于巴哈马东南部的矮林地，那里的作物生产技术都以壶穴耕种为基础。但是，猫岛某些地区的"白土地"上自由移动的土壤非常适合洋葱和土豆的种植，而红色土壤"赤陶土"已种植菠萝几十年了。猫岛的小规模农场主生产效率很高，因为他们平均耕种约 66 英亩的土地，而全国平均水平为一个小规模农场主耕种 20 英亩。猫岛农民的生产效率是全国平均水平的三倍。

与阿巴克斯相比，猫岛的大部分土地掌握在大型的离岸农业企业手中，数千英亩的土地用来种植柑橘和冬季蔬菜。此外，还有以前种糖料作物的土地，该土地一度由巴哈马农业产业有限公司用来生产蔗糖（25 000 英亩），该公司是美国一家木材公司——欧文斯-伊利诺斯公司的子公司。304 名小规模农场主的种植面积要比猫岛小规模农场主少得多。

到 1994 年，总生产面积下降了 44%，从近 90 000 英亩降到 50 249 英亩。这次减少影响到了所有主要的生产岛屿，大巴哈马岛除外，那里种植面积扩大了217%。大巴哈马港务局大片的土地被租赁出去，用于种植果园作物（柑橘、牛油果）和蔬菜。阿克林斯岛的产量也增加了，因为这个农业小区不得不去生产非易腐物质，如玉米和木豆。耕种和养鱼之外，除了几个飞绳钓鱼小屋的小众旅游，那里几乎没有任何经济活动。阿克林斯岛和崎岖岛上的人都在很大程度上从事农林活动，收获苦香树皮，以出口欧盟市场。

2006 年该行业进一步出现大幅下跌，种植面积不到 6 000 英亩。到 2010 年，即四年后，生产有所恢复。这主要是由于伊鲁萨拉缺乏农业之外的就业机会，该岛当时重新崛起成为领先的岛屿，380 个农户种植着 8 000 英亩的土地。

粮食生产

巴哈马粮食产量至少可以说是一直不稳定。1985 年，产值达到 3 400 万美元，这是自部门有统计数据以来所达到的最高水平。到 1988 年，产值减少 3 000 万美元，1991 年增加到 5 300 万美元，然后 1994 年再次减少到 4 200 万美元。这种情况一直持续到 2001 年，达到最高值 6 200 万美元。然而，2004 年再次下降到

3 800 万美元。截止到 2008 年，产值重新奠定了自己的位置，达到 7 800 万美元。

本地产值与进口粮食形成了鲜明对比，无论经济状况或游客人数的变化如何，进口粮食一直都在稳步增长。1995 年，进口粮食的价值为 2.08 亿美元；到 2007 年，即约 20 年后，这一数字已经翻了一番还多，达到 5.02 亿美元。粮食进口对粮食进口商（批发者、超市经营者、美国的特许经营权者、酒店业、美食和本地餐厅）来说是一个 5 亿美元的产业。

随着人口的增长和旅游产业的扩张（即巴哈马项目），按照目前的趋势，到 2027 年，粮食进口将是一个价值达 10 亿美元的行业。难怪一个重要的超市运营商对政府的减税政策方针表达了其喜悦之情；他认为，这预示着他的生意形势会很好。

关税调整或减税，对一个地方来说影响显而易见。当关税或税收较高时，会刺激当地生产；当它被降低后，本地生产便会停滞。在第一种情况中，粮食安全性得到了提高。

我最近在粮农组织-加勒比-农业讨论平台上分发了文件《粮食的地缘政治》以及我对减税的意见，该平台是一个电邮讨论平台。罗宾·菲利普斯先生是该地区最突出的农业企业家之一，同时也是加勒比家禽协会的一位同事，还是特立尼达和多巴哥的家禽协会主席，提出以下意见：

> 如果有人怀疑消除/减少税收对当地生产商及国家粮食安全带来的消极影响，我们可以提供两个案例作为参考：
>
> （1）圭亚那鸡肉。a. 1992 年，对鸡肉的关税降低到 25％，进口占总消费量的比例上升到 72％。b. 2003 年，关税提高到 100％，当地产量占总消费量的比例增加到 100％，过去 4 年多一直没有进口。
>
> （2）特立尼达和多巴哥鸡肉。a. 2001 年以前，总关税为 137％，进口量占不到总消费量的 2％。b. 2006 年，关税削减到 40％，截至 2010 年 12 月，进口量占总消费量的 33％，并在不断上升。
>
> 在这两种情况下进口的主要产品是美国鸡腿，该产品被中国政府 2009 年的调查认定出口价格低于生产成本的价格。2009 年 9 月，中国对美国鸡肉实行 105.4％ 的进口关税。我们加勒比共同体地区必须在两个相互冲突的方法之间做出选择：
>
> （1）与 1957 年 3 月 25 日定于罗马的《欧盟条约》第 39 条规定相一致的农业政策。

（2）布洛克学说——美国农业部部长约翰·布洛克1986年9月在乌拉圭关贸总协定会议上的建议。

不幸的是，选项2在许多情况下成了优先选项。

当地粮食产量反复无常，在一个不断萎缩的小规模农场主社区里有其不确定性。诸如那些从事家禽养殖、食品加工、商业果园开发、高科技农业（温室生产）、水培种植和基因组生产（组织培养和胚胎移植）的农业企业要么对是否应投资巴哈马农业企业犹豫不决，要么不愿投资。迄今为止，政府不与利益相关人协商，而是采用高压战术制定政策，如降低税收，但这可能会破坏商业实体，如罐头工厂、阿巴克斯大鸟公司、巴哈马家禽公司，甚至会使得实体企业停业，比如格拉德斯通农场。另一个因素是农田数量的急剧下降。农业是一个动态的活动，将新的土地投入生产是农业和畜牧业的一个组成部分。

这种情况的结果是，巴哈马将自身的粮食供应外包，依赖美国、加拿大、欧洲联盟（欧盟）、巴西、墨西哥、智利、哥斯达黎加和阿根廷、亚洲的泰国、太平洋国家澳大利亚和新西兰。

现状为何如此？

到20世纪60年代中期，巴哈马的经济已经从农业为主转变为服务业为主，特别是旅游业。这种转变也表明巴哈马成为一个城市社会。拿骚和自由港的经济发展刺激了国内大规模的人口流动，成千上万的人离开家庭群岛的陆地和大海，转而走向城市生活。

巴哈马得益于处于支配地位的美国经济刺激起来的第二次世界大战后的经济繁荣。美国农业的新体系正在形成，即基于廉价的化石燃料、合成肥料、化学除草剂、杀虫剂和新的杂交种子品种的低成本/高产量的产业化农业。这使得美国成为世界粮仓。这个系统产生了大量的剩余收成，美国成为世界上首要的粮食出口国。农业产业化成为全球模式。半个世纪后的今天，鉴于原油价格上涨，环境有恶化的可能，对水资源、污染、全球变暖的担忧，化学径流和农场动物污水处理对生态系统带来的影响，人们存在一种疑问：这种模式是否可持续。

世界银行和国际货币基金组织推动像巴哈马这样的发展中国家的政府将进口"廉价粮食"作为一项政策，而不是争取更大的粮食自给自足，以改善自己的粮食安全状况。像大多数发展中国家一样，巴哈马实施了这种"廉价粮食"的政策。如今，缺粮国已成为粮食出口国家（如美国、加拿大和欧盟）一个价值万亿美元的市场。

巴哈马现在正与中国和印度等粮食需求不断增加的新兴经济体竞争，这些新兴经济体人均收入不断上升。我们将食品供应链与暴发性疾病如猪瘟、禽流感、疯牛病以及最近欧洲蔬菜和牛肉大肠杆菌疫情的易感性联系在一起。依靠他人使得一个国家易受其他力量操控，巴哈马恰好将自己置于这种位置。

上面是近30年来全球贸易体制的做法，像巴哈马这样的国家与加勒比这样的地区现已成为粮食短缺的飞地，其中进口粮食量已经超过了当地的粮食产量。

到2010年，世界银行、国际货币基金组织、粮食及农业组织等全球机构和美洲农业合作研究所等半球机构开始推动一个以国家和区域粮食安全为主的议程。

美国前总统比尔·克林顿在海地突出强调了地震灾难善后中粮食不安全的现实。克林顿做出了如下道歉：

> "自1981年至最近一年左右我们开始反思时，生产大量的粮食是美国一直遵循的政策，即我们富国应该把生产的大量粮食卖给穷国并减轻他们自己生产的负担，以帮助他们直接跃入工业时代。这居然没有奏效……它是一个错误……
>
> "这个政策在它涉及的每个地方都失败了。你是无法把食物链与生产分开的。而且它也损害了很多的文化、生活的结构、自决意识。"

这就是背景，它使巴哈马陷入粮食不安全状态，创造了数百万美元的进口粮食市场，代价是牺牲小规模农场主和刚起步的农业企业。

为什么会下降？

除了小规模农场主的可能消亡、农业企业发展的不利因素和农业生产种植面积的减少，另一个重要因素是缺乏公共和私营部门对农业部门的投资。

在一个高级别专家论坛开幕式上，对于"如何在2050年养活世界"，粮农组织总干事雅克·迪乌夫做出以下回应：

> "农业部门别无选择，只能提高生产效率……而这将需要大幅度增加对该部门的投资——更好地获得现代生产物资，更多灌溉系统、机械和工具，更多阅读材料和更好的农村基础设施，以及更多有技能和受过更好培训的农民。

"国家之间的技术差距需要弥合，通过知识转移实现的能力建设……
应加强，以实现可持续增长的农业生产和生产力。"

对于全球农业以及国家和地区的农业部门和／或系统来说，21 世纪的第一个十年是举足轻重的十年。回顾第一个十年国家预算可知，农业部获得的周期性预算分配，在过去的十年里仅仅增加了 150 万到 170 万美元。大多数的部门资金都用来支付主要是拿骚员工的工资了。在 2002—2003 年的预算中，农业部获得的分配只占周期性资本预算的 0.55％，部门总体只占资本预算的 1.35％。这种情况并没有显著改变。整个农业部门获得的国家周期性支出小于 2％，资本支出不到 2％。为了落实粮农组织总干事的建议，现有的预算可能不够，如果我们(作为一个国家)和政府严肃对待提高粮食安全性的话。

私营企业对粮食生产的投资在 2002—2006 年间少得可怜(1 000～1 500 万美元)。2008 年，央行年度报告指出，商业银行对农业的贷款额为 1 100 万美元(2007 年)和 1 500 万美元(2008 年)。2010 年的年度报告指出，农业给银行的还款仅为 60 万美元，而旅游业为 6 150 万美元，建筑业为 1 160 万美元。

加勒比地区，从 20 世纪 60 年代到 90 年代农业增长率还不到 2％，同一时期农业贡献占国内生产总值(GDP)不足 1％。这种趋势的原因是政府缺乏对农业的投资，因为他们相信布洛克学说及"廉价粮食"理论，而这两者已经不利于该地区的农业，当然除古巴、圭亚那、伯利兹和牙买加之外。巴哈马农业对国内生产总值的贡献率已经下降到不足 1％。

未来之路

因为面临的挑战，巴哈马的农业正处于一个十字路口，政策制定者必须确定农业将选择何种道路并确定采用何种战略指导该行业与利益共享者度过这个时期。利益共享者正在并且一直面临着贸易自由化和 WTO 标准、全球粮食模式竞争、气候变化和全球变暖带来的问题、对农业劳动力的需求、获得资金甚至农业盗窃等一系列问题的压力。

最现实的挑战是为农业加入 WTO 做准备。小规模农场主、观赏苗木业、家禽养殖场和加工厂、当地的罐头厂、装瓶公司、食品加工者、当地家庭小工业和其他人将如何为加入 WTO 做准备呢？

做好加入 WTO 的准备不是一个简单或廉价的命题。它需要人力资源培训和发展。与此相关的就是建设基础设施，如建立一个标准局，再就是培养专门人才来翻译和应用农业协议法律法规，如保持卫生与植物检疫的措施。

我们一直在与我们面对的环境玩俄罗斯轮盘赌，因为我们依靠美国农业部作为粮食、植物和动物进入巴哈马的第三方结算所。这种依赖性在我们加入WTO时将结束。目前巴哈马是这个半球唯一不是WTO成员的国家。此外，巴哈马落后西半球的所有国家16年，要赶上还要付出很大努力。

另外一个重要的挑战是气候变化，这是专家眼中农业生产力所面临的最复杂的问题。农业生产方法可能要改变，因为小规模农场主和农业企业可能不得不通过改变种植日期、转换作物和品种、采用新技术来适应。典型的例子是加勒比家禽协会，其禽肉产量要在该地区具有全球竞争力才能在"廉价粮食"政策带来的挑战中生存下来。如今，加勒比家禽协会是加勒比共同体最大的农业综合企业，产值5亿美元，雇用10万名工人，并把该地区的禽肉安全储备定为4个月。

巴哈马农业要在这个技术驱动的生产环境中发挥作用，科学研究将不得不发挥重要的作用。目前，农业部门在应用性、基础性方面没有任何研究。

农业能给予这个国家的太多了，过去的20年里，历届政府都未能释放这种自然资源的巨大潜力。这是一种财富，通过气候、水资源、多样的植物群和动物群，最重要的是它的人民，被赋予这片土地。

粮农组织总干事呼吁21世纪要建立更高效的农业部门。巴哈马现在准备好了迎接这一挑战；然而巴哈马政府和人民必须相信，农业能够在经济中发挥有意义的社会经济作用。为了实现这一目标，必须兑现金融承诺。

世界正在远离低成本/高容量的全球农业模式，因为其可持续性在许多地方受到质疑。鉴于此，巴哈马就像其他有勇气改变的发展中国家一样，可以基于发展有竞争力的农业部门来设计一个模式。这种模式必须围绕鼓励农业企业发展和使小规模农场主户通过科技、创新、环境友好和研究型粮食生产系统纳入农业综合企业网络。

粮食生产是一个颇具争议的热点问题。美洲农业合作研究所与哥斯达黎加政府合作，将于2011年10月举办一个关于粮食生产的农业部部长的半球会议。亚伯拉罕部长说："说起农业，我们谈论气候变化、物价上涨和销售体系，但我们忽略了创新的主题。如果我们谈论粮食生产，特别是未来的粮食生产，它将在其中起到关键作用。"本次会议的口号"播下创新，收获繁荣"使人们注意到政府需要投入更多的资源进行创新，使农业更具竞争性、可持续性和包容性。

有了这个新的巴哈马模式，粮食生产的效益将为我们所有，因为我们不能再让每年5亿美元从我们国家流失，必须共同努力来留住其中大部分资金。现在我们的前景一定是：

◆ 粮食生产将会创造就业机会。

◆ 粮食生产将会利用科技。

◆ 粮食生产，使我们能够挣得（出口农业）外汇，并节约（国内农业）外汇。

◆ 粮食生产将维持家庭岛农业社区的地方经济。

◆ 粮食生产将阻止人们从家庭岛往拿骚和自由港移民。

◆ 粮食生产将改善我们的生活质量，提高数千人的生活水平。

这个目标可以实现；我们需要的不仅仅是政治首长的承诺，而且是作为一个民族，在这个粮食供应不被重视的世界里实现自己影响世界的使命。

巴哈马和加勒比的农业政治

巴哈马人在食品方面的花费占其收入的 50%～60% 以上。几个星期内，巴哈马人会去投票选出新政府。整个加勒比地区，在竞选宣传的时候政客们才乐于倾听民众的意见。随着食品花费的不断增加以及很多加勒比国家粮食生产政策框架的失效，粮食应该成为选举的一个议题。加勒比国家中处于某些收入范围的人连基本食品都负担不起。这就是巴哈马的情况，在这一收入阶层，食品的花费高达 50%～60%。在巴哈马，菠萝的商业化早已开始，菠萝在全球市场上销售可追溯到 19 世纪初。然而，对成千上万的巴哈马人而言，菠萝是吃不起的。食品店菠萝的售价每个为 7 美元。

在我看来，在粮食公共政策方面我们正在走错路。自从 20 世纪 90 年代中期以来，我们依靠"廉价粮食"的进口，即美国高额补贴的商品，如禽肉，其副产品在加勒比地区的市场上倾销，随后动摇了加勒比地区内部的生产，如家禽农业企业。这项政策对于实现该国的最大利益来说是行不通的，因为：

（1）这是在耗费我们的外汇；

（2）成千上万的粮食生产和附加值的工作都被外包给像哥斯达黎加、巴西、美国、新西兰、斯堪的纳维亚国家和远东的泰国这样的国家；

（3）我们已经放弃了对生产投入的责任；

（4）我们已经成为陈旧过时产品、过期产品、冰冻多年的肉食及新型"仅供出口"的商品的倾销地；

（5）我们正在因为吃太多糖含量高的、加工过的、"便宜"的快餐食品而得病，从而产生非传染性疾病健康危机；

（6）我们没有通过创新、科技开发这些岛屿自然资源的潜力；

（7）我们经济的多样化被抑制，从而制约了经济的扩张和新的就业机会的增加。

食品和收入

我从一个叫史蒂夫·都德的朋友那里收到一封邮件。他正经营全球谷物供应和运输农业综合企业。这是一封关于食品的成本及其与财富和健康关系的邮件。

1932 年，美国人花费在食品上的钱占收入的 25％；到 2009 年，这一数字下降到 10％。随着工业化农业的引入和家庭农场的衰落，研究和技术创新带来了更高的效率。最近的微软全国广播公司的节目政治国家与牧师夏普顿中，有人指出，美国 18.6％的人——将近 6 000 万的美国人称买不起食品。经济衰退可能已经是因素之一。美国是全球最大的食品出口国之一，美国人却发现自己面临着严峻的食品问题。迎合穷人的食品银行美国各地都有。

金砖四国（巴西、俄罗斯、印度和中国）中，巴西人花费在食品上的钱占收入的 25％，这是金砖四国中最低的。另一方面，中国占 40％，这在四个国家中是最高的。欧洲四国（葡萄牙、爱尔兰、希腊和西班牙）中，爱尔兰为 10％，是最低的，希腊 20％是最高的。希腊当前正处于在金融危机和经济困难时期。

在食品上花费最低的国家是丹麦——5％。法国、德国和新加坡徘徊在 10％上下，日本为 14％，土耳其为 30％。许多国家像加拿大、澳大利亚、新西兰、阿根廷和其他国家不属于调查对象。

巴哈马以及和我们情况相似的加勒比国家的食品花费占收入的百分比是多少呢？从 20 世纪 80 年代开始，美国一直在加勒比国家推进其"廉价粮食"计划。然而在巴哈马，家庭食品平均花费占收入的 50％～60％。在一些加勒比国家这一比例可能会更高。2008 年，海地发生粮食骚乱，因为海地人买不起"廉价粮食"了，这一骚乱将总理撵下了台。

对经济的贡献

几十年来，加勒比政客信奉"廉价粮食"这个理念，对农业部门的发展只给予口头支持。目前对农业投资很少。在我的书《新加勒比：转型之地》中，我想指出，作为国内生产总值的一部分，加勒比共同体政府的开支 2001—2002 年从 6.8％（圣卢西亚，2001 年）到 0.6％（巴哈马，2002 年）不等。

一名年老的小规模农场主描述了对加勒比青年毫无吸引力的产业。最终的结果是缺粮区出现了。巴哈马粮食生产成为维持巴哈马人在我们的许多岛屿，特别是在巴哈马东南部岛屿存在的公益活动。

作为大多数加勒比国家经济的一部分，农业对国内生产总值的贡献率为0.5%～2%。在巴哈马，贡献率小于1%。2007年，巴哈马粮食进口突破了5亿美元大关。到2015年、2016年，随着凯布尔海滩巴哈马项目的竣工，加上现有的粮食生产方式，粮食进口可能达到10亿美元。

伊恩·艾维是瑞耐特博客出版商，他提供的数据表明非洲国家的农业都比这些加勒比国家要好：

> 今年国内生产总值预期增长率显示许多非洲国家都做得很好，如博茨瓦纳为7.1%，安哥拉10.8%，科特迪瓦为8.3%，加纳为7.5%，卢旺达为7.0%，赞比亚为6.7%，肯尼亚为6.0%，乌干达为5.7%。

都市生活和旅游

加勒比政客已经听凭粮食生产政策受城市化和旅游业的影响。许多加勒比共同体国家的城市人口规模已超过农村。以巴哈马为例，85%的人口居住在拿骚和自由港的城市中心之间。这就造成了政府政策倾向于城市选民，忽略了提高农村（家庭岛）经济的政策措施，诸如发展农业的投资活动。

旅游业已成为推动许多加勒比国家经济的引擎。2005年，巴哈马旅游业产值20亿美元。酒店、美食餐厅和美国的快餐店在迫使政府推动粮食进口方面起到了显著的作用。粮食进口商控制粮食供应。在一些加勒比岛屿，如阿鲁巴，根本没有粮食生产。

作为对城市和旅游的效益的回应，政府已经采取了减税政策，以满足城市选民要求，因为选民的平衡已经转移，城市选民多于农村选民。旅游业由强大的特殊利益群体组成，他们通过游说使政府的政策对自己有利。对于酒店行业来说，食品是一个巨大的收入来源。城市化和旅游业改变了巴哈马等加勒比国家政府审视国内粮食生产和农业综合企业对经济发展作用的方式。一些国家的政府对于农业采取了"负电子"的态度。

艾维这样描述负电子："有些人纳闷为什么事情不能这么做或不应该这么做。对于为什么是错的他们会给出很多理由，但对于如何做得不一样或做得更好从来没有什么好的建议。他们总是想挑起事端或争论什么。那些人只会将组织的力量浪费掉。"长久以来，我们一直听说巴哈马农业没有竞争力。于是，就进口粮食。好吧，我们现在看到了依赖"廉价粮食"的结果。

新的全球议程

全球议程已经改变。过去的 25 年间，美国强化布洛克学说，推动发展中国家从美国进口粮食，从而突出了美国作为一个低成本的生产商和"廉价粮食"的供应商的角色。世界银行和联合国粮农组织等国际组织受到 G20 国家的支持，认为这是一个有依赖性、有缺陷的政策。这些机构重组政策和方案，以鼓励各国实现更高程度的自给自足；粮食安全是实现这一目标的途径。

这种新的全球议程与过去有很大不同，从而导致许多国家调整本国粮食生产的重点。巴哈马还没有进行调整。这种情况因为粮食税收减少而复杂化，也不利于私营企业对粮食生产和农业发展进行投资。

粮食供应是一个挑战，巴哈马等加勒比国家的政府将会继续面临挑战。有许多因素会加剧这些挑战，即金砖四国中产阶级的比例扩大，从而增加了对许多商品的需求。我们的政治家越早认识到这一现实，就会越好地给我们的农业部门定位来面对即将到来的挑战。

年　表

　　1994 年农业普查指出,50 250 英亩(20 350 公顷)的土地用作农场,占巴哈马的土地总面积(340 万英亩)的 1.5%。

　　哥伦布登陆巴哈马大约 500 年后,巴哈马的农业有了一个显著的变化,从阿拉瓦克巴哈马时期的维持基本生计变成了现在的农业工商业。在阿拉瓦克巴哈马时期,一些田间作物(如木薯)和谷物(如玉米)、水果(如椰子)一起种植。现在松树群岛可为当地市场生产近 7 000 万镑的农作物。

　　影响巴哈马农业增长和发展的巴哈马历史事件时间顺序表着重说明了农业的发展方式。

年代	影响农业的历史事件
1650 年	伊鲁萨拉冒险家将巴西木和棉花出口美国。
1784 年	保皇党及他们从美国南部带来的奴隶到达。
1785 年	每年平均数量出口。
1838 年	奴隶制废除和耕作措施不力加速棉花产业的衰败。
1855—1864 年	菠萝年均出口 2 000 吨。
1860—1878 年	1861 年大约出产 1 000 吨柑橘,平均每年 542 吨;美国内战开始;枪支时代开始。
1865 年	美国内战结束,枪支泛滥。
1890 年	种植 10 万英亩剑麻。
1892 年	剑麻试出口英国。
1906 年	报告表明剑麻清洗不净。

1911 年	剑麻需要检验。
1912 年	菠萝出口停止。
1914 年	剑麻价格低。
1915 年	剑麻价格高，因为墨西哥的剑麻生产遇到问题。
1916 年	剑麻价格暴涨 / 新普罗维登斯柑橘中发现蓝灰色蝇。
1917 年	新普罗维登斯柑橘产业灭绝，蓝灰色蝇到达伊鲁萨拉。
1919 年	美国《沃尔斯特德法案（禁止）》。
1920 年	柑橘出口停止。
1925 年	农业及海产委员会成立。
1927 年	质量低劣的剑麻和番茄出口/"西印度七大农学家"到达。
1942 年	新普罗维登斯缅甸公路暴动。
1951 年	只有 50% 的作物出口，因为美国市场崩溃，加拿大市场衰弱。本地罐头制造商以出口价格 30% 的价格购买了 40 000 英镑的货物（番茄）。
1953 年	飓风破坏了猫岛和南伊鲁萨拉的番茄作物。
1955 年	因为佛罗里达大量生产，所以价格低廉。
1958 年	当地罐头厂购买 80 000 蒲式耳番茄，这超过了出口量。新普罗维登斯总罢工。
1962 年	普选。
1964 年	组建内阁政府，并建立农业和渔业部。
1965 年	黄瓜成为主要出口农产品。
1966 年	巴哈马农业产业有限公司开始种植甘蔗。巴哈马货币从英镑换为美元。
1967 年	1 月 10 日，新进步自由党政府上台。农产品交易所移至波特礁。
1968 年	巴哈马农业大学毕业生返回。农业部部长转到贸易和工业部。
1969 年	内阁批准了国土资源大调查。第一个季度，12 474 英亩的土地产出 166 134 净吨的甘蔗，还有 14 896 吨的糖和 963 000 加仑糖蜜。10 000 吨原糖出口到美国市场，剩余部分出口加拿大。
1970 年	在新普罗维登斯格拉德斯通路建立中心农业站。

1971 年	土地的清理项目扩展——米勒路项目。
1973 年	巴哈马农业研究、培训和开发项目启动。开始在家庭群岛建造仓库。
1974 年	《合作社法》通过。
1975 年	巴哈马政府购买斧头湾农场。
1976 年	家庭岛专业官员。
1977 年	北长岛绵羊圈养项目。
1978 年	农业普查。
1981 年	番茄出口营销计划，组织方为新普罗维登斯阿巴克斯北安德鲁斯农业部门。开始在中心农业站开办食品科技和动物饲养单位。
1983 年	松树群岛农产品又开始出口。
1986 年	本·G. 哈蒙柑橘第一次种植。
1990 年	巴哈马出口第一茬红葡萄。
1991 年	以色列在巴哈马举办农业推广研讨会。
1992 年	新自由民族运动政府。
1993 年	《农业部（合并）法案》。
1994 年	农业调查。
1997 年	自由民族运动开始第二任期政府。
1998 年	巴哈马成为美洲农业合作研究所的成员。
1999 年	首届加勒比农业周——区域最早的农业活动。
2000 年	巴哈马第一任首相林登·O. 平德林爵士去世。
2001 年	卢卡亚热带农产品公司水培设施 8 月正式运行。巴哈马寻求加入 WTO。
2002 年	11 月格拉德斯通农场倒闭。
2003 年	戈弗雷被任命为巴哈马首任驻联合国粮农组织大使。
2004 年	3 月，巴哈马第一任总督约翰·保罗爵士去世。
2005 年	柑橘流浪汉在阿巴克斯暴动。
2006 年	3 月，北伊鲁萨拉传教士洞出土卢卡亚印第安人遗骸。
2007 年	《圣安妮宣言》：加勒比共同体关于粮食和农业政策及非传染性疾病肥胖症预防的倡议。

2008 年	《欧洲伙伴关系协定(EPA)》。10 月加勒比论坛和欧盟之间签署贸易协定。
2009 年	4 月,巴哈马向 WTO 提交了外贸管理备忘录。巴哈马胚胎移植项目 1 月份在格拉德斯通路农业中心启动。
2010 年	全国农业产业化博览会,包括在新普罗维登斯和九个家庭岛的小型博览会。

《孢子》杂志对《巴哈马农业历史沿革：1492—2012》一书的评论

在欧洲人 1492 年登陆巴哈马群岛之前，阿拉瓦克岛的居民已经形成了一套农业体系，包括利用迁移的方式耕种淀粉类和蔗糖类作物、在自家庭院种植日常所需的作物、捕鱼打猎以及采摘水果。此后，巴哈马的农业就处于不断的发展变化之中。

《巴哈马农业历史沿革：1492—2012》一书的作者曾于 1973 至 1982 年任巴哈马农业部部长。他在书中回顾了哥伦布到来之前以及殖民时期的农业状况，追溯了从勉强自给到庄园经济的发展所带来的社会和制度方面的转变。1950年之前，农业是巴哈马主要的就业机会提供者和外汇创收者。今天，旅游业的繁荣带来了城市经济的快速增长，为大规模地进口粮食提供了资金。饮食依进口的偏好而定(毕竟佛罗里达距巴哈马只有 30 分钟的航程而已)，当地的农业则尽力去满足季节性的需求。

巴哈马的农业已经被压缩到一个不确定的状态，并且容易受到 WTO 的支配，在那里"富裕的工业化国家的利益重于小国的利益"。

这本书是爱的产物，它精心细致地论述了一个国家的农业发展史，同时也表达了对未来的担忧，"深深包围在未知方面所带来的各项挑战中"。多少个非洲、加勒比和太平洋地区的国家正在经历着类似的故事？

(《孢子》杂志，1999 年 2 月号　第 79 期)

DEDICATION

• This book[①] is dedicated to my late mother, Sylvia, who introduced me to the subject of history during my early childhood by reading to me stories from Greek mythology; and to my father, William, who directed me to the field of agriculture.

• To my wife, Sandra, who played an important role through her perusal of the various chapters and her critical comments. To my son, Geoffrey, an agricultural economist, who greatly assisted in the presentation of the book, and to my younger son, Timothy, a history graduate, who was instrumental in providing research expertise.

• Finally, to the late Dr Cleveland Eneas, author, dentist and uncle, who was a source of inspiration by his insistence on recording our history.

---

① 本书英文部分 2013 年由 Media Enterprises Ltd. 出版。

ACKNOWLEDGEMENTS

The first edition was a professional responsibility. It was a first, so it called for bringing a number of diverse resources into play. In this regard, I wish to acknowledge all those involved in the publication of the first edition.

This second edition was very different as it required substantial statistical updating and, for that assistance, I am grateful to Mr. Leslie Minns of the Department of Agriculture.

Over the twenty-year period (1992–2012), the agricultural landscape of The Bahamas has been changed with the introduction of new technology, i.e. green-house production. The leading figures in this area are Mr. Tim Hauber and Mrs. Joy Sweeting of Lucayan Tropical Produce and Dr. Leroy Santiago who pioneered this technology among homeowners and agri-entrepreneurs. All of the individuals were instrumental in providing information and photographs.

Photo: Presentation of Ambassadorial credentials to the Director General of the Food and Agriculture, Dr. Jacques Diouf, in 2003 by the author.

This edition also enabled me to provide some in-depth information on the sector during the decades of the 1970's, 1980's and 1990's as well as highlight some view-points on the impact of Trade Liberalization on the sector.

I would also wish to express my appreciation to key publisher Mr. Neil Sealey, whose persistent prodding was a factor in getting me to update the book. It was apparent that there was increased demand for the book, particularly among educators, agricultural researchers and students at all academic levels.

Recognizing the importance of agriculture in geopolitics, the government of The Bahamas in 2003 appointed me as its Ambassador to the United Nation's Food and Agriculture Organization (FAO), Rome, Italy. This was the first appointment of its kind to FAO by the government of The Bahamas.

Godfrey Eneas
August 2012

INTRODUCTION

The story of agriculture in The Bahamas has never been told in its entirety. This book is an attempt to present a new and comprehensive perspective on the subject.

Agriculture's historical role is closely tied to the socio-economic development of The Bahamas. At one point it was the main employer of Bahamians and the chief earner of foreign exchange. Powerful politicians sought to control it because they recognized its economic power and its importance to the economy.

Despite the extremely limited physical resources of The Bahamas, the yields from the soil generated enough wealth to sustain the colonial economy. With new knowledge and technology agriculture can again become a pillar of society, but its potential must be understood and appreciated before it can be realized.

In the 21st century, this resource will require greater attention and protection if it is to fulfill its expected potential. A new direction is paramount if this objective is to be achieved.

Farming is recognized as one of the major economic activities with a strong association to environmental and developmental issues. Within this context, the agricultural policies and programmes which will fuel the sector toward growth and development in the 21st century, must incorporate environmental concerns.

This objective is achievable only if a partnership approach is taken. Gone are the days when the weight of determining the national direction of an industry was left solely in the hands of government. Dialogue is fundamental between industry, government, indigenous agribusinesses, small farmers, consumers, foreign entities who supply inputs to our agricultural sector, and Bahamian and foreign food importers.

Farming is undergoing profound changes and no single organization has all of the solutions to the many challenges confronting us in the 21st century. Structural adjustment programmes are being enforced in developing countries by large international agencies, and the liberalization and opening of markets pose a threat to the future of many types of economic activities in Third World countries. Redirection in agricultural policy has resulted not only from a felt need but an economic need, such as the influence of the packing house system on Bahamian farmers, their way of life and incomes.

Yet many policies are formulated and decisions taken without any type of consultation with the farming and agribusiness communities. No one can dispute the fact that farmers are closest to the natural interface with the environment, and it is in the farmers' interest to assist in the successful management of our natural resources as this is fundamental to their existence and survival in the new 21st century.

Agriculture in The Bahamas: Historical Development 1492-1992 was first published in 1998 and reprinted with minor corrections in 2001.

In this second edition, three relatively lengthy and substantive additions have been made. In Chapter III, The Performance of the Agricultural Sector during the 1970's, 1980's and 1990's, when large investments were made by the Pindling administration and I felt these points should be sighted.

Chapter VI highlights the introduction of new technology, principally greenhouse farming through Lucayan Tropical Produce which was a major investment in the sector. In addition, greenhouse technology was also adopted by a number of small farmers thereby upgrading their technical skills.

A new chapter is added, Chapter IX which deals with Perspectives: Where Global, Regional and National Food Production Issues intersect. I interjected this chapter because Global Agriculture came into greater focus by me as a result of my appointment as The Bahamas' Ambassador to the Food and Agriculture Organization (FAO) from March 2003-May 2007 and, my selection to the Board of Directors of the Tropical Agricultural Research and Higher Education Center (CATIE) Turrialba, Costa Rica from 2005-2008.

CHAPTER 1

AGRICULTURE: EARLY DEVELOPMENT IN THE BAHAMAS

When Columbus landed in The Bahamas in 1492, he met a culture that was very different from the one he had left in Europe.

The Arawaks, recognized as the first inhabitants of The Bahamas, had their foundation in the environment. The Europeans encountered a subtropical climate with abundant marine life: green turtles, turtle eggs, conchs (*Strombus gigas*) and scale fish; a variety of land fauna: raccoon, herbivorous tortoise (*Geochelone sp*), iguana (*Cyclura sp*), agouti (*Dasyprocta aguti*), hutia, pigeons, doves, parrots, and several barn owls (including the giant barn owl, (*Tyto pollens*) which are now extinct. A rich vegetation included edible fruits: genip (*Genipa Americana*), sea grape (*Coccoloba invifera*), cocoplum (*Chrysobalanus icaco*), pineapple, pine fruits and palms; ground provisions: cassava, sweet potato, peanut, and flora with medicinal properties like the lignum vitae (*Guaiacum acinale*).

Columbus and his men also found a society (cacicazgoes) which had order and a hereditary hierarchy (caciques) with whom "he had most dealings and who treated him with respect". (Watts, 1987) The Arawaks possessed implements for use in food production, stone or flint-fashioned tools and weapons, and displayed expertise in pottery making, cotton and basket weaving, metal works and a wood technology to manufacture spears, darts, dugout canoes and housing with thatch-palmed roofing. Island Arawaks, like those in The Bahamas, were not familiar with the mining of gold, which was prevalent among Arawaks on the larger islands of the Greater Antilles such as Hispaniola and Cuba.

According to Watts, 1987, there is evidence that trading took place among the Island

Arawaks in the Greater Antilles. Arawak villages at the time of the Spanish landings comprised populations between 1,000 to 2,000 inhabitants and were generally situated away from the coast in the hinterland. Two interesting facts are to be noted about Island Arawaks (Arawak Bahamians). First, there was an absence of major native infectious diseases according to the Spaniards and second Arawak women held a privileged position in the society and the line of inheritance was matrilineal. (Watts, 1987)

Figure 1.1   Taino housing structures. (Watts, 1987)

TAINO OR LUCAYAN TAINO AGRICULTURE

The topography of The Bahamas in the days of the Arawaks was unlike any found in Europe. The land was essentially composed of pine and hardwood forests on shallow limestone soils.

The Land Resource Study, undertaken in 1971–1976, categorized the land on the basis of vegetation and capability which was closely linked to rock type and rainfall. The two main island groupings were designated Pine and Coppice Islands.

The Arawaks inhabited both the Pine Islands and the Coppice Islands, but seemed more abundant in the Coppice Islands which were characterized by mixed broadleaf and scrubby woodland. The islands themselves were narrow, rugged and undulating with hard rock. They farmed the sandy soils of the "whitelands", or the pockets of fertile black or red loam which can be found in potholes and solution holes.

Out of this growing environment, a system of pothole farming was developed based on Arawak agriculture where the techniques of shifting cultivation or slash-and-burn farming, the development of garden plots and the establishment of a "conuco" were fundamental aspects of the system.

The Spaniards were extremely impressed by the food production system which the Island Arawaks developed. The Arawaks cultivated several types of food crops from a system which they developed during pre-Columbian days and a system which the Spanish were able to observe, evaluate, record and, in some instances, practice.

Food was derived from three sources:

(1) *Shifting cultivation*—this was based on the creation and maintenance of "conuco" where starch and sugar-rich foods were grown.

(2) *Garden plots* for kitchen-type crops.

(3) *Hunting* of wild animals and birds and fishing—this provided meat along with the collecting of wild plants and fruits.

The centrepiece of the Arawak agricultural system was the development of the conuco as a mechanism to guarantee a dependable source of food and as an important technical development in the food production cycle of Arawak Bahamians.

TAINO CONUCO

An Arawak conuco was established in close proximity to the village provided the land was not steep or swampy and had good drainage and light soils. Once the site was selected, large trees were ringed (the bark was removed) and the trees were chopped down. The stumps were left to decay in the ground and the felled debris burned.

Watts writes *"immediately prior to planting, conucos presented the appearance of an unruly tangle of partly burned trunks and branches with a rich ash layer on the soil, intermingling with rotting stumps."* (See Chapter 5)

After the site was cleared, the area was prepared for planting by the use of a hand tool called the dibble, which has remained in use from Arawak times to the 20th century by subsistence and pot-hole farmers in The Bahamas.

The propagated crops were taken from cuttings which grew vegetatively and comprised mainly starchy tubers like the manioc and yucca (*Manihot esculenta*) and sweet potato (*Ipomoea batatas*), peanuts (*Arachis hypoger*) and lima beans (*Phaseolus lumatas*). Squash was also believed to be one of the cultivars used by the Island Arawaks.

Planting took place at the end of the dry season. Lacking irrigation equipment, the

Arawaks depended on seasonal rains to irrigate their conucos, hence the plantings at the end of the dry season.

Apart from the nutrients which resulted from burning, Island Arawaks used manure as a soil builder and fertilizer prior to Columbus' arrival.

The main crops which were cultivated were manioc (cassava) or yucca, of which there were two varieties—bitter and sweet.

The bitter variety had to undergo an extraction process which was performed by the women. The residue of the extraction was baked into an unleavened bread, called cassava bread. Several years ago, a portion of a large clay griddle used to bake cassava by the Island Arawaks was found on San Salvador, the first landfall.

The sweet manioc variety was boiled and baked by the Arawaks as a vegetable, and the other variety of sweet potato (*Ipomoea batatas*) was eaten as a dessert by the Spaniards because of its sweetness. The Arawaks favoured the less sweet variety.

Farm management, or conuco management, was based on the division of labour. The men were responsible for selecting and clearing the site and planting the crops. The women performed the mundane activities like weeding, animal caring and harvesting, which could be done any time providing the conuco was not threatened by flooding.

Crop husbandry work on the conuco started at daybreak and usually ended before noon.

Conuco farming was a long term activity as a site could stay in production anywhere between 15 and 20 years. After this period, the conuco was abandoned to lay fallow for 30 years. During this period, there would be a regrowth of the vegetation and a build-up in soil nutrients.

It took the Spanish a mere two or three decades after Columbus' first arrival to exterminate the Island Arawaks from The Bahamas. The Arawak Bahamians were taken to Cuba and Hispaniola to work in the gold mines, which eventually led to their extinction.

After the Taino Bahamians' forced removal from these islands, the history of The Bahamas is brief until 1647, when the islands began to be recolonized by the Eleutheran Adventurers.

ELEUTHERAN ADVENTURERS

The Eleutheran Adventurers came from Bermuda and comprised Puritans, mainly farmers and fishermen, who were seeking religious freedom in the wide-open New World. Under the leadership of William Sayle, a former governor of Bermuda, they set sail but the voyage ended when their ship struck a reef off the north coast of Eleuthera, where they settled.

Life in The Bahamas was not easy for the Eleutheran Adventurers. They began to suffer the adverse effects of crop failure in 1649, not long after their arrival. Luckily, they were able to obtain supplies from the Massachusetts colony.

The shipment consisted of about £1,000 sterling worth of corn and other necessities. This was paid from the money made from selling Braziletto wood which was the principal dyewood during this period. In 1650, 10 tons of Braziletto wood was sent to Boston and sold, of which £124 sterling was donated to Harvard College (now Harvard University), as a token of gratitude. One report indicates that this was one of the highest donations at the time.

The Adventurers made annual tours to the Turks Islands to rake salt, capture turtles and collect ambergris from whales. They also engaged in wrecking to augment their income.

During this period references were made to the Lords Proprietors who were said to be the technical owners of the Colony. The first reference was in 1670 in a letter to the Proprietors stating that it was possible to grow a higher quality tobacco in The Bahamas than on the mainland of America. However, there does not seem to be any indication that the inhabitants embarked on growing tobacco for the commercial market.

The other reference to the Lords Proprietors was in connection with introducing conservation measures in December 1671. It was recognized that there was a need to conserve and regulate the cutting of Braziletto wood and to protect the turtles.

THE LOYALISTS

After the Revolutionary War in America (1775–1778), many British Loyalists came from the United States and settled in The Bahamas; those from the South brought their slaves. The Loyalists also brought farming innovations which, at the time, changed the face of agriculture in The Bahamas. Prior to their arrival, there was no extensive cultivation of any crop. These people came from an agriculturally advanced area of America and, with their slaves, they were able to introduce large-scale farming. They were familiar with cotton in the southern United States and cotton was the obvious choice for them.

The influx of Loyalists into The Bahamas was significant in understanding the population growth, and agriculture was also given impetus by their arrival in 1783, when large tracts of land were given to them and cleared for cotton.

Cotton became the most extensively cultivated crop on these islands, the Coppice Islands especially. One report states that on Crooked Island there were 40 plantations and about 2,000–3,000 acres of cotton being grown. On Long Island there were about 4,000 acres, and between 1703 and 1785 it was reported that the export from Long Island and Exuma together was about 600 tons of cotton a year. Cotton planting lasted for about 20 years until the crops began to fail due to the attack of insects, the scarcity of the soil and poor tillage methods.

The depth of the soil on these islands has decreased considerably since the days of the Loyalists, when the islands were heavily forested. The reason for this decrease was the continual cutting, felling and burning of the vegetation, which left the soil unprotected so that a considerable amount of it was eroded away.

Apparently the Crown was aware of the danger of soil erosion and depletion. In 1787 the Crown purchased the rights of the original proprietors of The Bahamas and then made grants and sold plots of land. The purpose of this was to encourage people not to burn the land continuously but to farm for a few years before moving to another area in order to eliminate shifting cultivation.

The plan was not totally accepted but some evidence of success can be seen today in Cat Island in the stone walls, track roads and footpaths that were developed.

From the latter part of the 18th century until the early 20th century, Bahamian agriculture became a successful competitor in the world market. During this period the principal crops, apart from cotton, were sisal, pineapples, citrus fruits and tomatoes, with the Bahamian farmer competing against farmers from Florida, Cuba, Puerto Rico, Hawaii and, later, California.

Various reasons have been given for the decline of agriculture in the 1920s. Official reports point to the soil erosion and its depletion, the high tariffs which were placed on

Bahamian exported products, and the high cost of Bahamian labour. No one can deny that the underlying problem was that farmers were still using traditional methods of cultivation and not keeping up-to-date with advances in technology. As a result, Bahamian agriculture became stagnant.

EXPORT AGRICULTURE

The Bahamas has always demonstrated the capability to produce large volumes of produce for both the domestic and foreign markets. During the latter part of the 19th century, Bahamian produce and agricultural products competed on the world market.

Records show that 542 tons of citrus were exported annually to the United Kingdom between 1860 and 1877. This peaked in 1879 when 1,241 tons of oranges and 166 tons of grapefruit were sent abroad to both the European (UK) and North American (US and Canada) markets. (Martin, 1981)

The citrus export industry died by 1920 because of bad handling, poor quality of fruit being shipped to the markets and destruction of the groves as a result of the blue-gray fly. It would take almost 60 years before citrus production would regain its export potential.

The pineapple, which is primarily produced for local consumption today, was introduced to The Bahamas by German refugees around 1720. In 1844 pineapples were shipped to Britain in large quantities. Exports between 1855 and 1864 ranged around 2,000 tons annually and emerged as the chief agricultural export of The Bahamas. By 1900, pineapple was an important export crop and in 1907, £30,000 sterling worth of pineapples was exported. The colonial reports recorded pineapples as the chief export crop but, after that date, the pineapple industry was confined to the home market.

The downfall of the industry stemmed from the inability of the industry to compete internationally, coupled with poor husbandry practices and the lack of reliable means of transportation. By the 1920s pineapples for export were virtually non-existent.

By 1920 citrus fruits and pineapples were grown primarily for the local market; then tomatoes came to the forefront. Between 1920 and 1927 tomato exports for the US markets almost doubled from just over 2,000 to some 4,000 tons.

This production capability had been developed chiefly in Eleuthera and Cat Island. The other islands like Exuma and Long Island were producing, but not in such large quantities as in Eleuthera and Cat Island.

While losing the export markets in citrus and pineapple, Bahamian farmers produced a wide variety of tropical fruits and vegetables for the domestic market. Being an archipelago, one of the constraints farmers faced was getting their produce in an acceptable condition to the Nassau market, which was the only urban market until the early '60s.

Sisal was introduced to the islands from the Yucatan in 1845 by Mr C.R. Nesbitt, the Colonial Secretary, but Sir Ambrose Shea, then Governor of The Bahamas, is given credit for promoting the crop. By 1929 sisal production had declined to the point where the value of exports represented barely a tenth of a decade earlier. By 1931 the sisal industry had become marginal as a result of the poor earnings from exports. The reason given for its failure was high labour costs, which precluded the operation of plantations and factories. The Sisal Inspection and Marine Products Board Amendment Act 1931 was established to provide better grading and packing of sisal, but this legislative measure came too late.

Today, Eleuthera remains the main production centre of pineapples. Cat Island is also a high producer. In 1964 an offshore company began to grow 500 acres for export and by the 1965 season the export value of pineapple was £3,900 sterling. The 1966 figures were more impressive and encouraging. Fresh pineapples obtained about B$8,000 on the export market and preserved pineapples valued about B$135,000. The subsequent failure of the pineapple industry was due to deterioration of the stock and failure of the soil. The adoption of innovations, such as the use of chemicals, has contributed to the resurgence of pineapple production for domestic consumption.

Citrus fruits were exported in large quantities to the United States until 1900. When Florida started to produce citrus on a large scale the US government imposed a tax of 1.5c per lb. on Bahamian citrus, which forced The Bahamas out of the market. Another reason for their inability to compete was due to the invasion of the blue-gray fly.

In 1965, citrus production received a setback when Hurricane Betsy inflicted a great deal of damage on the recovering industry. Almost all of the areas recovered, however, and by the end of 1966 local fruit was in fair supply.

Citrus production is important to the home market and is in great abundance from around November to February each year. There were limitations to the expansion of the industry in the Coppice Islands because of the lack of irrigation facilities. Instead the favourable growing conditions on the Pine Islands have given impetus to the industry.

In recent years the Ministry of Agriculture has embarked on a scheme of introducing improved varieties of citrus fruits from Florida. The results have been most encouraging. In 1995 citrus accounted for 86 percent of total crop exports.

The tomato industry emerged as one of the most important export commodities of The Bahamas during the 1920s. In its early stages of development, exports amounted to about £39,000 sterling, and within a relatively short period reached £100,000 sterling. During this time, agriculturalists in Florida discovered that they could produce early tomatoes and this posed a threat to The Bahamas. However, the supply of tomatoes has remained plentiful; approximately 90,000 bushels were sold to local canneries in 1965 and smaller quantities were sold as fresh fruit in the local market. The export market was supplied by the large offshore companies in Andros and Abaco, as small Bahamian farmers were not able to compete on the export market. The primary outlet for tomatoes grown by the small farmer has been through the packing houses and local fresh fruit and vegetable distributors who supply the supermarkets, hotels and restaurants.

OFFSHORE COMPANIES

After World War II, The Bahamas entered a new era of economic development. Tourism had become the engine that propelled the economy and agriculture was emerging from stagnation as a new agricultural system was gradually being introduced.

In the latter part of the 18th century, the Loyalists had emigrated to The Bahamas and brought their highly developed technological skills. In the early 1950s a second wave of technology swept into The Bahamas in the form of large offshore companies that were highly capitalized and commercial agricultural enterprises.

One of the first of these large companies was the Colonial Development Corporation, an agency of the British government, which was located in Andros and Eleuthera. Three Bays Farm in Rock Sound, Eleuthera, was one of the farms owned by the Corporation. However, the Corporation abandoned its enterprises in 1952–1953.

Also prominent at this time were two other enterprises, namely, 21st Century Agricultural Ltd. in New Providence, and Eleuthera Limited in Hatchet Bay, Eleuthera.

In 1958, the principal large scale enterprises were Eleuthera Limited; Bahamian

Livestock Company, Rock Sound, Eleuthera; Heveatex Plantations, Marsh Harbour, Abaco; The Andros Island Growers, Mastic Point, Andros, and Franklin Farms Ltd., Mastic Point, Andros.

Heveatex Plantations grew a large variety of fruits, including citrus, papaya, avocados, mangos, bananas and sugar cane for the local market; and cucumbers, tomatoes and sweet peppers for export to the United States. The Andros Island Growers grew similar high-value crops for export. They consisted of cucumbers, tomatoes, cantaloupe and sweet peppers. Franklin Farms Ltd., however, produced strawberries, tomatoes and papaya for export.

After 1960, several more companies joined the ranks of the large scale agricultural enterprises. Companies such as Scott Matson, Andros (formerly Abaco) grew fruit and vegetables for a specialized winter trade in the United States where they operated a large production and marketing organization. Parker Farms also produced fruit and vegetables; Harrisville Company, Hatchet Bay, Eleuthera, developed a productive dairy and poultry enterprise; the Pedigree Charollais'Ranch, Rock Sound, Eleuthera; the Golden Isles Dairy, New Providence; the New Providence Development Company; and Owens-Illinois/Bahamas Agricultural Industries Limited (BAIL), in Abaco produced sugar. The trend continued through the 1970s, 1980s and 1990s

CHAPTER 2

BAHAMIAN AGRICULTURE AND
BRITISH COLONIAL POLICY

The Bahamas came under British rule in 1629 and remained a colony in the British Empire until 1973. For 344 years, British policies dictated the course of economic development in The Bahamas and influenced the role which the economic sectors would play in the development process. To appreciate the development of agriculture in The Bahamas, the impact of British colonial policies on this sector of the Bahamian economy must be understood.

Later, political advances in the form of universal adult suffrage, abolishment of the company vote, and constitutional change, brought about internal self-government in 1964 under a United Bahamian Party (UBP) government. In 1967, the colony experienced another political change when the Progressive Liberal Party (PLP) won the general election. In 1973, the PLP administration gained independence for the people of The Bahamas under the new prime minister, Mr. Lynden Pindling. The PLP governed The Bahamas for 25 successive years until it was defeated in August, 1992 by the Free National Movement (FNM) under the leadership of Mr. Hubert A. Ingraham.

FEATURES OF COLONIAL ADMINISTRATION

The fundamental ideology of the British Empire was based on the belief that the colonies should be complementary to the metropolis, contribute to British trade, and its inhabitants abide by British law.

British colonial administration was structured to achieve these objectives in the far-reaching British Empire. It was bureaucratic, immune to political pressure, endeavoured to be consistent in its policies, and its procedures were based on law. The hallmarks of British colonial administration were that it was efficient, impartial, incorrupt and non-interventionist.

Within the structure of the administration there were priorities which centred around the maintenance of law and order and the ability of the colonies to sustain themselves financially. British economic involvement required the installation of infrastructure in order to enhance the economic and social life of the colony to the extent where the colonies were able to pay and support the amenities. British capitalists would utilize the infrastructure by developing the natural resources of the colony, thereby facilitating the expansion of British wealth and power. The by-product of this approach was the creation of opportunities for its colonial "subjects".

It is important to see The Bahamas in the context of a British West Indian colony. In the 1940s, the Labour Government in Britain examined infrastructure development in the colonies, which resulted in social and economic regeneration through infrastructural development taking precedence over the attainment of self-government for the colonies of the Empire.

This led to a Commission of Enquiry into the socio-economic conditions of the British West Indies, which recommended to the Labour Government that legislation be introduced for the specific purpose of providing grants and loans for the construction of infrastructure, such as roads, bridges, waterways, clinics, hospitals and schools. The Labour Government passed the Colonial Development Acts (1940 and 1945), but there is little evidence that the Acts achieved their objectives in the Caribbean. If they did, The Bahamas did not benefit.

A healthy socio-economic environment with minimal problems was important for the colonies, and most colonial officials lacked training in industry and commerce to manage the economies of their colonies. They relied instead on elementary fiscal measures to guide them on policies related to economic growth and development.

Economic development was a matter of concern to the Labour Government in the 1940's because it feared that private investment would exploit the resources of the colonies. As a result, the Colonial Development Board was created to initiate economic development activities which would benefit the colonial subjects and the colonies themselves.

From 1950 to 1953, the Colonial Development Corporation operated farms in The Bahamas located at Rock Sound, Eleuthera and Staniard Creek, Andros. The Colonial Development Corporation's reasons for terminating their operations in The Bahamas were probably due to high operating costs, which made their products non-competitive. Offshore farming operations from the US filled the void left by the Colonial Development Corporation's withdrawal and went on to successfully export large volumes of agricultural produce to the US and Canada, which high-lighted the Colonial Development Corporation's ineffectiveness.

The colonial authorities recognized that there were prerequisites for economic and social development. In The Bahamas, the agricultural sector was chosen to initiate economic activities which would facilitate development. In other colonies, it may have been the construction of railways and harbours to enable the transportation of raw materials or a telecommunication system to improve communications.

The need for a reliable supply of water and a dependable source of electricity was often critical for the development of the region. Emphasis was also given to social services, the maintenance of an educational system at least to the primary level, and a health care system to eradicate endemic diseases. These formed the fundamental ingredients in the colonial development programme and were areas with which agriculture had to compete.

In reviewing colonial policy there are many explanations regarding its objectives. Some policy analysts believe that every aspect of imperial policy was intended to open up the dependencies to economic development by market forces, relying on the dynamics of the capitalist system in an "open economy" to transform "backward" into "modern" societies. At the same time, it was generally hoped to tie the colonial economies to that of the mother country and so wrench each from its geographical setting and integrate it into one imperial economy.

AGRICULTURE UNDER COLONIAL ADMINISTRATION

Colonial administrators viewed agriculture as a productive activity with substantial economic gains which would benefit the British Empire. Within this context, agriculture was the basis of all tropical economies and provided the mainstay of export trade. It paid for imports on which tariffs were also levied to meet the cost of operating the government in both the metropolitan country and the colonies themselves.

To ensure the success of agriculture in the colonies, the British established an elaborate scientific network to support this worldwide industry which they owned and controlled by virtue of their imperial authority.

The premier training institution for British advisors who were dispatched to the colonies to man the various departments of agriculture was the Imperial College of Tropical Agriculture (ICTA), St Augustine, Trinidad. ICTA became world famous through its emphasis on research in tropical agriculture, which was critical for the expansion of colonial agriculture if the colonies in Africa and the Caribbean were to continue British dominance of many tropical crops on the world market.

The officers who completed their training at ICTA were usually graduates of British universities like Cambridge, Reading, and London's Wye College, although there were others. These colonial officers were the individuals who would eventually be responsible for advising peasants and small farmers in colonies like The Bahamas.

In addition to ICTA, there was the Commonwealth Agricultural Bureau and other support agencies like the Commonwealth Institute of Biological Control; Commonwealth Institute of Entomology; Commonwealth Mycological Institute; Commonwealth Bureau of Horticulture and Plantation Crops; Commonwealth Bureau of Soils; and the Department of Scientific and Industrial Research; to name a few. During the waning days of the Empire, the Department of Overseas Development came into play both as an aid agency and as an instrument of foreign policy in economic development issues for former colonies, who had now become Third World countries with struggling economies.

Well into the 20th century the elements of a successful agricultural sector in The Bahamas were still absent and this became a matter of great concern to the Colonial Office in London. This was evident in the Colonial Secretary's 1930 memorandum entitled *Agriculture in The Bahamas*, which stated:

> "We [Colonial Office] cannot be blind to the fact that the productivity of the Colony has diminished nigh to vanishing point and that The Bahamas stand almost alone among the British Colonies as a territory that has gone back rather than forward in productivity and contribution to British Trade.

"Retrogression has in late years gone so far that the Colony now imports even tropical fruits and a great part of the staple food supply of the mass of the people. There might be no very serious consideration if the populace had other available means of subsistence, but in point of fact the opportunities of the people to earn their living have diminished rather than increased."

Agriculture was seen as the sponge to absorb an expanding labour force, and The Bahamas concerned the British Colonial Office because agriculture was not producing food nor was it generating jobs.

LAND AND LABOUR IN COLONIAL AGRICULTURE

Colonial administrations usually faced two labour problems: either labour was available but land was in short supply, or land was available but labour was in short supply. (Fieldhouse, 1981) These difficulties were manifested in colonies where the following conditions prevailed:

(1) When there was a substantial population willing to produce on their own land;

(2) When there was ample under-utilized land but a shortage of willing labour, as in The Bahamas;

(3) When there was a substantial group of British permanent settlers who wanted to operate farms but encountered a shortage of land and labour.

In The Bahamas the situation was addressed with the export of citrus, pineapples and tomatoes in the early 1800s. The Colonial government, however, saw the sisal industry as the main agricultural mechanism of providing employment and generating trade to support government operations and various farming entrepreneurs. To encourage this some 100,000 acres of land was earmarked for production in 1890.

By 1931 the export viability of sisal was gone, although attempts were made to revive it. By September, 1950, the Colonial Office in England was so concerned that the Secretary of State for the Colonies communicated through the Colonial Secretary's Office with the Chairman of the Agriculture and Marine Products Board regarding the state of the sisal industry, particularly the mechanical cleaning of sisal and its presentation on the export market. Earlier that year in February, the Colonial Secretary had also expressed his concern about local agricultural production in the colony, and a monitoring system was established.

The 1951 Annual Report stated that there were no new acreages planted, and old plantings had produced 196 tons valued at £19,422 compared with 252 tons in 1950 valued at £16,376.

In 1958, the Secretary of State for the Colonies, accompanied by the Governor and Director of Agriculture, toured the Acklins, Crooked Island, Long Cay district in order to inspect farming activity in the southeastern Bahamas.

Colonial officials in The Bahamas realized that the agricultural sector could not accommodate the surplus manpower. In response, a migrant farm worker's programme was organized with the United States. In 1918, about 3,000 Bahamian men had gone to work in Charleston, South Carolina, and the annual reports of the Agriculture and Marine Products Board showed that migrant work was important to maintaining a balance in the employment market.

Also in the 1950s, the attraction of offshore US multinational corporations to the islands of the northern Bahamas was also critical in terms of providing employment in the lumber industry and cash crop production on the islands of Andros, Abaco and Grand Bahama—the Pine Islands.

TYPES OF AGRICULTURAL PRODUCTION IN THE COLONIES

Agricultural production in the colonies was generally of two types-capitalist and non-capitalist. The capitalist system comprised individual European-style farms, plantation farming, neither of which occurred in The Bahamas, and the development of forestry through large-scale forestry companies such as Owens-Illinois in The Bahamas.

The non-capitalist type of farming was made up of small cash crop farmers who cultivated sisal, citrus, tomatoes and pineapples for the export market.

Another type of non-capitalist farming was subsistence farming. The annual reports of the Board referred to this type as peasant farming. This was the group of farmers who produced not only for themselves but supplied the Nassau market with fruits, vegetables, grains, mutton and pork from the various farming communities in the Out Islands.

COLONIAL POLICY INTEGRATION

Colonial agricultural policy was implemented mainly through the Governor via the

Colonial Secretary's Office. Prior to 1930, The Bahamas had no agricultural staff. The situation changed in the 1950s as greater integration of colonial policies began to take place in a number of areas, particularly in the recruitment of colonial officers as technical officers.

In July, 1952, the Board accepted an invitation for its Senior Agricultural Officer, who at the time was the highest ranking professional officer to attend a Conference for Agricultural Directors at Wye College, scheduled for July 6 to 9, 1953, where The Bahamas was represented. The Agriculture and Marine Products Board of The Bahamas also made a request through the Colonial Secretary's Office to send an observer and apply for membership in the British Caribbean Advisory Council for Agriculture.

Figure 2.1   An Out (Family) Island farm around the turn of the century. Crop cultivation utilized a horse-drawn plough, and transport of inputs, produce and labour was by horse-drawn wagon.

Agricultural development in The Bahamas was greatly influenced by colonial policies. The importance of the export marketing aspect was a key ingredient in generating foreign exchange for financing the administration of government and providing employment.

Tropical agricultural production had become a significant factor in the economic stability of the British Empire. The output was not only a source of food but also an important source of raw materials for British industry. Colonial administrators utilized these mechanisms and maintained their influence and control over agricultural development in The Bahamas.

CHAPTER 3

ADMINISTRATION OF THE AGRICULTURAL SECTOR

Prior to regulating agriculture in The Bahamas, legislation was passed to protect specific natural products.

In 1882, an Act was passed to protect the sponge industry. Legislation was passed such as the Wild Bird Protection Act in 1905, the Sisal Protection Act in 1915 and the Fibrous Plants, Fruits and Vegetable Act in 1917. It was not until 1925 that an umbrella act, encompassing both Agriculture and Fisheries, was passed to establish a Board.

The creation and implementation of agricultural policy in The Bahamas has come under three types of administrative bodies—the Board of Agriculture, the Agriculture and Marine Products Board and the Ministry of Agriculture and Fisheries.

Various colonial administrators introduced different bodies either to consolidate colonial administrative authority or for constitutional advancement in the governance of The Bahamas. Both agriculture and marine products played significant roles in the economy of The Bahamas, particularly in providing employment and generating foreign exchange through exports.

Prior to 1926 there were two boards, one for agriculture and the other for marine products, whose reports are available from 1909.

THE BOARD OF AGRICULTURE (1916–1924)

An interesting factor about the board's annual reports during this era was the lack of mention of the board's members. The only individuals mentioned were the Boards' two chairmen who signed the reports, Messrs L.G. Brice and Gilbert A. Albury.

After the chairman prepared and signed the reports they were sent to the Colonial Secretary who forwarded them to the Governor for transmission to the Honourable House of Assembly, which was the elected body in the parliamentary machinery.

Mr. L.G. Brice's Chairmanship (1916–1918)

World War I was in progress and a number of young Bahamian men including John Henry Saunders, the author's grandfather, had gone to Europe to fight for king and country. Meanwhile in The Bahamas, citrus, one of the main export crops, had been adversely affected by the white fly and blue-gray fly, consequently depriving the colony the ability to earn foreign exchange. As a result several initiatives were taken to revive the colony's food production capability.

A spraying programme was implemented to combat the white and blue-gray fly problem in New Providence and Eleuthera. A nursery was established in the Botanic Station (presumably the Botanic Gardens, later to be called the Experimental Station in Chippingham, New Providence).

To generate interest in, and encourage pineapple production, an important crop since 1855, the board identified contracted "cultivators" or growers to whom they supplied slips and fertilizer.

Attention was also focused on sisal production, the main agricultural export for its fibre, which was on the increase. However, there was concern about the "ruinous practice called plugging where the leaf and stem are dug out from the trunk to obtain as much fibre as possible, thus leaving it bare to all weather."

The other major export crop was tomatoes. The price was excellent in 1916 and reliable transportation enabled the crops to be shipped to New York. The following year, however, export suffered due to poor transport and extremely cold weather in New York.

Crops such as onions, sweet potatoes and corn were also encouraged. The Board imported seeds to stimulate the planting of "war gardens" (to combat food shortages because of the War) in homes and the Board of Education held competitions for school gardens.

A programme was established to distribute sprouted coconut seeds to encourage coconut production as a source of fats for cooking oil. Apparently imported and local cooking oils were both very expensive.

The Board also took a great deal of interest in mutton and pork production by introducing improved breeds. Two Southdown rams were purchased for the colony; one was sent to breed in Long Island since Long Island was one of the major mutton-producing localities; and the other was kept in Nassau at the Botanic Station where livestock owners were encouraged to bring their ewes for breeding on a gratis basis.

Despite the outbreak of hog cholera at the Botanic Station in 1916, a large Black Berkshire pig was obtained from Jamaica for breeding purposes. In addition to fresh pork, salt pork was also utilized from local pork.

There is no mention of an agricultural staff, even though there was manpower for the spraying of fruit trees and the inspection of fruits

Mr. Gilbert A. Albury's Chairmanship (1920–1924)

The Board was concerned about sustaining an export market for Bahamian tomatoes, the centrepiece of the agricultural programme. Tomato production meant jobs, income for the farmers and a source to earn foreign exchange for the colony.

Tomato production was chiefly undertaken on Eleuthera, and there was a continual push to bring land into production. In 1920 a high profile advertising programme with posters was conducted in New Providence to bring 400 acres into production. In 1924, Cat Island was looked at as an island with the potential to grow export-quality tomatoes.

The financing of the export marketing programme was conducted through foreign buyers, who provided the funds to purchase inputs needed to produce a crop. A contractual agreement was arrived at between the growers and the "foreign capitalists".

In 1922, local growers were extremely disappointed with the price that they were paid for tomatoes by foreign buyers. The years 1923 and 1924 were excellent years for tomato production. In 1924, Florida experienced severe flooding which resulted in a high price for Bahamian tomatoes.

Transportation was a critical factor in the export of tomatoes as New York was the main market. Shipments generally were a situation that was further complicated by the fact that Eleutheran tomatoes had to get to Nassau for onward transshipment.

When transportation ran smoothly, Bahamian farmers generally received a good price for their crop. Vessels like the SS *Maple* and the Miami Steamship Company were the main sources of transportation.

Ripe tomatoes were processed by J.S. Johnson Company and canned tomatoes were shipped to Cuba and Jamaica.

Efforts were continuously being made to revive the citrus industry which was affected by the white and blue-gray flies initially in New Providence and eventually in Spanish Wells, the Current and the Bluff, Eleuthera.

The Plant Protection Act of 1916 was enforced, a spraying programme was implemented and, as a last resort, infected trees were destroyed. A nursery was set up in the Botanic Station as well as on Cat Island for the purpose of propagating seedlings.

Through the introduction of an improved variety of seeds, the board was interested in promoting crops for the Nassau market by encouraging a variety of different vegetables to be grown. Garden contests and exhibitions were held throughout The Bahamas.

There was a firm policy on introducing improved breeds of livestock to upgrade the quality of local livestock. Three Southdown Shropshire rams were imported, and Berkshire and Devon hogs were purchased to improve the hog line. Rhode Island Red poultry was introduced to encourage poultry production, and a bull was imported from Jamaica in order to expand beef production.

One area of success was in honey production. Four colonies of Italian bees were imported in 1920. By 1922 there were 10 apiaries (New Providence, 5, Exuma, 2, Long Island, Eleuthera and Spanish Wells, 1 each). By 1924, local honey production was in over supply.

The board continued to encourage sisal production and attempted to revive cascarilla bark production on Crooked Island and Acklins, and cotton production on Cat Island.

The Board of Agriculture era came to an end in 1925; the annual report for 1925 could not be located. The reports from 1916 to 1924 were consistent in their objectives despite the lack of professionally trained manpower.

AGRICULTURE AND MARINE PRODUCTS BOARD (1925–1963)

On May 14, 1925, the Agriculture and Marine Products Board Act came into existence. This Act would be the governing authority for the agricultural sector for almost 40 years. When The Bahamas eventually moved to ministerial government, a new authority figure would introduce a new era in the administration of the sector.

An interesting feature of the Agriculture and Marine Products Board was that the

Governor would annually appoint a board consisting of not more than five persons and which would include two members of the House of Assembly and one chairman.

The principal duty of the board was "*to make all such inquiries, experiments and researches, and to collect and distribute all such information as they may think important for the purpose of promoting the most profitable methods of cultivating the soil and of disposing of the products and also the purpose of promoting the breeding and raising of livestock and poultry…*"

In reviewing this Act, the Colonial Secretary wrote in his 1930 report "*Agriculture in The Bahamas*":

"The Bahamas alone of all the West Indies and perhaps as one may conjecture, of all British Colonies, have no Agricultural Staff.

"The Board of Agriculture has need of funds to employ an efficient staff of instructors and helpers; they should be in a position to supply very cheaply seeds, plants and fertilizers and maintain nurseries. They ought to collaborate most closely with the Board of Education and assist the Board in the management of school gardens. At present, many school gardens are of doubtful value. The need for propaganda, advertising and provision of facilities for production is no less urgent than are similar aids to the tourist traffic and more particularly urgent is the need during the next few years.

"It is not suggested that the Colony should seek the services of a scientist of the first order or devote substantial sums to academic research. What is obviously needed, however, is the service of a trained agriculturist possessed of practical knowledge of the economic side of agriculture on whom the active field work of direction and the advancement of production would principally devalue…"

The Colonial Secretary knew exactly what he wanted and no doubt he was determined to do it. An interesting aspect of this is that he probably preferred a cadre of Englishmen from the Colonial Agriculture Service. He probably compromised with the Board to bring in West Indians, who were usually considered to be cheaper than Englishmen. The House of Assembly may have thought that by being black they would also integrate and relate to the farming community better, thereby achieving overall better results.

In 1928, the Colonial Secretary with the approval of the Board made arrangements with the Government of Jamaica to provide The Bahamas with its first contingent of technical agricultural officers.

With the assistance of the Board of Agriculture, seven agricultural teachers were recruited to teach and demonstrate modern farming methods to Bahamian farmers and school children.

The late Mr. Cleveland H. Reeves recalled in correspondence that "*I, being the Secretary and Business Manager of the Board of Education, had the honour to meet these teachers at the dock on their arrival and getting them temporarily settled down in Nassau pending their permanent assignments.*"

They were assigned as follows: Mr. Haallan Ryan (Trinidad) to Whymms Bight, Eleuthera; Mr. J.T. Wint to George Town, Exuma; Mr. P.J. Powell to Clarence Town, Long Island; Mr. R.W. Brown to Arthur's Town, Cat Island; Mr. I. Deveaux to Andros; Mr. N.M. Leach to Sandilands Village, Fox Hill, New Providence; and Mr. L.A. Jervis to Government's Experimental Gardens, Chippingham, New Providence.

No doubt these men made their marks in the agricultural communities where they were teaching. There is evidence that they assisted in the grading and certification of produce for export on behalf of the Board of Agriculture. These men made a tremendous contribution in plant propagation, especially in citrus, avocado pears and mangos, and in banana production.

It should be borne in mind that these were difficult times for The Bahamas as the United States was experiencing problems with its economy. Shortly after the arrival of these agriculturists from the West Indies, the Great Depression was about to occur.

With no work in The Bahamas, large numbers of Bahamians were moving to the United States, especially Miami, which became a matter of concern. In 1920 the population of The Bahamas was 57,800; by 1928 the population had decreased to 53,000. Agriculture was seen as one of the areas to generate employment and farming was that avenue. The policy of the Colonial government was to promote agricultural production and this attitude towards agriculture was consistent with that policy.

They saw the achievement of this policy "*not so much the creation of a new prosperity as the retrieving of conditions of rural (Out Island) prosperity that once existed and have been forfeited.*"

The employment of these agricultural teachers was an attempt to make farming a viable economic activity. The development of small farmers on a full time basis was the ultimate objective.

The "West Indian seven" arrived in 1928. It would take another 23 years before The Bahamas would have its first university-trained agriculturist.

The Functioning of the Board

The amalgamation of the Board of Agriculture and the Marine Products Board in 1925 ushered in a style of government which was new to The Bahamas. Even though Bahamians elected their representatives to the Honourable House of Assembly, it was a modified form of democracy because the right to vote was tied to land ownership; adult suffrage was not universal, making women ineligible to vote; companies could vote; elections were not held on the same date throughout the country; and constituencies were not strictly based on the numbers of registered voters.

The Colonial Governor not only represented the British monarch in The Bahamas but wielded awesome executive authority in these islands. In order to allow locals to engage in some of the decision-making aspects of governing, the Parliamentary organization was structured around the House of Assembly where elected representatives sat, and the Legislative Council which was, in effect, the upper chamber to which members were appointed for a period of ten years with reappointments for five years each.

The members of the House of Assembly ensured that the policies of the House were carried out. According to the Minute Book of the board, a situation arose in the tomato industry where the board's views conflicted with those of the House of Assembly. The minutes of the board's meeting of May, 1950 states:

> "The second interim majority report by the Select Committee of the House of Assembly regarding the tomato industry was then read and after deliberation the Secretary to the Board was directed to invite members of the committee to meet with the Board for the purpose of clarifying their recommendation in order that the Board might conform to the wishes of

the House."

In 1926 the chairmanship of the Agriculture and Marine Products board continued under Mr. Gilbert A. Albury. The direction of the board's agricultural programme did not change as emphasis was still placed on tomato exports. The sisal crop was damaged by a hurricane and had to be exported as a grade two product. Attempts were being continued to revive the citrus industry. Seeds were still distributed to encourage vegetable production.

Between 1926 and 1949 the Board's annual reports could not be located.

In 1949, the records show that the Hon. R.T. Symonette was the chairman. No significant changes had been made in the programme. However, the Board had hired a full-time veterinary officer and made provisions in the estimates for a Director of Agriculture and Senior Agricultural Officer.

Livestock production was emerging as an important sub-sector and the livestock numbers of sheep, goats, horned cattle, pigs and horses were increasing substantially. This made animal health an important issue as well as improving the livestock capacity of The Bahamas by establishing improved pastures. The Board's programme of introducing improved breeds of livestock had obviously begun to pay dividends.

As tourism was evolving into the sector which would provide the engine for the growth and development of The Bahamas, initially by being a seasonal economic activity and eventually year-round, Mr. Roland T. Symonette's presence as the Chairman of the Agriculture and Marine Products Board emphasized the importance the colonial government placed on farming and agriculture.

Mr. Symonette was a powerful political figure. He was leader of the United Bahamian Party, which was the party in power when The Bahamas gained internal self-government in 1964. He was knighted in 1959 and also had the distinction of becoming the first Premier of The Bahamas (1964–1967).

The Symonettes' political influence and power were not confined to Sir Roland. His son, Robert (Bobby) was Speaker of the House of Assembly during the UBP era, and his younger son, Brent, held two portfolios in the Free National Movement government which came to power on August 19,1992. Mr. Brent Symonette served as Minister of Tourism from 1992 to 1994, and as Attorney General from January to May, 1995.

Because of their great wealth the Symonette family was and has remained a powerful political force in The Bahamas. Like the British patrician, Sir Roland understood that land was the key to riches and status and this formed the basis for their economic and political power, thereby institutionalizing the political influence of the Symonettes for decades and possibly generations.

The Executive Council over which the Governor presided represented the executive branch of the government. In today's context it would be synonymous with the Cabinet. The Council was a nine-member body comprising the Colonial Secretary, the Attorney General, and Receiver General and Treasurer, all ex-officio members.

The other six members were appointed by the Crown based on the Governor's recommendation, and were usually powerful politicians from the House of Assembly.

This was an era when the Governor was characterized as the "First Gentleman" of the colony and the Speaker, the "First Commoner". This was the British Colonial government at its peak and in its purest form.

It would seem that the creation of an Agriculture and Marine Products Board was a colonial administration mechanism to provide elite political figures with a foot in the door to executive power. In this way, they expanded their power from lawmaking and budgetary approving to the ability to influence and make policy in vital areas of the economy, and to ensure the implementation of programmes which would reflect these policy decisions.

The annual report for 1950 could not be located. However the annual report for 1951 showed that in addition to the Agriculture and Marine Products Board, an Advisory Committee was established in that year. It was chaired by a member of the Executive Council and the other members came from the House of Assembly, including Mr. Henry M. Taylor and Mr. W.W. Cartwright, farmers, fishermen and businessmen.

There was a great deal of political agitation among the black masses. Messrs Taylor and Cartwright and several others were the charter members and founders of the Progressive Liberal Party, which 16 years later won the government from the United Bahamian Party which was led by Sir Roland Symonette. Mr Taylor was knighted by the Queen and became the third Bahamian Governor-General.

The technical capability of the Board was in the process of being professionalized. In 1949, the staff establishment showed where budgetary provisions had been made for a

Director of Agriculture and a Senior Agricultural Officer, expanding the staff which now had a full-time veterinary surgeon.

The post of Senior Agricultural Officer was filled by Mr. Oris S. Russell, who obtained his BSc and Master's degrees in Agriculture from the University of Florida. He took up his appointment on September 1, 1951, and in 1954 was promoted to the post of Director of Agriculture.

During Mr. Russell's tenure as Director of Agriculture he broadened the work of the department by convincing the board to employ more technical staff. This ushered in the era of the British colonial officer and began the post-war redirection of agriculture in The Bahamas.

Professional officers were hired in several sectors, including veterinary medicine and fisheries, and an ornamental horticulturist was hired as curator for the Botanical Gardens. In addition livestock and crop officers, and a marketing officer to oversee marketing in the public sector, were appointed.

Many of these officers had previous experience in other British colonies. When Mr. Russell was promoted to Permanent Secretary, Mr. Charles Lynn replaced him as Director. Mr. Lynn had extensive experience in tropical agriculture; he was a well respected officer in the Colonial Service and was instrumental in organizing the Land Resources Survey.

Apart from being an outstanding agriculturalist, Mr. Russell was also acknowledged for his skills as a public administrator. On his promotion to Permanent Secretary, he became the first Bahamian to attain that status in the public service. Because of his early experience in the Colonial Secretary's Office, he acted as Chief Secretary to the Colonial Governors on numerous occasions prior to The Bahamas'attaining independence in 1973. After Independence, he was transferred to the Ministry of External Affairs as its Permanent Secretary.

Even when Mr. Oris Russell was not professionally involved with the sector, he always maintained a keen interest in conservation and environmental matters and provided strong support for the activities of The Bahamas National Trust.

When Mr. Russell was appointed Senior Agricultural Officer in 1951, changes were made which can be seen in the annual report. The work of the Board was more defined. The Advisory Committee also seemed to have helped the technical staff of the Board with identifying the problems the farming community was facing.

Figure 3.1   Mr. Oris Stanley Russell, B.Sc. (Agr.), MAgr, was the first
Bahamian to hold the post of Director of Agriculture. He was Director from
1954 to October 5, 1965, when he was promoted to the post of Permanent
Secretary. In 1982, he was awarded the OBE.

Apart from the distribution of seeds, livestock and new fruit tree varieties, the importance of extension work was acknowledged through technical advisory visits to the Out Islands and development work in the form of improved pastures for increased livestock production.

This was a progressive step in changing the official outlook of agriculture in The Bahamas. The Introduction to the 1951 annual report states:

> "With the exception of the Colonial Development Corporation's farms at Rock Sound, Eleuthera and Andros, the Andros-Bahamas Development Co. and the Twenty-First Century Agriculture Ltd. at New Providence, farming as in the past was conducted as a peasant industry."

The task ahead in the second half of the 20th century was to convert a "peasant industry", which was primarily oriented towards domestic production, to an agribusiness-propelled sector.

AGRICULTURE IN THE 1950s

In conjunction with the Board of Agriculture and Marine Products, an Advisory

Committee was also established in 1951. Its numbers were drawn from the same group of individuals as the Board. This Advisory Committee functioned from 1951 to 1953, when it was abruptly curtailed.

Figure 3.2 The Central Agricultural Station. Colonial Agricultural Officer, Mr. Ian Dingwall, harvesting carrots from a plot trial. Mr Dingwall left The Bahamas for Costa Rica, where he died.

With a Director of Agriculture, the work of the Agriculture and Marine Products Board became centred around the Experimental Station in Chippingham, Nassau, where emphasis was directed in the following areas:

Plant Propagation

Priority was given to the propagation of budded citrus trees, grafted avocado pears, and mangoes for sale to the farming community and gardening public.

The Bahamas'citrus industry continued to be plagued by the white and blue-gray flies. It was also planned to extend the short season of avocado pears and introduce new and improved varieties of mangoes.

In addition to fruit tree propagation, ornamental plants were also introduced and propagated for wider distribution to the public.

Varietal Trials

The board was the main distributor of seeds for small farms in the Out Islands.

The introduction of new varieties of seed was an important responsibility for the Board, and conducting trials on the various seed types became a significant aspect of the board's work.

Trials were continuously being undertaken on seed varieties of onions, sweet corn, tomatoes, papaya and cantaloupe, the output of which was sold at the Produce Exchange.

Figure 3.3   The old Market on Woodes Rogers' Walk. The slaughterhouse is the building immediately behind and to the left, and typical sloops that brought the animals to Nassau are in the foreground.

Livestock

Much of the work in the area of livestock husbandry centred around the identification of various grasses for pasture utilization, particularly on the coppice islands of Cat Island and Long Island. Improved breeds of sheep and goats were also introduced, as well as new breeds of pigs. In addition, there was a substantial increase in poultry, particularly in Eleuthera and New Providence, and in South Eleuthera, the Wood-Prince Cattle Project had brought some 300 acres under pasture and developed a 300-head Aberdeen-Angus herd.

With a veterinarian as a part of the technical staff, the animal health of the colony was constantly being monitored in order to prevent animal diseases from reaching epidemic levels.

The slaughterhouse was located behind the market range. The animals were brought from the Out Islands in small sloops and taken to holding pens nearby. Recognizing the build-up in livestock, funds were allocated under the Public Works Act of 1955 to construct a new abattoir. The facility was completed in 1958 after delays in finding a reliable source of water, and the same facility has been in use since, with improvements being made to keep up with technology.

International Collaboration

In 1952 an agreement was made with the Florida Agricultural Experimental Station to use their staff as consultants to the board, which would cover transportation costs and provide a subsistence allowance.

Plant Protection Programme

A vigilant watch was maintained on insect and plant diseases. A spraying programme was organized and headquartered at the Experimental Station where requests could be made for a spraying service.

Extension and Out Island Visits

The limited size of the board's technical staff made it difficult to provide a high-powered extension programme. However, it was recognized that this was needed in order to introduce new crop and animal husbandry techniques to the farming community.

One of the most significant innovations took place in pineapple production with the introduction of calcium carbide, which forced the pineapple to ripen early, and the season to be expanded to meet the demands of the domestic market.

Export Crops

The board continued to encourage small farmers to grow for the export market which was dominated by okras and tomatoes during the 1950's.

Bahamian tomatoes were still being shipped to Canada and the United States, but Florida had entered the market and became a major competitor. A lack of transportation at this critical time contributed to the Bahamian tomato growers' problems.

Tomato production in The Bahamas was reaching a state where the local canneries in Eleuthera and New Providence were absorbing more of the tomato crop (75,000 bushels in 1955 and 80,000 bushels in 1956) than the exported quantities.

Small quantities of cascarilla bark were also still being exported, but citrus, pineapples and sisal were no longer competitive export crops of The Bahamas on the world market. It was just a matter of time for okras and tomatoes.

Domestic Marketing

The main conduit for the marketing of local produce from Out Island farmers was the Produce Exchange, which was located in Nassau but which had no cold-storage facility and limited storage space for crops with a relatively short shelf life.

In 1951, the Produce Exchange was purchasing slightly more than £30,000 sterling in produce, which covered almost 50 types of fruits and vegetables, some of which created a seasonal problem with over-supplies which glutted a relatively small local market. Thirteen of the major islands in the Bahamian archipelago shipped produce to the Exchange.

In 1955, pigeon peas were the single largest crop shipped to the Exchange. Pigeon peas were in such abundance that 55-gallon drums had to be used for storage.

Figure 3.4   The Market (right foreground) when donkey drays, wagons, and carriages were the principle mode of transport. Left of the Market is the Ice House, and to the right of it was the straw vendor's section.

Agribusiness

Apart from subsistence and small cash crop farms, there were several foreign entities in operation. In addition to those mentioned earlier, Eleuthera Limited, Hatchet Bay, Eleuthera; the Crockett Development, Marsh Harbour, Abaco; Andros Growers Ltd., Mastic Point, Andros, and Wood-Prince Cattle Development Project (Bahamas Livestock

Company), Rock Sound, Eleuthera, had established themselves in The Bahamas.

These eight businesses represented large-scale commercial farming in The Bahamas. They employed substantial numbers of Bahamians, introduced new technologies, displayed new management skills and generated foreign exchange for the colony, particularly those entities which were engaged in exporting.

Infrastructure Improvements

In 1953, the office building at the Experimental Station was destroyed by fire and a modern office complex was constructed as a replacement. In 1957–1958, funds were allocated to expand the Experimental Station by adding a section for a Botanic Gardens.

In December, 1954, the Board and its staff moved into new offices in the Market Range on Bay Street. These included a small laboratory, a boardroom and space to sell agricultural supplies. The offices were built on the second level of a building which housed a modern fish market on the ground floor. The office accommodation was the first permanent home of the Board in over 50 years.

Figure 3.5   The white building behind and to the right of the Market is the building that housed the headquarters for Bahamian agriculture during the periods of Board, Departmental, and Ministerial Administrations.

Labour

Throughout the 1950s, thousands of Bahamian men were being recruited to work in the United States as farm labourers. Reports state that *"a number of workers who otherwise would have been engaged in agriculture in the Colony continued to be recruited as agricultural labourers in the United States"*.

Working on the "Project", as it was called by Bahamians, provided an opportunity for some Bahamians to become exposed to large-scale farming and earn excellent wages which they repatriated to their families back home.

Employment opportunities were limited in The Bahamas just after World War II, as tourism was still seasonal and only just developing into a year-round economic activity.

AGRICULTURE IN THE 1960S

The 1960s was a period of phenomenal change in The Bahamas, especially change in political affairs. Like the colonies in the far-reaching British Empire, The Bahamas was also caught up in the spirit of achieving constitutional advances in order to attain greater control of its national affairs.

In 1964, at a Constitutional Conference in London, The Bahamas was granted internal self-government, which also meant the introduction of ministerial government. Three years later, in perhaps the most momentous general election, the minority white-controlled United Bahamian Party was defeated at the polls by the majority black Progressive Liberal Party on January 10, 1967. For the first time in the political history of The Bahamas, the Party which reflected the 85% composition of the population had gained the right to govern The Bahamas through the democratic process under the Westminster system of government.

The new government initiated new policies and programmes, meaning that the agricultural sector would play a different role in the economy under the new Progressive Liberal Party than in the past.

The Agriculture and Marine Products Board was changed to the Ministry of Agriculture & Fisheries in 1964 with its Bahamian Director becoming the Ministry's first Permanent Secretary. A number of colonial officers had been recruited to fill several technical positions, and in 1968 Bahamian agriculturists began to replace the colonial officers and expand the level and scope of technical expertise.

With the increased number of professionals, the agricultural sector was propelled on a new economic development course.

Policy

Before 1960, farming by Bahamians was referred to as a peasant industry. In the 1960s, agriculture was viewed as an economic activity.

The general policy of the Board was to promote the agricultural development of the Colony and the breeding and raising of livestock and poultry.

Other objectives of the Board included: ① To make the Colony as self-sufficient as possible in food for man and beast; ② To encourage, where feasible, the production of cash crops for export; ③ To import, select, produce and distribute improved seeds of selected varieties of food and livestock aiming at the improvement and encouragement of the production of food crops and livestock to improve the welfare of the farming community and the nutrition of the people; ④ To investigate and introduce practical methods of pest and disease control; ⑤ To protect, as far as reasonable, local agricultural products from competition by imported products of the same type.

In reviewing the board's Minute Book, there is no indication that this policy was initiated by the board. It must have been the decision of the Director of Agriculture to project a new policy direction for agriculture in The Bahamas.

The work of the Board centred around:

Crops and Livestock Production

Farmers were producing a wide range of vegetables; fruit trees; and livestock, such as sheep, goats and pigs. Small farmers in the Out Islands shipped their fruits and vegetables to the Nassau market through the Produce Exchange.

Sheep and goats were the primary livestock species in the Out Islands by the traditional farming community. Pigs were essentially a small farmer activity in New Providence, where abattoir facilities were available along with a market for fresh pork.

Poultry and beef were oriented toward commercial enterprises. There was a poultry association and between the broiler and layer populations production was approaching 1,000 tons of dressed meat and 12 million eggs.

Beef production was carried out by The Bahamas Livestock Company in Eleuthera, where in 1963 the herd exceeded 700 impressive Aberdeen Angus, and Aberdeen Angus crossed with Charollais. A small portion of this beef was made available on the local market.

The export market was supplied by several American offshore entities, namely Abaco Farms, Ltd. in Mastic Point, Andros; S & H Farms, Franklin Farms, Golden Acres Farms, and Green Cove Farms in Freeport, Grand Bahama.

These offshore operations in 1961 had some 3,500 acres under production in winter vegetables such as cucumbers, tomatoes, squash, eggplant, sweet pepper, and fruits such as cantaloupe and papaya.

Experimental Station, Chippingham, New Providence

At the station, concentration continued on plant propagation, varietal trials, the sale of budded and grafted fruit trees as well as ornamentals. Improved breeds of livestock were sold to the public, and work was being undertaken on the development of the Botanic Gardens.

Development Activities

The establishment of pastures in Cat Island and Long Island were major programmes for the board. Thirteen sites were identified for pasture development in Cat Island. In Long Island, feeder roads were being built in order to make more bush pastures available for sheep grazing.

Veterinary Services

Visits by the Board's veterinarian to the various livestock-producing communities were an integral part of the board's work. Animal health was an aspect of great concern, and in 1960 great effort was made in getting the Animal Contagious Diseases Act passed.

MINISTERIAL GOVERNMENT: ESTABLISHMENT OF THE MINISTRY OF AGRICULTURE AND FISHERIES/MARINE RESOURCES

Cabinet government came into existence in The Bahamas on January 7, 1964 under the new constitution which granted The Bahamas internal self-government.

Under the new constitution, the Hon. George Baker, who had served as chairman of the Agriculture and Marine Products Board for several years, became the Minister of Agriculture and Fisheries. His portfolio included Fisheries, Agricultural manufactories; Animal Health; Wild Bird Protection; The Commission Merchants Registration Act; Plant Protection; the Animal Contagious Diseases Act; Public Markets and Slaughter Houses.

No new policies were initiated by the new Ministerial government, but an attempt was made to prepare a five-year Agricultural Development Plan which emphasized the need for technical staff, demonstration units in the Out Islands, and research on the major crops which involved new varieties and fertilizer requirements.

In order to adjust to this new form of government, administrative changes were made throughout public service. The Director of Agriculture, Mr. Oris Russell, was transferred to the Cabinet Office for several months and in 1965 was promoted to the newly created position of Permanent Secretary.

This promotion also meant that the post of Director became vacant along with the positions of Deputy Director and Senior Agricultural Officer. In 1966, these positions were all filled by colonial officers, who occupied all professional positions until 1968.

The major activity of the sector in 1965 was the establishment of Owens-Illinois' operation in Abaco through its subsidiary, Bahamas Agricultural Industries Ltd. In 1966 the marketing infrastructure was upgraded when a new Produce Exchange and retail outlet were opened on Potter's Cay.

The Progressive Liberal Party became the new government under the leadership of Mr. Lynden Oscar Pindling on January 10, 1967.

Extension Work

The Board did not have an extension unit, although there was a need to perform extension functions. Only periodic visits were made to the farming districts primarily for advisory purposes because of the limited number of technically trained personnel on the staff.

In 1963, after 38 years, the Agriculture and Marine Products Board ceased to be the government's administrative arm for agriculture in The Bahamas.

AGRICULTURE IN THE 1970s, 1980s AND 1990s

Background

Prior to the 1970s, the food production system in The Bahamas was principally on a part-time basis with a technology which was essentially traditional. Apart from a poultry industry of four units, two or three pork producers, the two dairy farms, one in New Providence, the other in Hatchet Bay, Eleuthera and two offshore American operations, the Bahamian food production system was at an extremely low level of technical development with an output which was purely seasonal and declining in some respects.

In 1973 two significant events took place, firstly The Bahamas Agricultural Research Training and Development Project in North Andros came into existence and secondly, several hundred acres of new land in various parts of The Bahamas were cleared for production (through government assistance). In conjunction with this, factors such as expanded duty-free concessions, the availability of credit through commercial banks, placement of extension officers in the Family Islands and the development of specific crop and livestock production programmes came on stream.

The Bahamas Agricultural Research Training and Development Project, BARTAD as it was commonly known, dealt with three specific aspects of Bahamian Agriculture.

Research: Prior to BARTAD very little research work had been done on the agricultural capability of Bahamian soils. The intention of the BARTAD programme was to indicate a wide range of agricultural activities in which the Bahamian farmer had an opportunity to compete with imported products at world market prices.

Training: In order for BARTAD to function as an efficient research facility, it was necessary to train Bahamians at every level. This training programme, in conjunction with the Government's scholarship programme, had resulted in 28 Bahamians being professionally trained in agriculture. The majority of these individuals also received post-graduate qualifications and experience. This was a dramatic turnaround in that in 1968 there was only one Bahamian professional officer in the Ministry.

Development: In order to improve the technical capabilities of Bahamian farmers it became necessary to develop family farm units in the 40-80 acres range on which a combination of enterprises (vegetables, livestock, orchard trees) would be organized to such an extent that those individuals occupying one of the farms would be able to earn an income comparable to that of workers in the tourism or construction sectors.

The Bahamas Land Resources Survey indicated that there were approximately 238,000 acres of land which was ideal for agricultural development. In 1973 only about 5% or 12,000 acres of land were under production. With this resource available, the government subsidized an extensive land clearing programme throughout The Bahamas. Even though approximately 124,000 acres of this land is on Andros (134,000), Abaco (50,000) and Grand Bahama (30,000), the traditional farming island of Eleuthera, Exuma,

Long Islands and Cat Island still received the bulk of the land clearing subsidy. A special programme was designed for the southeastern Bahamas, specifically Acklins, Mayaguana and Crooked Island.

Sectoral Performance in the 1970s

As a result of agricultural infrastructural improvements and manpower development, a significant growth pattern in the sector began to emerge. The National Food Bill of The Bahamas (exclusive of live animals) was escalating as indicated in Table 7.2. This expanding food import bill stemmed from the growth in tourism.

Visitor arrivals in The Bahamas had surpassed the million mark by 1971 as The Bahamas attracted 1.5 million visitors. This was a period when stopover or air arrivals comprised the majority of visitors when compared to cruise ship arrivals. The increase in arrivals fueled domestic food consumption. Tourism would continue to have a substantial impact not only on food imports to feed the visitors but also on the transformation of the Bahamian diet.

Tourism propelled food imports on the one hand while an aggressive policy framework pushed local production. In 1974, the value of local food output was $10.5 million and by 1977, output had grown to slightly more than $16.5 million. The new policy direction was taking hold and having a positive effect on the sector.

The above trend represented a compounded average growth rate of 16.4% per year; growth for the total economy (GDP) over the same period was 5.4% per annum with total value increasing from $685 million to $802 million.

Steady advances in output were made by the poultry and the fruits and vegetable sub-sectors as the following figures show:

Value of Local Poultry Production	Value of Fresh Fruit Vegetable Production
1974—$7,074,200	1974—$1,738,200
1975—$8,697,600	1975—$2,173,400
1976—$9,600,000	1976—$3,279,000
1977—$11,184,000	1977—$4,726,738

This increase in poultry production, no doubt, has contributed to the decline of the livestock and poultry component of food imports from 44.4% in 1973 to 35.4% in 1977.

The value of local fruits and vegetables increased from $1.7 million in 1973 to $4.7 million in 1977. This represents a compounded average growth rate of 39.6% per annum. With such an increase, it is not surprising that fresh fruits and vegetables imports have remained steady or may have actually declines in real terms over the period.

The export of agricultural products has been increasing steadily. Whereas in 1974 agricultural exports amounted to some $389,652, the figures for 1976 were $1,075,640. There was a decrease, however, in 1977 when exports dipped to $688,967. Thus while agricultural exports were less that 1% of total exports in 1973, they had increased to 6.2% in 1976.

Statistical projections estimated that based on the growth over the period 1973–1977 by 1985 the value of local production would be in excess of $34 million with fruits and vegetables accounting for $15 million and poultry being worth about $18 million.

The GDP in 1977 had been projected by various sources at around $802 million of which the Agricultural Sector contributed about 2%. With continual growth and development it was reasonable to expect that by 1985 this should have increased to about 3%–3.5%.

When the 1970 Census of population was taken the labour force in the Agricultural Sector was 3,099 which represented 4.4% of the total labour force of about 69,791. In 1978, the agricultural census revealed that the agricultural labour force had jumped to 5,561 and this represented 6% of the total labour force of 93,450. This 82.7% increase of agricultural employment over 8 years was in comparison to a 33.9% increase in total population over the period and thus the rate of increase of agricultural employment had been greater than the rate of increase of population. One could therefore, conclude that either agriculture had become more attractive as a means of employment or alternative employment had become less available or attractive. It also demonstrated that the sector was able to maintain Family Island farming communities with sustainable employment.

Marketing Infrastructure

The potential of the Bahamian Agricultural Sector was as evident then as it is today, almost four decades later. However, one cannot escape the fact that increased production must be channeled not only at import substitution but also at the export markets of North America and Europe. It is necessary, whether for domestic or foreign consumption, that a high quality product is made available. As a result of this outlook, steps were taken to improve the marketing infrastructure for locally grown produce. The main answer for this improvement was the establishment of packing houses in the production centers. The concept was to make it easier for the farmer to deliver crops in his farming community and receive prompt payment. Eight packing house on the islands of North Andros, Eleuthera, (2) Exuma, (3) Cat Island and Long Island (2), were constructed along with a wholesale Produce Exchange outlet in Freeport, Grand Bahama.

Agro-Industrial Development

An aspect of agriculture which had not been given the proper impetus was the development of agro-industries. Agro-industrial activity has been confined to food processing in the 1970s and 1980s. There were three canneries in The Bahamas—two in Nassau and the one in Eleuthera which is now closed. These canneries utilize a substantial amount of local raw material like tomatoes and okra. The canneries would like to diversify and expand their operations but in some cases, the supply of local raw material was not available and, in other instances, the cost was prohibitive. Agro-industries have also been negatively impacted by the decision to harmonize duties as was the case in 1996. This initiative resulted in the duty reduction of a number of commodities, i.e. broiler production, pigeon pea, guava and tomato processing and the Light Industry and Manufacturing Sector.

As the sector expanded, the industrialization of the sector should have become more pronounced. If this had occurred a different clientele of worker would have come into existence as well as other agro-industries would have been developed. This aspect of Bahamian agriculture has been badly neglected. The government's Food Technology unit had not had the desired impact on the overall sector.

Decade of the 1980s

In the 1980s the Agricultural Sector was expected to play a more dynamic role in the economy. This dynamic role called for expanded growth and development which meant a greater involvement in agricultural by the private sector. For the past twenty years, almost all of the attention and emphasis was given to the small farmer. In order to achieve a "take-off" growth position, the private sector will need to provide the necessary growth catalyst. Capital intensive, mechanized production technology and agribusiness development were fundamental ingredients for the exploitation of the agricultural potential on the Pine Islands of Abaco, Andros and Grand Bahama. Economies of scale had to come into play in the agricultural sector in order to ensure a higher level of efficiency and greater utilization of financial and manpower resources, in essence to improve the competitiveness of the sector.

The Department of Agriculture had projected a minimum Annual Growth Rate of 10% . In order to attain this level of growth, reliance of the public sector for financing would be totally unreasonable as this would increase the burden of the Bahamian tax payer.

The Ministry encouraged the private sector to take a closer look at the potential which existed in the area of food processing but more specifically the processing of pork and pork products for local consumption. In the 1980s there was a potential market of some $4-5 million annually awaiting exploitation. Similarly, the processing of fruits and vegetables had not been exploited to the fullest extent. It was felt that joint involvement both in the large scale production of the raw material and processing for both exports and the local markets: Again a potential market of $4-5 million annually was available.

Another area would be a public/private sector arrangement in the development of some 20,000 acres of prime agricultural land in Abaco for the production of export crops. The decade of the 1980s was to usher in the era of developing the potential of the southeastern Bahamas. Islands like Mayaguana, Acklins, Crooked Island and Cat Island were to receive unprecedented attention and agriculture was supposed to be the vehicle to bring about this growth. Greater attention was to be given to the production of nonperishable commodities like pigeon peas and to the agro-forestry item like Cascarilla Bark to initiate a processing industry with Acklins as a center.

Agricultural Decline: The 1990s

The value of agricultural production, during the second half of the 1980s decade, has been inconsistent and cause for concern. In 1985, the value of production was $34 million; in 1991, it rose to $53 million of which about $35 million was derived from crop production. This dramatic increase stemmed from the farming activities of offshore growers whose output peaked at $21 million. Delete offshore crop production from the totals and the figure is reduced by about 60%.

Export production accounted for 16,470 acres of high capability land being farmed. Abaco had five highly mechanized industrial agribusinesses in operation on 14,670 acres followed by Grand Bahama with 2,400 acres and Andros with 600 acres. There was also an additional 1,200 acres on South Eleuthera where avocado pears were grown for the US market.

Offshore growers were providing substantial employment for the farming communities in North Andros and Abaco, particularly in northern Abaco. It is this large scale industrial agriculture which was responsible for the influx of Haitians to that island as farm labourers. Several Haitian communities sprang up as a result of the need for farm labour. Unofficial reports have it that Haitians now outnumber native born Abaconians. The sociological impact of the Haitian farm labourer has brought a new dimension to demographic conditions on Abaco. This scenario is vastly different than that in North Andros where Androsians provide the labour and in Grand Bahama which has an urban centre with a mixed labour force in Freeport.

Meat production in 1985 was approximately 0.55 million dollars in value; in 1991, the figure was 0.53 million dollars. This resulted from the fact that the local animal production is declining and is reflected in the number of animals being slaughtered at the government's abattoir. Ten years ago in 1982, 6,000 animals were slaughtered at the abattoir; in 1991, the figure had shrunk to 2,200 animals a little more than a third of the 1982 figure. The largest decline was in swine production where the figures had gone from 5,112 in 1982 to 1,850 in 1991. Declining figures are the same for cattle, sheep and goats production.

The poultry industry was an exception even through it was always the belief that the poultry industry had the potential to make The Bahamas self-sufficient in eggs and broiler meat. The value of poultry production in 1985 was $20 million; in 1991 the value was $17.4 million, a decline of $2.6 million over a six year period.

New Government, New Policies

Under the new government's reorganization, the Departments of Agriculture and Fisheries were placed under the Ministry of Trade and Industry and, until 1969, there was no Ministry of Agriculture and Fisheries. The restoration of the Ministry took place on January 13, 1969*(*see sectoral investments).

A new Board was appointed under the chairmanship of Mr. George L. Thompson, who was the Member of Parliament for Central Eleuthera, where he engaged in farming and operated a cannery which specialized in pineapple products.

The new government, through the Minister of Trade and Industry and the Agriculture and Marine Products Board, wasted little time in enunciating a new agricultural policy, which was:

(1) To sustain and improve local production of foodstuffs for the benefit of primary producers and to diversify the economy; and (2) To plan the future development of agriculture and fisheries in order to secure a greater measure of national security in food supplies consistent with keeping living costs as low as possible; In conjunction with the new policy direction, the Ministry was reorganized into five divisions:

① Headquarters—responsible for administration, planning, coordination, direct services and regulatory functions;

② Field Services—responsible for surveys, investigation, advisory work and the Botanic Gardens;

③ Animal Health—for disease control, public abattoir and dog control;

④ Fisheries—for surveys, investigation and advisory work;

⑤ Economics and Marketing—including the Produce Exchange and retail outlets.

With a cadre of technical officers now on the staff, and the addition of Bahamian professional officers, the Ministry was in the best position in its history to service the agricultural sector.

Under the new organization and with the additional technical staff, the work of the Ministry was more defined. However, the colonial officers recognized that basic information and data were lacking for planning the growth and development of the sector.

A paper entitled "Proposal for a Land Resource Survey and Land Capability Assessment of The Bahamas to Provide a Basis for Development Strategy" was presented to the Cabinet of The Bahamas on January 7, 1969. It was approved and would cost between $1-1.3 million for the UK's Ministry of Overseas Development to conduct the survey, which started in March, 1969.

The Ministry also wanted a new, modern research facility, as the Experimental Station was outdated and was being developed into a Botanic Gardens. In 1968/69 a site was selected for the proposed Central Agricultural Station and construction began in 1970.

It should be noted that a great deal of the Department of Agriculture's work centred around its Field Services Division, where the Senior Agricultural Officer emphasized advisory work which included aspects of the principles of agricultural extension education.

Farming in The Bahamas was classified on the following basis:

◆ Subsistence farming.

◆ Small scale farming.

◆ Medium and large scale non-mechanized farming.

◆ Medium and large scale farming on ploughed land (offshore growers, Pine Islands).

◆ Farming and gardening on New Providence.

◆ Sugar cane production on Abaco.

The pasture development programme declined because of the inability to recruit an experienced livestock officer.

In its extension activities, a very popular radio programme, Farm Forum, made an impact in the various farming communities in the Out Islands.

The Ministry's marketing programme came under criticism, bordering on hostile, from government members of parliament representing farming communities in the Family Islands.

Positive steps were being taken to bring new impetus to the agricultural sector.

Sectoral Investment:

Major Agricultural Developments by the Pindling Administration

YEAR	ACTIVITY	COST
1969	Construction and Establishment of the Central Agricultural Station, Gladstone Road, New Providence.	$2,000,000
1970	Land Resource Survey Total evaluating of the physical resources of The Bahamas—land capability/soils, water resources.	$3,000,000

(*to be continued*)

YEAR	ACTIVITY	COST
1971–1979	① Land Clearing Programme ② Miller's Road Agricultural Settlement Scheme (Land Allocation)	$480,000/yr. N/A
1973	① Bahamas Agricultural Research Training and Development Project (Joint USAID/Bahamas Govt.) ② Government Scholarship Programme Introduction to train agriculturalist (28 in program)	$10,000,000 N/A
1973–1980	Construction and equipping six (6) Packaging Houses: N. Andros, N. Eleuthera, Central Eleuthera, S. Eleuthera, Cat Island, N. Long Island and Wholesale Outlet, Freeport.	$1,000,000
1974–1975	① Establishment of the Cooperative Movement via Cooperative Societies Act, particularly Agricultural Cooperatives. ② Purchase of the Hatchet Bay Plantation, Hatchet Bay, Eleuthera and its properties in N.P.	N/A
1976	Placement of professionally trained Agriculturalists as Extension Office in the Family Islands, namely Eleuthera, Exuma, Long Island and Grand Bahama	N/A
1978	Census of Agriculture	N/A
1979–1980	Sheep in-Confinement Project, N. Long Island to research mutton production under bush pasture conditions (Joint project between FAO/Bahamas Government).	N/A
1981	Construction and Establishment of Food Technology and Animal Feeds Unit (EU Dev. Fund)	+$20 Mil-plus

Number of Persons in Agriculture (1978–2006)

Year	Census—1978				Census—1994				Census—2005				Census—2006			
	Male	Female	Total	A/C	Male	Female	Total	A/C	Male	Female	Total	A/C	Male	Female	Total	A/C
Farmers	2,976	1,238	4,214		1,192	535	1,727									
Farm Workers			1,276		2,852	766	3,618									
Family Members	2,272	1,955	4,227		555	795	1,350									
Total			9,717	80,000			6,695	50,000			1,242				943	6,000

Note: A/C census of agriculture years (1978–1994) *Acres under consultation Source: Statistical Unit Department of Agriculture

CONCLUSION

The agricultural sector of The Bahamas has been bedevilled by policies which have been short-sighted, inconsistent with the economic realities of the day, and superficial in scope and nature.

Prior to the 1960s, agriculture for the indigenous population was regarded as a peasant industry. After the 1960s some economic importance was given to domestic production from a protectionist perspective—offshore producers were viewed as entrepreneurs and investors attaching financial importance to their activities.

The protectionist attitude also affected the offshore growers. The minutes of board meetings show how offshore growers were denied access to the domestic market. It was the boards' view that offshore growers were in The Bahamas to produce for the export market solely. Only under unusual conditions were they able to put their produce on the local market and only with the approval of the board.

Throughout the life of the board there were continuous investigations into administrative matters. The board was constantly concerned about the granting of duty-free permits, approval of applications for offshore entities to engage in farming, personnel matters such as promotions and salary increases, responding to complaints and other correspondence from the farming community, and recommending the recurrent and capital budgets to the Executive Council and ultimately to the House of Assembly.

The protectionist view was enforced by the boards' authority to recommend the introduction of an increase or decrease in the tariff rates for imported fruits and vegetables depending on the quantity which was available to the market from local producers. The board never seemed to be interested in establishing a comprehensive development policy for agriculture in The Bahamas.

Defining a comprehensive policy for agriculture in the 1960s was extremely difficult as The Bahamas achieved internal self government in January 1964 and, three years later, a new administration took over the reins of government.

For productive agriculture to take place in The Bahamas the elements of a comprehensive agricultural policy should have comprised the following:

◆ Food for local consumption.
◆ Raw materials for agro-industries.

◆ Employment which generates income.

◆ Greater income, which encourages other industrial, commercial and service activities.

◆ Export market development in order to generate foreign exchange and foster growth in output.

◆ Saving foreign exchange through import substitution.

◆ Opportunities for increased taxation through the development of agribusinesses which also provide a base for employment expansion.

These seven elements are still the keys to developing a dynamic agricultural sector today and can be achieved through a motivated farming community, a competitive group of agribusinesses and resourceful and competent professional and technical manpower.

The seven points must be packaged to propel the sector to new heights in order to lift the sector's significance in the Bahamian economy.

The concluding paragraph in the Department of Agriculture and Fisheries 1970 Report states:

"Unless and until government formulates a forward looking agricultural policy, and differentiates between the requirements of the consumer in a sophisticated modern society, and the social requirements and cost of retaining the settlements in the Out Islands, much of this frustration and criticism will remain.

"Modern mechanized agriculture and the social welfare of the vast majority of the present producers are two entirely different things, and both in themselves are worthy of attention."

The decade of the 1970s saw great progress in the agricultural sector as a result of approximately $20–25 million in public sector investment. These investments were directed to manpower training and development as well as improving the infrastructure for marketing and research. Investment potential of the sector was highlighted as US agribusinesses saw The Bahamas as a production locale in view of the fact that Florida was experiencing severe cold spells and farming was competing with resort development for land. The 1970s represented a high water mark for Bahamian agriculture.

During the decade of the 1980s, local output varied between $20 million in 1980 and $34 million in 1989. This period was one of stagnation and is reflected not only in output but also in the decrease in acreage under production, farm labour and small farmers.

The 1994 Census of Agriculture provided the data to verify that the agricultural sector had shrunk to unprecedented levels. Bahamian agriculture was in serious trouble. Output fluctuated during the decade between $36 million and $55 million. Imports were mounting as The Bahamas became an urban society. The situation would be further compounded by the fact that the global trading environment was becoming increasingly liberalized. By 1995, every country in the hemisphere was a member of the World Trade Organization (WTO) except The Bahamas.

By the end of the 20th century, the global population would surpass 6 billion, against less than 3 billion twenty years ago and is projected to reach 9.5 billion by 2050. The world's agricultural sector must be able to produce the food needed for an expanding global population, 90% of which is in developing countries like The Bahamas. Almost 50% more food would have to be grown in the year 2000. Additional food supplies will be needed by the end of the century to conquer famine and malnutrition and to accommodate the requirements for improved nutrition as well as meet the demands for higher incomes which are being generated in the emerging economies of India, Brazil, China, Russia and South Africa.

As a result of the economic downturns over the past three or four decades, the scourge of hunger and malnutrition has appeared in pockets of our Bahamian society, particularly in the inner city communities of New Providence.

Our capability to produce our own food is being threatened by a declining agricultural sector. During the next decade, we should establish enlightened agricultural policies to meet, not only domestic demands, but by making it possible for Bahamian agribusinesses to exploit export markets.

As The Bahamas and the rest of the Caribbean emerge from the first decade of the 21st century, food production in the region as a whole is in serious decline to the point where the region has become a food deficit locale. With a burgeoning tourism industry, food imports will increase.

On the global scene, food production is being challenged by issues like global warming, water security, population growth, the need for a second "green" revolution and the escalation in the need for fossil fuel. National and region food production policies must be successful in addressing the issues of food security.

CHAPTER 4

ORGANIZATION OF THE AGRICULTURAL SECTOR

Historically, farming in The Bahamas was a fundamental activity. It provided food from an environment where the growing conditions were extremely different and difficult for Europeans. Food production for subsistence was the first order of business and, as production became more refined, surpluses could be exported.

The capability to export food would take more than 300 years after Columbus' arrival even though braziletto wood and cotton were being exported in the late 1600s and 1700s.

Lacking a plantocracy, agriculture in The Bahamas was organized around essentially medium and small farmers growing for subsistence purposes with several cash crops for the domestic market and a few crops like sisal, pineapples, tomatoes and citrus for exporting.

After this capability was demonstrated, The Bahamas became an attractive place for foreign agricultural entrepreneurs. In the early 1900s, the Board of Agriculture's annual report states:

> "The agricultural year began with the brightest prospects. Before the crop of the previous year was disposed of, foreign capitalists were on the scene, taking up land and making contracts with local growers, prepared to advance the necessary funds to secure the largest crop of tomatoes ever produced in the Colony."

This trend of foreign agricultural entrepreneurs has continued throughout the century. With its close proximity to the US mainland, a frost-free climate and growing conditions similar to the rockland areas of Homestead, Florida, growers from Florida saw their Bahamian operations as *"an insurance against the complete loss of winter crops from frost damage"*.

The attraction of offshore agricultural enterprises has always been part of the programme to attract foreign investors to The Bahamas. These foreign agribusinesses have brought in new farming technology, have provided training and jobs, and assisted the country in saving and earning valuable foreign exchange.

Incentives included duty-free permits for equipment and supplies, repatriation of profits, liberal and long-term lease arrangements for high capability farmland, and the availability of work permits for specialist manpower.

Apart from the offshore operations, the remainder of the Sector was in the hands of Bahamians.

FARMER GROUPS

Farmer groups are an integral part of agricultural development, and the establishment of these entities have long been attempted in various forms in The Bahamas.

In the 1920s reference was made to *"the formation of a farmers union for the western localities which it is hoped may be associated with the Farmers Union of Fox Hill. Much could be done through these unions in the direction of organization"*.

The unions were seen as a means of channelling farming information to the farmers, teaching new training husbandry practices and most of all the medium through which farmers could market their produce collectively.

The details on these farmer unions are sketchy and brief. In the Board's annual reports of the late 1940s and 1950s, there is a standard section which states:

> "There were no cooperative societies other than 20 Tomato Growers Associations on the islands of Eleuthera and Cat Island. These associations are assisted by the Board of Agriculture to the extent of advancing seed and fertilizer, etc. for the tomato and other crops. The Board markets the crops and deducts the advances from the proceeds of each consignor until the entire indebtedness is liquidated. The Produce Exchange also markets and sells farm produce for 65 Farmers' Associations situated throughout the Colony." (Barnett, 1984)

These Associations played important roles in both domestic and export farming. Even though on the export side, "foreign buyers" had to deal with many small farmers, the associations then became the mechanism to bring the farmers together into a body. The unity of these associations is hard to determine; likewise the ability to ascertain their control over the growers.

From time to time, produce from the associations to the Produce Exchange arrived in an immature state, thereby causing losses, sometimes quite severe losses. It was known that there was a difficulty in getting the growers to grade their tomatoes properly and because of their inability to discipline themselves, the board had to employ tomato inspectors.

The cooperative movement as an economic tool for farmers did not come into practice until the 1970s, after the Cooperative Societies Act was passed in 1974 and the Department of Cooperatives Development became operational in 1975.

As a result of The Bahamas Research, Training and Development Project, the North Andros Agricultural Cooperative came into existence. Since then, a number of agricultural cooperatives have sprung up all over The Bahamas: Long Island (1978), Exuma (1979), North Cat Island (1979), Mayaguana (1984), Grand Bahama, Abaco (1990), and New Providence (1995).

The roles of the various cooperatives vary according to the needs of the farming community or the farm group (such as livestock, crops); however, under the Cooperative Society Act, cooperatives are granted benefits, which are viewed as incentives by the farmers, to form these entities. The most prominent incentive is the ability to import items duty-free as well as earn exemption from stamp tax.

In addition to cooperatives, farmers were encouraged to participate in fairs and expositions. From as far back as the 1920s, there are references to events where farmers from the various islands competed against each other.

The Board of Education was the one governmental entity which encouraged essay competitions among the schools, specifically those in the Out Islands. Garden exhibitions and, competition for fruits and vegetables produced by these schools, were also held. The "West Indian Seven" were very influential in heightening the national interest in these school garden events.

During the 1970s the Commonwealth Fair came into existence. This fair was unique in that farmers from all of the islands were urged to participate. Individual on-island competitions were held before the national event, where the best from the islands were judged and sent to Nassau to compete in the national event.

Categories were not confined to agriculture alone but also to handicrafts, cottage industries, manufacturing, art, and displays from manufacturers.

The event was organized during the directorship of Mr. Claude Smith, a British-trained agriculturist who had worked in sugar cane breeding on the sugar estates of Jamaica. Mr. Smith returned home to work for The Bahamas Agricultural Industries Ltd., which established 25,000 acres of sugar cane on the island of Abaco in 1966. When BAIL went into liquidation in 1971, Mr. Smith joined the Ministry of Agriculture as Director of Agriculture. He was the second Bahamian to hold that post.

In 1993, the Commonwealth Fair was replaced by the National Agricultural and Industrial Exposition, whose aim was to diversify the Bahamian economy by emphasizing both agriculture and manufacturing. The Exposition came under the aegis of the Ministry of Agriculture's National Advisory Committee on Agriculture, which coordinated its efforts in organizing the Exposition with the Ministry of Agriculture and Fisheries, The Bahamas Agricultural and Industrial Corporation (BAIC) and The Bahamas Chamber of Commerce.

Farmer groups in The Bahamas have not been effective from the perspective of being able to influence agricultural policy. There is no national body representing the farmers of The Bahamas. However, farmers recognize the need for such an entity.

AGRICULTURAL EDUCATION AND TRAINING

Bahamian professional agriculturists have been trained all over the world. During the last 20 years, most have studied in the United States, the United Kingdom, and the Caribbean.

During the 1970s, most trained agriculturists sought employment in the public service. As the sector expanded opportunities grew in agribusiness, but encouraging young Bahamians to seek career opportunities in the field of agricultural science was not an easy task initially. With limited employment opportunities, and an activity which was located in the Out Islands away from the urban centres of Nassau and Freeport, the call was not heard by many.

The Bahamian government recognized that there was a need for trained agriculturists and the government figure who supported this effort was the Hon. Carlton E. Francis, an educator who entered politics and became Minister of Finance in the PLP government in 1967.

As an educator, Mr. Francis was very familiar with Dr. Booker T. Washington's philosophy on the education of black people. Under his aegis, Mr Francis organized an agricultural training programme for high school graduates at the Central Agricultural Station on Gladstone Road in Nassau. As a former teacher, Mr. Francis was aware of the work the West Indian Seven had done in the various Out Island schools.

Official visits were made to a number of institutions like the University of Florida, the University of the West Indies and several historically black US colleges. Agreements were made with Tuskeegee University in Alabama and Prairie View A & M University in Texas to reserve places for Bahamian students to enter their agricultural programmes. Scores of young Bahamians came forward to participate.

The Bahamas had had a long relationship with Tuskeegee University which had deteriorated. In 1936, six Bahamian teachers were sent to Tuskeegee Institute for summer school to study agriculture, domestic science and woodwork. This was to be an annual programme but it was interrupted when World War II broke out. The relationship was revived in the early 1960's, and several outstanding students graduated in agricultural science and went on to earn PhD degrees.

Figure 4.1   Author with Mr. George Heastie at the Department of Agriculture's booth at the Agricultural Show in New Providence circa 1970.

Figure 4.2   Fenced area for School Garden at the Government's S.C. McPherson Secondary School, April, 1996.

Dr. P.K. Biswas, Professor of Agricultural Science at Tuskeegee, took keen interest in these early students and over the past 40 years he has advised and counselled scores of Bahamians.

Dr. Biswas' early students included Dr. P. A. Bonamy, who was a graduate of the Jamaica School of Agriculture, and acted as Director of Agriculture in The Bahamas, and then went on to become an Under Secretary in the Ministry of Agriculture and Fisheries; Dr. Robert Taylor, who became a Professor of Agriculture specializing in Soil Science at the Alabama A & M University in Huntsville, Alabama and now Dean of Florida A & M University; and Dr. Gershwin Blyden, who became a pharmacologist/physician practising in Florida. Drs. Taylor and Blyden were apprenticed under Mr. Palestine Michael at the Experimental Station in Chippingham. Other Bahamians who followed were Dr. Selma Campbell, Hamber and Dr. Erecia Hepburn.

Since the early 1960s, The Bahamas has developed a strong, well-trained group of veterinary surgeons in both the private and public sectors. More than 85 percent of the veterinarians in The Bahamas have been trained at Tuskeegee University. Dr. Keith Campbell, chief government veterinary officer, was the first to graduate from Tuskeegee in the mid 1970s.

In addition to the arrangements that Mr. Francis made for Bahamians to attend Tuskeegee University and Prairie A & M, while on a visit to Guyana he arranged for a

Bahamian, Morlan Webb, to attend the Guyana School of Agriculture.

Figure 4.3   School garden being prepared by Government High School students as part of their agricultural course, February, 1983.

The Bahamas Agricultural Research Training and Development Project was another important avenue through which Bahamians were trained. Its staff and trainees were sent to Penn State University in Pennsylvania for professional training in a variety of disciplines at both first and advanced degree levels.

When the College of The Bahamas was established in the mid 1970s, agriculture was started as part of its Natural Science Division. Many graduates of the two-year programme have gone to pursue bachelor degrees, and many have gone to Tuskeegee University.

The Ministry of Education has established an agricultural science curriculum in the government schools to introduce agricultural science to school children. The tradition which was started by the West Indian Seven continues today.

Practical courses or field days as part of an extension education programme have been absent in upgrading the technical skills of farmers and women in agriculture. As the sector expands, new and different levels of agricultural expertise will be required, and professionals will be needed to provide this expertise. The Bahamas has come a long way in developing its agricultural manpower and over the last 70 years a wide range of professional skills have become available.

Figure 4.4   Hon. George A. Smith, M.P., Minister of Agriculture and Fisheries, holding a book from a set which was donated by the British Government through the British High Commission in The Bahamas. To the left of the Minister is Mr. Claude Smith, then Director of Agriculture, with the author at Mr. Smith's left. Also pictured are Mr. Ronald Thompson, Director of Fisheries, and Mr. Roosevelt Finlayson, Director of Cooperatives, 1975.

AGRO-INDUSTRIALIZATION

The agricultural sector of The Bahamas imports all its inputs such as seeds, fertilizers, pesticides, animal feeds, started pullets, hatching eggs and others. Millions of dollars leave the country to buy inputs which are mainly supplied by US manufacturers.

To maintain a level of competitiveness with imported foodstuffs, a duty-free exemption is granted on request and in law depending on the input in question.

Under the Tariff Act, animal feeds are allowed duty-free exemption. If a farmer requires a farming implement, he has to apply to the Department of Agriculture for a duty-free permit which may or may not be approved. If approval is given, then a duty-free permit is issued for the item in question. This facility is available to all bonafide farmers and farming entities.

In order to accommodate the small farmer, the Department of Agriculture operates a supply store which sells a wide range of agricultural inputs which are purchased by the farmer at a subsidized rate. This has been an aspect of the Ministry's responsibility for decades. In the 1960s, this became one of the policies of the ministry and continues today.

There are occasions when the supply store's inventory on certain critical inputs like fertilizers are low. This has created a degree of instability in farming as many of the small farmers depend solely on this facility for supplying their inputs. The supply store does not operate independently, as the revenue generated from sales is deposited in the country's consolidated account, which is controlled by the Treasury. However, replenishment of supplies is made on request to the Treasury as well as payments to suppliers. New orders cannot be placed without a purchase order from the Treasury, which controls the funding, and the Ministry of Agriculture is unable to dictate spending priorities to the Treasury. The small farmer gets caught in the middle and suffers in the long run. To prevent the small farmers from depending heavily on the government's facility, they have been encouraged to form cooperatives.

Figure 4.5   Agricultural Extension Officers—(Pictured left to right) Mr. Charles Lloyd, Exuma; the author; Mr. Earl Deveaux; Mr. Cecil Dorsett, Eleuthera; and Mr. Komal Smith, Long Island; September, 1980.

Fertilizer is a major input in crop farming because of the nature of Bahamian soils. Despite this fact, there is no commercial manufacturing or blending of fertilizer. In the mid 1970s, a blending facility was started in New Providence, however poor quality control measures led to it going out of business.

Large operations like Bahama Citrus Growers Ltd. blended its own fertilizers on the farm. Using liquid fertilizers in its citrus groves, the company constructed a facility which mixed and stored its fertilizer on site.

The Bahamas is reaching a point where the manufacturing or blending of fertilizer should be undertaken to serve the needs of the sector. The continued importation of expensive fertilizer as a finished product in bags is too costly, and this makes it exceedingly difficult for the small farmer to compete. The manufacture or blending of fertilizer is an aspect of agro-industrialization which is very feasible for The Bahamas.

Figure 4.6   Dr. P.K. Biswas (centre) with author to the right, and author's son, Geoffrey, in front of Milbank Hall, the location of the School of Agriculture at Tuskeegee University.

In animal production, feed represents 60 to 65 percent of production costs. Animal feeds are a $20–25 million business in The Bahamas with the poultry industry being the largest importer and consumer.

In the past 30 years, several US-owned feed suppliers have investigated the possibility of constructing feed mills in The Bahamas. New Providence was usually selected as the site but, in recent years, Grand Bahama and Abaco have developed modern poultry facilities. There are infrastructural deficiencies and environmental concerns that inhibit the erection of a feed mill facility in New Providence, even though the bulk of the industry is located there.

One major limitation is the unavailability of a dockside holding facility to accommodate the off-loading of raw materials like corn. Feed is currently imported as a duty-free item, generally in bulk for the poultry industry and one or two pork producers.

Smaller livestock farmers, particularly those in the pork business, buy their feed in bags which are very expensive and marginalizes pork production at this level.

The Hatchet Bay operation constructed a mill on its property and would transport its feed ingredients to Eleuthera, where they were then blended into feed products for its broilers and layers. This facility soon became obsolete because the performance level from the locally blended feed was considerably lower when compared to the performance of poultry producers using imported finished feeds.

This aspect of local feed manufacturing has stirred up concern for some producers. Being able to keep abreast of new industry trends is essential, particularly when producers are competing against not only themselves but also imported products. There is a view that a locally manufactured feed may lag behind in technology. The local manufacture of animal feeds is still under consideration and this aspect of agro-industrialization will be a reality in the near future as expansion in the livestock industry continues and economies of scale come into play.

Food processing has always been an integral part of the agricultural sector. However, food processors have not received the level of recognition which would have given them the incentive to expand their operations. This is particularly the case of the canneries which have had to fight an uphill battle to stay in business and remain competitive with the giants of the processing industry like Heinz, Campbell and Del Monte.

Local canneries have had difficulties in obtaining a regular supply of fresh raw materials, and as a result have had to resort to importing concentrates and other ingredients. The best examples have been with pigeon peas and tomatoes. Pigeon peas are grown throughout The Bahamas and are a staple part of the Bahamian diet. In order to maintain a pigeon pea product line, canneries have imported pigeon peas from countries in East Africa. In 1960, The Bahamas exported almost 1,300 cases of pigeon peas as an excess of 4,000 bushels were produced by small farmers.

Bahamian farmers only grow tomatoes for the fresh market. The processing varieties of tomatoes are not grown. The canneries are not the primary market since they pay a substantially lower price per bushel than the fresh market. In order to achieve the desired thickness in purees and pastes, the canneries have to use two and three times as many tomatoes of the fresh variety compared to canneries utilizing the processing varieties. To supplement local supplies, tomato concentrate plays a big role in the process.

The processing of fruits and vegetables by Bahamian canners is a declining activity. In the 1950s and 1960s a cannery was located in South Eleuthera, one of the major tomato growing areas in The Bahamas. By the early 1970s, its doors were closed. This Rock Sound Cannery was owned by the Baker brothers, Useph and George. Both brothers served in Parliament as representatives from Eleuthera. Mr. George Baker was the first Minister of Agriculture and the final one in the United Bahamian Party government. During the 1950s, the canning of tomatoes was a very important agro-industry and in 1960 the local canners processed 84,000 bushels of tomatoes at a value of £41,000 sterling and spent £12,500 on wages to cannery workers.

In Gregory Town, Eleuthera, a prime pineapple production area, the Thompson brothers processed pineapple wine, juice and jam. However, after the death of Mr. George Thompson, also a representative in the House of Assembly for the area, the factory went out of business.

By 1995, only two canneries existed and they were both in Nassau—P.W. Albury & Sons and Sawyer Food Products. They produce foods such as tomato paste, whole tomatoes, pigeon peas and jams.

Through the facilities of the Food Technology Unit at the Central Agricultural Station, efforts have been made to encourage the development of cottage industries using local fruits and vegetables as the raw materials. Several operators have put a variety of outstanding products on the market, both for local consumption and as souvenir products for the three million tourists who visit The Bahamas annually. The Bahamas Agricultural and Industrial Corporation has established a small business development unit to assist individuals who may be interested in this type of business.

Bahama Citrus Growers Ltd. developed an excellent fresh squeezed juice from its orange and grapefruit groves. The product had a shelf life of about ten days and was well received by both locals and visitors. With the closure of the operation, the further development of citrus processing, not only of juices but also as jams, jellies and marmalades, never came to fruition.

Local dairy products made little impact on the market because dairy production was always an inconsistent activity, even though Hatchet Bay made a gallant effort in attempting to compete with imported milk and ice cream. Eventually, they withdrew from the business and began producing a milk as a product from powder.

Golden Isles Dairy Ltd., owned by Mr. E.P. Taylor, developer of Lyford Cay, came on stream in the 1970s but eventually folded. Bahamas Dairy Farms, Ltd. was also established in Grand Bahama in 1991; however this operation experienced problems and could not sustain the production of a high-quality fresh-milk product.

Dairy products produced from local dairy cows never developed into a substantial agribusiness. In 1995, a new twist was introduced in the production of dairy products, specifically fresh milk. Holiday Farms located in New Providence introduced the Farm Fresh brand name. They began to turn out a fresh milk product by importing raw milk from the United States. This raw milk would then be processed into fresh milk and other dairy products. The approach of this operation was new but it was unable to sustain its place in the market.

The development of industries tied to agricultural production either from the input or the output end should play a significant role in this century. The area will open new job opportunities, assist farmers in producing more competitive products, and will deepen the prospects for economic diversification of the economy through agriculture.

BAHAMAS AGRICULTURAL AND INDUSTRIAL CORPORATION

In 1981, the government of The Bahamas decided to disband The Bahamas Agricultural Corporation and The Bahamas Development Corporation and to form The Bahamas Agricultural and Industrial Corporation (BAIC), which became a functioning entity in March, 1982.

As a statutory body, it was essentially the private sector arm of the government for a number of activities, one of the more important being the ownership of commercial operations in agriculture, light industry and manufacturing; or to engage in joint venture activities encompassing these activities.

Prior to the formation of BAIC the government purchased Eleuthera Limited, Hatchet Bay, from the Levy Estate and placed it under the aegis of The Bahamas Agricultural Corporation (BAC). This created a great deal of controversy, particularly in political circles.

Figure 4.7   Hon. Paul L. Adderley, former Chairman, Bahamas Agricultural Corporation and Minister of Finance. Mr. Adderley articulated the Government's position in the purchase of Hatchet Bay and the role it would play in the agricultural sector. He is pictured (centre) with Mr. Cyril Stevenson of The Bahamas Information Services (left) and the author (right) at a BAC press conference.

Eleuthera Ltd. was a major employer in Eleuthera and represented substantial real estate in both Hatchet Bay and Nassau. The primary reason, according to the government, was to preserve about 200 jobs between Nassau and Hatchet Bay but primarily in Hatchet Bay, which attracted workers from nearby settlements like Gregory Town, Alice Town, James Cistern, and as far south as Palmetto Point. In addition, the area represented the settlements which comprised a constituency which was held by a government member. Alice Town was also the largest polling division in the constituency and a government stronghold. There was extreme political pressure on the government to purchase the facility.

The operational aspects of the facility came under great public scrutiny as the farm and its various divisions generated substantial debts both locally and abroad. The Public Treasury had to step in and bail out the operation of its debts on numerous occasions.

This became a recurring facet of the operation. Opposition politicians made it an issue by labelling it as gross mismanagement of a government entity which had become a financial burden on the Bahamian tax payer. Further, it was an activity, they claimed, in which the government should never have entered.

Numerous articles appeared in the press surrounding the government's involvement and the problems which the operation was facing. A strong defender of the government's involvement with Hatchet Bay was the Hon. Paul L. Adderley, Minister of External Affairs with the responsibility for The Bahamas Agricultural Corporation.

In defence of BAC's involvement, Mr. Adderley stated that "*the corporation has a responsibility to play its part in the production of food in The Bahamas toward the attainment of the goal of agricultural self-sufficiency.*" This was the role that he, as chairman of BAC, saw an entity like Hatchet Bay playing in the agricultural sector.

Hatchet Bay was problematic, but many of these problems were inherited by the government. A run-down, outdated facility had been purchased, and it would have taken a substantial amount of capital to upgrade the operation. In addition, the operation was overstaffed in many divisions and highly inefficient.

Many elements in the Bahamian business community, including the press, were gravely suspicious of the government's excursion into the private sector. In November, 1978, these critics were answered by Mr. Adderley when he pointed out that there were attempts "*to destroy the goodwill and credit of the Hatchet Bay operation and the economic viability of the Government-owned facility and the jobs of approximately 135 Bahamians now employed in Nassau and Hatchet Bay… The Corporation is not a Government-owned monopoly but is engaged in business in competition with private enterprise.*" (PRP)

Hatchet Bay as an agribusiness never became a financially viable entity. When the owner died his heirs abandoned the business and the government took it over. It sits there awaiting the rediscovery of its role in the Bahamian economy.

The Bahamas Agricultural Industrial Corporation has entered several joint venture agricultural projects since it came on stream in 1982. The most notable was the B.G. Harmon Company citrus project in Abaco. BAIC was able to negotiate a lease package which paid them close to $1 million in fees during the life of B. G. Harmon and Bahamas Citrus Growers Ltd's sojourn into farming in The Bahamas.

When the government decided to place The Bahamas Agricultural Research Training and Development facility into private hands, BAIC became the joint venture partner with Agro-Andros, the Israeli group that grew winter vegetables. This operation failed miserably and was subsequently taken over by a Florida group, operating under the name Morgan's Farm.

BAIC's role in the agricultural sector has been primarily in joint venture projects with the private sector. Attempts are being made to broaden the role it plays in the agricultural sector by delivering farm management skills to small and medium-sized farms.

CHAPTER 5

FARMING SYSTEMS

The Bahamas Land Resources Survey categorized the land resources of The Bahamas on the basis of vegetation and capability. Two types of vegetation were identified and were closely linked to rock type and fresh water availability. On the basis of vegetation, the two main types of islands were designated Pine and Coppice Islands, respectively.

The Survey report referred to Abaco, Andros, Grand Bahama and New Providence as the Pine Islands, which comprise two thirds of the total land area of The Bahamas. (LRS 1977)

The distinguishing features of the Pine Islands are that they have large reserves of fresh water which support Caribbean pine (*Pinus caribea*), and thin layers of brown soil and parent material can be broken down mechanically to produce free-moving soil.

The remaining islands make up the Coppice Islands. Their characteristics are a vegetation of mixed broadleaf and scrubby woodland. The islands themselves are narrow, rugged and undulating with harder rock. There is some fertile soil of black or red loamy nature which can be found in potholes and solution holes.

Under the land capability aspect, the land has been divided into classes, 191,700 acres which have been identified as having agricultural potential. The Pine Islands of Abaco (50,000 acres), Andros (134,000) and Grand Bahama (30,000) are the islands where this tillable land is in the greatest abundance.

The Colonial Secretary, in his 1930 report, was bewildered by this type of topography and stated:

"The main obstacle to modern forms of cultivation in The Bahamas is probably to be found in the uncompromising character of the land which, at first sight, seems utterly impossible for cultivation and which in its natural state cannot give a high return per acre… Any attempt to develop agriculture to an advanced stage on this sort of land, … one is even surprised that anything can be extracted from what appears to be more or less barren rock." (Colonial Secretary, 1930)

Despite the Colonial Secretary's negative view, he knew that

"scientific aids have never been applied to agriculture in The Bahamas; in other words the potentialities of the colony have never been exploited. We have a means by which the chief obstacle to agriculture may be overcome and until it has been tried we cannot claim to have put the capabilities of the colony to the test."

Unfortunately, the Colonial Secretary did not have the information which the *Land Resource Study* provided but he knew that there had to be a way to unleash the agricultural potential.

Either through sending to or visiting Florida, the Colonial Secretary remarked that:

"the defects described have been overcome in Florida where rocky lands have been scarified and otherwise treated and converted into fertile soil, and there is no apparent reason why the same process should not be successfully applied in The Bahamas."

The 1920s method entailed

"breaking up of the surface rock with minute charges of dynamite, rather as dynamiting has been resorted to elsewhere in substitution of ploughing. Thereafter would follow the scarification and mingling of existing soil with the pulverized rock… the process is of course relatively expensive and to be an economic undertaking it must be carried out over more or less large acreages."

Over the last 70 years, land clearing, in conjunction with the Land Resources Survey information on land capability has developed into a highly technical field, and, perhaps, it is technology that has had the most impact on the metamorphosis of agriculture in The Bahamas.

One technique of clearing land mechanically is using a tractor (a D-8 Caterpillar). A rock plough is attached to the tractor and the rock is shaved by the plough cutting 2 inches deep into the rock on each pass. This is performed until a depth about 8–18 inches is achieved, depending on the crop to be grown. A heavy Rome disc is then passed over the land, and this along with the tracts of the tractor helps to pulverize the soil further. The more the land is worked, the better it becomes.

Figure 5.1   Land clearing in the Pine Islands. A D-8 Caterpillar tractor cleared this pine forest in North Andros for farm land. This picture shows the final phase in the land-clearing process—a state of readiness for planting.

The land clearing technology by mechanical means revolutionized agriculture in The Bahamas. This technique is a far cry from the technology described by the Colonial Secretary. It would take almost 20 years after the Colonial Secretary's observation for this technology to become a reality in The Bahamas. It would take another 25 years for it to become an integral part of the farming system in The Bahamas.

POTHOLE FARMING

Pothole farming is perhaps the oldest system of farming in The Bahamas. It is a system which began with the Arawak Bahamians and has been passed on and perfected by 20th century Bahamian farmers. It has been very successful and is based, until the recent introduction of commercial fertilizers and pesticides, on what is called the "art of farming".

It is a system which has been ridiculed even by the Colonial Secretary. In his 1930 report he describes it as follows:

> "Cultivation of most of the land in The Bahamas might be described as a sort of flower pot cultivation and the pots, varying as they do in breadth, depth and soil composition, are not all suitable for plants of the same species and so it comes in one and the same field one finds the most varied assortment of growths.
>
> "There is no sort of ordered cultivation: here we find guinea corn side by side with a melon plant, then a citrus tree next to it a few peas, a mango tree occupies one pot-hole while a tomato plant fills the next, in short an agricultural potpourri in more than one sense."

Many farmers on the Coppice Islands have been successful practitioners of pothole farming which is unique in many respects because of the environmental conditions on those islands.

Farmers in the Coppice Islands have also developed production practices adapted to the peculiarities of their islands. On North Eleuthera, for example, the farmers would clear a piece of the land by cutting and burning away the underbrush. After a period of time, they would plant annual crops like tomatoes and cabbages, which would take 90 days to mature and an income for the farmer.

The vegetables would be followed by bananas on an intercropping basis, and in two or three years after bananas "die back" fruit trees would then follow. After the fruit trees reached their mature height, sheep would be introduced. The cycle would continue, resulting in a substantial acreage of mixed farms.

This system had grown from a subsistence level to small and medium-sized farmers producing for a highly urbanized domestic market, comprised of both tourists and indigenous Bahamians.

Figure 5.2   Area cleared by cut and burn technique for the pothole farming system.

In the 1950s the government commenced a subsidized land-clearing scheme where the government and the farmers shared the land-clearing costs on a 50/50 basis. The land was cleared mechanically; farm feeder roads were also constructed in most farming communities for pick-up trucks which enabled the farmer to transport his inputs to his holding and retrieve his harvest to take to the dock or packing house. These trucks were usually enjoyed duty-free entry for bonafide farmers with a certain acreage. From 1971–1979, the land-clearing programme was allocated $500,000.

This pothole system allowed farmers to support their families, build houses, educate their children in Nassau or abroad and allowed them to enjoy a relatively high standard of living.

LARGE-SCALE FARMING

The Loyalists, unknowingly, chose the Coppice Islands with the least agricultural production potential according to the *Land Resource Study*. The amount of high-quality land on those islands was lower than the amount under cotton production. It was not until the late 19th century that the more fertile Pine Islands began to produce export crops. A problem for the earlier settlers was the difficulty of clearing the fire-resistant pine forest, which only became possible with the use of machinery in the 20th century.

Around the 1880s sisal emerged as an important crop with export potential. This industry survived for almost 40 years and created jobs and generated a fair amount of foreign exchange.

Authorities at the time indicated that the new product was outstanding itself and of exceptional strength. However, the product developed a bad reputation on the world market as a result of poor preparatory habits and the lack of quality inspection and grading.

One expert opinion suggested "*mechanical decorticating would undoubtedly be of greatest advantage, and the practicability of using portable decorticators should be put to the test.*" This apparently never occurred.

Figure 5.3   Author with Agricultural Superintendent George Dorsett in North Eleuthera with cabbages ready for harvesting under the pothole farming system, January, 1974.

Figure 5.4   Field of cabbages under pothole farming system, January, 1974.

Figure 5.5   Bananas thriving in potholes—"Banana Holes"—on North Andros.

Other crops such as pineapples, citrus and tomatoes were exported in large quantities. The competition, utilizing improved husbandry practices, soon left The Bahamas behind. Pineapples became synonymous with Hawaii; the same with citrus and Florida.

Land clearing by mechanical means enabled large acres of the Pine Islands to be brought into production. After World War II, this new wave of agricultural technology brought farming entrepreneurs to The Bahamas.

Some of these operators were land speculators; others were bonafide farmers hoping for a freeze in Florida so they could make a killing on the US markets by supplying produce from a warm weather neighbour.

In the 1950s these operations saw the opportunity to produce high-value luxury crops such as squash, cucumbers, sweet peppers, cantaloupes and tomatoes for export. The Heveatex Plantation was started in Marsh Harbour, Abaco, by a Mr. J.B. Crocket of Massachusetts. Mr. Crocket eventually sold the operation to Scott and Matson of Ft. Pierce, Florida under the name Abaco Farms Ltd., subsequently to become the Key-Sawyer farm and then as Bahamas Star Farm.

The operations in Andros were located in Mastic Point, a region then stretching as far as present day San Andros. The Andros Growers and Franklin Farms Ltd. also produced strawberries, papayas and tomatoes. Foreign agricultural entrepreneurs also made substantial investments in Eleuthera. Mr. Austin T. Levy of Rhode Island established his agribusiness in Hatchet Bay and called it the Hatchet Bay Plantations and

Eleuthera Ltd. It was a highly diversified operation as the production activities centred around poultry (broilers and layers) and dairy products (600 gallons of milk daily in 1952).

Figure 5.6   Newly cleared pine land with recently planted row crops demonstrating large-scale mechanized farming on a Pine Island.

Hatchet Bay evolved into a company-like town as inhabitants from nearby settlements were employed either on the farm, at the marina (which occupied a very picturesque location), or as seamen on the vessel which transported the finished products and passengers to the Nassau market.

An elaborate docking and distribution facility was built by the Levy Group. The Nassau side of the operation included a holding facility where the eggs, broilers and other dairy products like ice cream were warehoused for distribution to depots which were owned by the company and strategically located throughout Nassau. In the 1950s it was the most sophisticated agribusiness operation in The Bahamas.

By the 1970s, the Hatchet Bay operation could not compete with the more specialized poultry or dairy operations in Nassau and the imported competitive products being sold in modern supermarkets, and the depots folded.

Technically, Hatchet Bay was not the best site for this type of farming activity because the area experienced extreme water shortages. The potable water supply was limited and over-pumping caused salt intrusion into the water lens which fed the farm.

Figure 5.7   Large scale farming on mechanically prepared land in the Pine Islands—a Potato Field.

The poultry operation began to experience high mortality rates from the birds drinking water of a high salinity level. Eleuthera, being a long narrow island, does not lend itself to the formation of fresh water lenses of any great depth like the broader Pine Islands.

By the mid-1970s The Bahamas government took the decision to purchase the entire Hatchet Bay operation from the Levy Estate. This was the government's first venture into commercial farming and their efforts to return it to profitability failed.

Several private entities attempted to lease the facility from the government with no success. The entire facility now sits deteriorating in the Eleuthera sun.

Mr. William Wood-Prince of Chicago, Illinois, started a cattle ranch in Rock Sound, Eleuthera. Mr. Wood-Prince was the president of Union Stock Yard and Transit Company and had expertise in cattle rearing. In 1952 he established the Bahama Livestock Company, which developed a herd of 600 Aberdeen Angus cattle to supply the local market with beef.

By the 1970s beef production had declined and the operation utilized the site as a quarantine station for Charollais cattle being exported from France to the US via The Bahamas and Canada.

Table 5.1   Agricultural Exports from 1901 to 1995

MAJOR AGRICULTURAL EXPORTS 1901–1995

CROP		UNIT	1901–1910	1911–1920	1921–1930	1931–1940	1941–1950	1951–1960	1961–1965	1966–1970	1971–1975	1976–1980	1981–1985	1986–1990	1991–1995
CITRUS	ORANGE	short ton	4.97	1.21										359	4,040
	GRAPEF-RUIT		2.66	2.28									2,130	19,764	61,668
	LEMON												1,123	24,968	17,437
	PRESIAN LIME												2,875	8,221	130,215
	TANGELO											7,976		391	325
FRUIT	PINEAP-PLE	dozen	42			2,672	6,450	20,911	14,785	653					
		case	22.6												
		$					1,924	11,175	3,900	44,188					
		box						1,050	1,050						
		$						1,369		134,306					
	AVOCADO	(EG)										1,208,000	357	697	1,405
	PAPAYA								6,885				1,479	3,187	1,701
	SQUASH	bu.							38,136	1,523					
		$						34,223		66,110	351,220				450,260

(*to be continued*)

MAJOR AGRICULTURAL EXPORTS 1901–1995

CROP	UNIT	YEAR	1901–1910	1911–1920	1921–1930	1931–1940	1941–1950	1951–1960	1961–1965	1966–1970	1971–1975	1976–1980	1981–1985	1986–1990	1991–1995
	ONION	short ton						356							
		lb.									90,865				0.03
		$						15,089							60
	TOMATO (crates)	bu.	9,611	348											20
	TOMATO	$		342,997	995,928	101,920	1,196,000	62,000	8,382	4,225,593					
							139,158	500,337	17,431	50,384					1,787,240
	TOMATO	case							6,475						
	Canned	$							11,838						
	TOMATO								10,970						
	Juice	$							10,751						
VEGET-ABLE		bu.							81,800						
	EGGPLANT	lb.							905,000						
		$							89,613	26,623					
	SWEET	bu.							17,453						
	PEPPER	$							13,398	5,324					621,480

(*to be continued*)

MAJOR AGRICULTURAL EXPORTS 1901–1995

CROP		UNIT	1901–1910	1911–1920	1921–1930	1931–1940	1941–1950	1951–1960	1961–1965	1966–1970	1971–1975	1976–1980	1981–1985	1986–1990	1991–1995
VEGETABLE	OKRA	bu.						3,241,600							417,420
	OKRA	$						92,800							183,870
	CUCUMBER	bu.						83,271	23,411,944						
	CUCUMBER	$						37,958	1,383,993	488,725	7,294,363				10,481,900
	CUCUMBER	lb.								30,834,715		120,000			31,430,560
	PIGEON PEAS	case						1,298						13,641 Shton	
	PEAS	$						1,932						18,811	90,946
	OTHER FRUIT & VEGETABLE						Ckra,7,980 (cwt)				8,238,847	30,840,938			
							19,356				775	4,525	6,239	29,422	61,386
	EDDOE	bu.													
	EDDOE	$								5,081					
	SUGAR	short ton								22,873					
	SUGAR	$								2,591,426					
	SISAL	ton					252	676							
	SISAL	$	365,816	764,290	197,948		16,886	26,586							

US companies were able to secure long-term leases for timber rights to cut lumber from large sections of the forests on the Pine Islands. One of these companies was Owens-Illinois and in 1966, Bahamas Agricultural Industries Ltd., an Owens-Illinois entity, started a sugar-cane operation on 25,000 acres of Abaco land and invested $18 million to start the sugar production and $10 million to construct a sugar mill. Personnel were brought in from all over the Caribbean, including Mr. Claude Smith, a Bahamian working on Jamaican sugar estates. The minutes of the Agriculture and Marine Products Board Meeting on April 17, 1950, stated that a research scholarship had been awarded to Mr. Smith for Cambridge University, England, under the vocational training scheme for colonials released from war service.

The government of The Bahamas in cooperation with Owens-Illinois, its parent company, and BAIL were able to obtain a sugar quota with the US government, thereby ensuring a market for Bahamian sugar. But several factors came into play which impacted negatively on the operation. The yields were low and production costs were high; the technology of growing sugar on limestone rock land presented difficulties; and rainfall was lower than necessary in the early stages of growth. In addition, the price for sugar on the world market dropped as Cuba dumped huge quantities of its sugar on the market and this upset the pricing trends. In 1971, BAIL shut down the operation and sugar cane production was never revived.

The BAIL estate remained abandoned for almost 20 years until the B.G. Harmon Group started its citrus export business.

CAPITAL INTENSIVE FARMING

The Bahamas consumed approximately 25 million pounds of broiler meat and 60 million eggs in 1995. The local broiler industry supplied 60 percent of total demand whereas egg producers supplied almost 100 percent. Currently between 400–500 individuals are employed in broiler and egg production and the investment in the poultry industry is approaching $50 million.

The poultry industry in The Bahamas is an important agribusiness activity and is the most capital intensive farming enterprise in the agricultural sector of The Bahamas. The industry is confined to three localities in The Bahamas: the two main urban centres of Nassau and Freeport and the third most populous island, Abaco.

In the 1950s the poultry producers were Eleuthera Limited in Hatchet Bay, and Sunshine Farms, Gladstone Farms, Godet's Poultry Farm and Soldier Road Farms in New Providence. During this decade, there was a vibrant Bahamas Poultry Association which met once each month to discuss the problems facing the fledgling industry. Rocky, Rainbow and Ponderosa farms came on the scene later in New Providence; likewise in Grand Bahama, Gray's Poultry, Sunshine Farms and Bahamas Poultry Ltd. began operating after the '60s.

In 1995, many of these operations folded and only Sunshine and Rainbow Farms have survived in New Providence as layer units with Gladstone Farms in broiler production. Sunshine Farms producing eggs and Bahamas Poultry with broilers have remained solvent in Grand Bahama.

The per capita consumption of broiler meat is extremely high, almost 85 pounds per annum, which has allowed the broiler industry to grow substantially in the past 40 years.

Gladstone Farms has grown from a 300 broiler per week operation in 1959 to about 60,000 birds per week in the 1990s. In November 1988 it opened its own hatchery rather than continue importing live chicks from the United States.

Both broiler and egg production units in Grand Bahama are Bahamian owned and operated, as in New Providence. Sunshine Farms has been in the egg business for 40 years and its competitor, Rainbow Farms, has had more than 25 years in layer production. The Abaco broiler operation came on stream in 1995 to meet the needs of an expanding market on that island.

Figure 5.8   Broiler chickens at Hatchet Bay in 1981.

In its desire to expand and make The Bahamas more self-sufficient in chicken meat, Gladstone Farms has embarked on a contact growers programme, which is aimed at broadening the ownership and involvement in the poultry industry.

In 1994, O.T. International, a Canadian agribusiness group, became part owners and managers of Gladstone Farms. The new management was able to improve the efficiency levels of the farm and produce a better quality bird which had gained wide acceptance among the local consumers and food importers.

DEMISE OF POULTRY PRODUCTION

Pork production has remained a small farmer activity and capital investment in this industry is very small when compared to the poultry industry. The largest pork producers are 100-sow units in both Nassau, Freeport and North Eleuthera.

The constraints to pork production in The Bahamas are several. They include the high cost of feed, the lack of processing facilities, the high cost of land (particularly in New Providence), and the threat to the environment by the disposal of waste materials.

However, the market for fresh and processed pork is substantial and growing. The level of technology was improved by a joint venture pork production project between the governments of The Bahamas and one of China's provinces, i.e. Taiwan Province.

Advancements are also being made in the nursery industry. Several highly capitalized units are producing high quality ornamentals for landscaping and seasonal potted plants for household indoor and outdoor display. The Bahamas is now self-sufficient in poinsettias, and the scope is expanding for other types of flora.

Capital intensive agriculture in The Bahamas will have a brighter future on the islands of North Andros, Abaco and Grand Bahama. This type of production is limited on New Providence where the pressure for land, water resources, and concerns for the environment are acute. In the next few years the entire poultry industry may be relocated from New Providence to North Andros, where the overall environmental conditions are more favourable and the threat of urban spread is minimized. The same applies for pork production.

Table 5.2   Poultry Production and Value 1979–1996

YEAR	BROILERS		EGGS	
	VALUE ($)	QUANTITY	VALUE ($)	QUANTITY (lbs)
2010	11,858,276	9,656,961	10,744,461	6,036,214
2009	10,191,043	8,415,298	9,629,633	6,017,010
2008	10,515,012	9,111,192	7,450,512	5,476,200
2007	11,473,012	9,877,692	7,250,765	5,329,680
2006	7,298,580	6,239,897	7,250,765	6,437,370
2005	7,298,580	6,239,897	7,765,469	6,437,370
2004	7,298,580	6,239,897	7,765,469	6,437,370
2003	8,615,181	7,356,141	7,764,906	6,438,330
2002	17,065,290	15,191,057	7,397,796	6,130,470
2001	17,148,067	15,282,021	7,094,549	6,012,330
2000	17,834,318	16,589,504	6,478,801	5,490,510
1999	16,191,901	14,406,242	6,186,683	5,242,950
1998	21,039,840	18,986,273	5,232,580	4,434,390
1997	22,403,774	21,323,401	4,986,869	4,226,160
1996	20,990,000	19,440,000	5,260,000	4,460,000
1995	18,150,000	16,350,000	5,200,000	4,350,000
1994	15,180,509	14,457,708	5,084,457	4,345,690
1993	15,510,483	14,038,033	4,853,174	4,148,012
1992	10,700,000	9,150,000	4,350,000	4,070,000
1991	12,711,160	10,860,000	4,616,982	4,200,000
1990	11,230,000	9,590,000	4,470,000	4,060,000
1989	14,405,747	13,195,264	3,989,138	3,499,244
1988	17,440,000	16,000,000	4,000,000	3,600,000
1987	18,200,000	16,900,000	5,000,000	4,900,000
1986	16,200,000	14,800,000	5,000,000	4,200,000
1985	15,500,000	14,200,000	5,000,000	4,200,000
1984	16,700,000	1,500,000	5,000,000	4,100,000
1983	14,500,000	13,300,000	5,000,000	4,100,000

POULTRY INDUSTRY STATISTICS

（*to be continued*）

POULTRY INDUSTRY STATISTICS				
YEAR	BROILERS		EGGS	
	VALUE ($)	QUANTITY	VALUE ($)	QUANTITY (lbs)
1982	12,500,000	11,500,000	4,000,000	4,000,000
1981	16,800,000	15,400,000	5,000,000	4,200,000
1980	14,800,000	13,600,000	5,000,000	4,500,000
1979	14,100,000	12,900,000	4,000,000	3,900,000

Source: Planning and Statistics Unit, Department of Agriculture.

Table 5.3   Sheep and Goats Slaughtered 1970–2010

SHEEP AND GOATS SLAUGHTERED AT THE GOVERNMENT ABATTOIR			
YEAR	SHEEP	GOATS	TOTAL
1970	2,160	1,414	3,574
1971	1,765	3,285	5,050
1972	981	971	1,952
1973	959	712	1,671
1974	873	544	1,417
1975	110	737	1,840
1976	668	670	1,338
1977	886	566	1,452
1978	808	615	1,420
1979	692	539	1,231
1980	590	502	1,092
1981	568	321	889
1982	480	304	784
1983	357	262	619
1984	195	216	411
1985	133	122	255
1986	118	188	306
1987	107	202	309
1988	127	165	292
1989	133	206	339

(to be continued)

SHEEP AND GOATS SLAUGHTERED AT THE GOVERNMENT ABATTOIR			
YEAR	SHEEP	GOATS	TOTAL
1990	151	178	329
1991	172	186	358
1992	177	176	353
1993	109	255	364
1994	155	193	348
1995	172	237	409
1996	159	188	347
1997	169	103	272
1998	199	146	345
1999	199	130	329
2000	195	111	306
2001	208	120	328
2002	72	106	178
2003	69	96	165
2004	86	92	178
2005	172	155	327
2006	0	0	0
2007	88	124	212
2008	210	120	330
2009	133	73	206
2010	169	55	224

Table 5.4   Sheep and Goat Herds for 1958, 1974 and 2010

YEAR	SHEEP	GOATS	TOTAL
1958	22,300	14,300	36,600
1974	10,945	13,244	24,189
1994	6,292	13,580	19,872
2006	1,497	812	2,309
2010	4,901	6,290	11,191

EXTENSIVE LIVESTOCK PRODUCTION

Livestock rearing of sheep and goats has traditionally taken place on bush pastures in Exuma, Eleuthera, Long Island and Cat Island. The bush pastures are comprised of broadleaf vegetation including jumbay and guinea grass.

In 1958, livestock statistics showed that there were 22,300 sheep and 14,300 goats. The Department of Agriculture embarked on a programme to establish improved pastures for commercial use in the main livestock producing communities. After extensive trials of various grass types at the Experimental Station in Chippingham, the Department established communal pastures with pangola and coastal Bermuda grasses. Based on the available statistics, this was probably the high point of sheep and goat production under the traditional husbandry methods.

Sheep production by small farmers under traditional husbandry practices has been declining drastically for almost 40 years; goat production has been relatively stagnant.

New livestock production measures have been introduced periodically in an effort to improve production. In the 1950s the communal pastures with improved varieties of grasses were set up to expand production, but the lack of a maintenance programme caused the pastures to deteriorate on Cat Island and Long Island.

The sheep in-confinement project was designed to revive mutton production nationally but here again this project never really got established, which has resulted in a decline in the number of livestock.

Figure 5.9   Goats on a farm in North Andros in the BARTAD period of the 1970s.

Figure 5.10   Tomato plant growing on top of a "pothole" on coppice land in the southeastern Bahamas.

BIOTECHNOLOGY AND INDIGENOUS AGRICULTURAL KNOWLEDGE

As The Bahamas was securing its political rights through majority rule leading to Independence in 1973, scientists were grappling with food production challenges which were facing mankind. The results of their efforts yielded the Green Revolution.

The technologies introduced by the Green Revolution during the 1960s and 1970s were geared towards accelerating the output of farmers, especially those in developing countries. The Bahamas benefitted from the increased availability of improved seed varieties, new chemical fertilisers, and pesticides. These expensive inputs were provided to farmers on a subsidized basis through the Ministry of Agriculture's Fish and Farm Supply Store on Potter's Cay, where imports were usually sold at cost or slightly less.

Table 5.5   Quantity and Value of All Bahamas Red Meat Production for 1989–2010

Year	Mutton	Goat	Swine	Beef	Total	
1989	85,197	71,083	240,763	17,096		LBS
	187	155	321	36	690	$1,000
1990	106,416	64,844	209,520	38,464		LBS
	233	139	274	82	728	$1,000
1991	117,673	63,783	184,281	53,377		LBS
	258	139	241	110	748	$1,000
1992	121,364	61,034	190,552	38,505		LBS
	264	131	240	78	714	$1,000
1993	76,800	92,923	276,686	63,105		LBS
	175	209	420	127	931	1,000
1994	107,703	67,139	330,296	26,519		LBS
	244	151	510	57	962	$1,000
1995	119,442	81,917	311,712	41,254		LBS
	265	181	482	92	1,020	$1,000
1996	110,044	65,558	310,141	30,627		LBS
	245	144	479	69	937	$1,000
1997	5,549	2,762	318,518	17,389		LBS
	259	79	580	78	996	$1,000
1998	7,048	3,795	353,517	13,634		LBS
	230	91	894	62	1,277	$1,000
1999	103,464	41,407	397,557	28,064		LBS
	226	63	864	73	1,226	$1,000
2000	96,162	33,822	418,647	37,494		LBS
	211	73	956	76	1,316	$1,000
2001	115,908	31,440	405,278	31,844		LBS
	230	68	912	66	1,301	$1,000
2002	35,642	23,923	393,087	23,087		LBS
	78	52	884	46	1,060	$1,000
2003	36,233	22,231	311,896	24,102		LBS
	59	36	704	40	839	$1,000

(*to be continued*)

Year	Mutton	Goat	Swine	Beef	Total	
2004	50,516	19,497	34,114	22,082		LBS
	76	29	767	35	907	$1,000
2005	91,329	32,891	313,819	22,513		LBS
	137	49	706	36	928	$1,000
2006	91,329	32,891	313,819	22,513		LBS
	137	49	706	36	928	$1,000
2007	69,161	32,770	360,220	11,197		LBS
	233	107	1,068	33	1,441	$1,000
2008	110,959	26,179	331,973	16,877		LBS
	193	45	747	32	1,017	$1,000
2009	244,409	233,813	4,876,985	209,535		LBS
	489	468	11,063	471	12,491	$1,000
2010	268,680	277,485	5,034,549	211,150		LBS
	537	555	11,418	475	12,985	$1,000

During the 1980s scientists evaluated the technological trends generated by the Green Revolution. Professionals changed their focus from input orientation to investigating farming methods, especially among resource-poor farmers.

In the 1990s, there has been a significant shift in scientific approaches. The orientation has now moved to farming systems and the application of both indigenous and western science-based technological knowledge.

It is interesting to observe a body of new information being developed to recognize indigenous crop and livestock practices under the broad area of biotechnology.

Countries with colonial backgrounds have experienced agricultural research geared towards export crops utilizing standard research techniques. The developed or industrialized countries, several of which were colonial powers, controlled the agricultural research institutions of the world. These entities were located in state-funded agricultural universities in Britain, Canada, United States, Europe, Australia and New Zealand. Examples include colonial research facilities such as Rothamstead, England, and Wageningen, Netherlands; international hemispherical regional research centres such as the former Imperial College of Tropical Agriculture (ICTA), St. Augustine, Trinidad;

private industries such as the Colonial Development Corporation and global agencies such as the Food and Agricultural Organization (FAO).

Crop and livestock practices successfully employed by indigenous farmers were ignored and regarded as having little scientific value, and therefore unfit for detailed scientific investigation.

The traditional agricultural techniques generally used by these farmers encompass the slash-and-burn method, where farmers cleared small areas of vegetation by burning the debris and planting crops into the ash-enriched soil. When the fertility of the ash from the burned debris was exhausted, subsistence and/or peasant farmers would then move on to another area which would be cleared. The abandoned land would then revert to its natural vegetation over a period of years.

Among academics and professionals in agricultural science, "indigenous knowledge" is a term with no universally accepted definition but with many descriptions, i.e. "local knowledge", "location and culture-specific knowledge" and "localized knowledge systems unique to a particular society or ethnic group" are some that are in current use.

"In practical terms these are the indigenous technologies developed by a local community to solve a particular problem taking into account all the local relevant factors. In the case of agriculture these solutions are developed by farmers.

"The technologies and knowledge are specific to the farms' environmental conditions and the farmers' needs, and help them to produce enough to feed their families and, in many cases, to provide surpluses for local markets."

In The Bahamas, no effort was being made during the colonial era, and none now in the post-Independent period, by administration or research agencies, to study the agricultural system used prior to the arrival of Columbus in 1492.

Pothole farming is perhaps the oldest system of farming in The Bahamas. It is a system which has been very successful and is based, until recently when commercial fertilizers were introduced, on indigenous subsistence farming. Farming practices were passed down from father to son, generation to generation.

During my tenure as Director of Agriculture, young graduates were placed in the island farming communities as Extension Officers and were instructed to study and appreciate the art of farming. In conjunction with the art of farming and their scientific knowledge of agriculture, they would develop a rapport to engender an improved system of farming which, in the long run, would enable the traditional farmer to accept new farming practices.

The scientific community has taken too long to recognize the scientific value of this body of information. It is only now that researchers are concluding that high-external-input agriculture (HEIA) has not had the dramatic impact on agriculture, particularly in developing countries, as was envisaged. The move towards low-external-input agriculture (LEIA) is growing and gaining importance in the research community because the high costs of commercial inputs are placing the small farmer in a non-competitive position.

Figure 5.11   Signing of the lease between B.G. Harmon (Bahamas) Ltd. (which eventually evolved into Bahamas Citrus Growers Ltd.) and The Bahamas Agricultural and Industrial Corporation (BAIC).

Figure 5.12   Mature citrus groves being sprayed at Bahamas Citrus Growers Ltd.

In the case of The Bahamas, pothole farming is a legitimate system of agriculture which developed as a result of the unique topography and growing environment. It is a system which warrants serious investigation in order to perfect it.

The Bahamas is not alone. There are other countries where indigenous agricultural systems have been developed but were ignored for the same reasons as pothole farming. As ethno-science legitimates itself in the eyes of the scientific community, systems like pothole farming will gain scientific credence.

Table 5.6   B.G.Harmon Citrus Production 1990–1999 (est)

BAHAMAS CITRUS GROWERS LTD. PROJECTED PRODUCTION (FIELD BOX EQUIVALENT)		
SEASON	RED GRAPEFRUIT	VALENCIA ORANGE
1990–1991	11,400	0
1991–1992	58,590	2,500
1992–1993	154,500	9,000
1993–1994	263,000	20,000
1994–1995	510,000	35,000
1995–1996	750,000	55,000
1996–1997	1,200,000	72,000
1997–1998	1,470,000	85,000
1998–1999	1,850,000	105,000

Figure 5.13   The late Mr. Carlton Francis, former Minister of Finance, meeting with the Hon. Doyle Conner, Secretary of Agriculture for the State of Florida, along with the late Mr. Lionel Davis and the author.

Figure 5.14   President Arthur Chung of Guyana is flanked by the late Mr. Carlton Francis, former Minister of Finance on the right, and the late Mr Lionel Davis, MP, and Parliamentary Secretary on the left with Mr. Oscar Phillips, Honorary Consul for Guyana in The Bahamas. The author is to the right of Mr. Francis, April, 1974.

The pace of agricultural development in many Third World countries would have been quicker and more easily sustained if conscientious attempts had been made by the international agencies to fund research programmes to study indigenous agricultural practices. The mistakes of the 20th century in this area should be rectified in the 21st century.

CHAPTER 6

MAJOR AGRICULTURAL PROJECTS
(1965–2001)

Successive governments of The Bahamas have realized that the economy is extremely vulnerable to external factors as a result of its heavy dependence on tourism and banking. Although economic planners in The Bahamas believe that tourism will remain the engine which drives the economy of The Bahamas, the agricultural sector was one of the sectors which was targeted for economic diversification.

Agriculture is seen as a way to provide new job opportunities and to earn and save foreign exchange. It has the ability to stem the flow of population movement from the Out Islands to the urban centres of Freeport and Nassau, and could accelerate the infrastructural development of the Out Islands by raising the income levels in the farming communities.

The dilemma facing Bahamian agriculture is the fact that no government has clearly defined the contribution which the agricultural sector should make to the overall economy. Over the last 30 years, the public sector has influenced the rate of agricultural growth and development through various governmental activities. The private sector, however, has played a secondary role in the development process, and this is perhaps the primary reason for the inconsistency in the growth and development of the sector.

For Bahamian agriculture to achieve its full potential, the private sector should become the initiator with the public sector assuming the role of facilitator. In the past, substantial sums of public funds have been invested in capital development projects for the sector. The projects in the public sector are valued at approximately $20 million; about $40 million has been invested by the private sector.

To understand the pattern of agricultural development in The Bahamas, a chronological account along with a description of the projects and the policy basis is given for major agricultural activities both in the public and private sectors, respectively.

BAHAMAS CITRUS GROWERS LTD.

Christmas 1983 was the coldest ever in Florida's history. Millions of dollars worth of citrus and vegetables were frozen causing considerable losses to Florida farmers.

The long-lasting low temperatures severely damaged orange and grapefruit groves in northern Florida when citrus farmers were already recovering from damaging freezes which occurred in January of 1981 and 1982.

Ben G. Harmon of Clearwater, Florida, had had enough of the freezing weather and decided to seek a warm weather destination. After careful deliberation of several locations, including the Dominican Republic in the Caribbean and Costa Rica in Central America, he chose The Bahamas.

Mr. Harmon's choice stemmed from several reasons, such as close proximity to the United States, a stable government, an international financial centre, excellent growing conditions, and an English-speaking, highly literate work force.

Initially, the project was considered for North Andros, which had considerable acreage of land conducive to large-scale mechanical cultivation like the sugar lands in Abaco. North Andros was also the location where the government had expended large sums of money developing wellfields to augment the water supply of New Providence.

The government felt that the project was important and Abaco would be a better site, because the need to clear land at considerable costs no longer existed. The sugar cane fields of the defunct Bahamas Agriculture and Industries Ltd. still sat there as they had for almost 15 years.

After the B.G. Harmon Group visited Abaco they were convinced that they had a good arrangement with the government of The Bahamas.

Two years after the Florida freeze, on November 7, 1985, the B.G. Harmon Group signed an agreement with the government of The Bahamas through The Bahamas Agricultural and Industrial Corporation. The agreement called for a $50-million investment to develop 20,000 acres into an integrated citrusagribusiness.

The first planting took place in 1986 and continued until January 1992 with a total of 1,870 acres of planted citrus. The plantings consisted of 1,710 acres of red grapefruit and 160 acres of Valencia oranges, representing the largest single acreage of citrus in The Bahamas. Around 1990, B.G. Harmon (Bahamas) Ltd. had an ownership change and the name was changed to Bahamas Citrus Growers Ltd.

Despite the project's potential, the owners abandoned it because of financial difficulties in 1994. Fees for the lease and for stamp tax on the duty-free importation of inputs increased and, along with the enforcement of an export tax, caused operating expenses to escalate. The most crippling financial burden came when the price of red grapefruit plummeted on the US and world markets due to the expansion of red grapefruit plantings in Florida and Texas in the US and Brazil in South America.

After eight years, a budding industry with all the ingredients to make economic diversification a reality in the agricultural sector succumbed to the same fate as the sugar industry which Owens-Illinois had tried to establish 20 years earlier.

BAHAMAS LAND RESOURCE STUDY

The winds of political change had dismantled the British Empire in India, Africa and the Caribbean, and in the late 1960s, The Bahamas remained one of the last bastions of colonialism. A significant segment of the upper echelon of the public service of The Bahamas were career colonial officers who had served in many of the early independent countries of Africa.

In 1968–1969 the senior officers in the Department of Agriculture and Fisheries were comprised of these officers who had broad agricultural experience, particularly in the promotion of British interests and know-how.

These savvy colonial officers convinced the newly elected government, composed of men with virtually no governmental experience, that a land resources survey was a major priority for the planning of agricultural development programmes in The Bahamas. This survey would cost the Bahamian taxpayers almost $1.5 million dollars.

The team which administered and conducted the survey were all British. Their Bahamian counterparts were all recent graduates with no experience.

A promotional piece stated "*the survey is a project carried out by the British Government for the Government of The Bahamas in cooperation with Bahamas Government agencies and research staff of the University of the West Indies.*"

Figure 6.1   Mr. Palestine Michael, Senior Agricultural Instructor, at the Experimental Station, Chippingham, with a group of trainees, including Dr. Robert Taylor, Dr. Gershwin Blyden and the author (kneeling).

The government of The Bahamas agreed to the survey because it called for *"investigating and describing the physical land resources of The Bahamas to achieve a national assessment of land capability to provide a basis for development planning by The Bahamas government."*

For a country such as The Bahamas whose physical resources are not only delicate but also extremely limited, a land resources survey is a useful tool for planning. The survey revealed physical resources, which included underground water; the soil and rock, which make up the land surface; pine forests; and other useful and significant vegetation such as hardwoods and cascarilla. The recording of agricultural activities, assembling of meteorological data, and the mapping and classification of land according to capability were also undertaken.

The survey was completed in the early 1970s and, over the years, it has made a significant impact as a water resource reference source, despite its omission of Inagua, San Salvador, Mayaguana and New Providence.

EXPERIMENTAL AND RESEARCH FACILITIES

The Bahamas has never had a tradition in research agriculture, probably because there were no important export crops that required constant monitoring for new varieties, pest and disease control measures, improved yields, establishment of fertilizer regimes or an evaluation of limestone soil performance in tropical agriculture production. Today, research activities are generally confined to applied work, field trials and livestock breeding.

The Colonial Secretary expressed his concern in his 1930 report *"Agriculture in The Bahamas"* about the lack of research and scientific capability. He wrote:

> "But the sine qua non for success is, I am firmly convinced, more expert direction.There is no justification for the supposition that of all agricultural countries,The Bahamas can dispense with scientific knowledge and direction.
>
> "Before proceeding with any agricultural project, I am inclined to think that we should obtain a thorough survey by a competent agriculturist and economist with a view to determining the prospects of agriculture and ascertain what focus of production could be most profitably undertaken."

The Colonial Secretary's observations were accepted first in the Colonial Office in Whitehall, London, and second by the legislature of The Bahamas. The colony took steps to rectify this situation and scientific investigation into Bahamian agriculture commenced.

Government Experimental Station, Chippingham, New Providence

The government's experimental station was situated on the site of the present Botanical Gardens. It was essentially a place where plant propagation activities took place, as well as production of livestock (pigs and sheep) for upgrading stock to be sold to farmers in the Family Islands and New Providence.

The plant propagation work encompassed both ornamental and economic horticulture. The usual techniques of budding, grafting, cuttings and air layering were used to propagate the various types of Bahamian flora. During the 1950s a great deal of trial work was done on fodder grasses, chiefly pangola and Bermuda grasses, for improved pasture.

A small citrus grove was established and other orchard crops such as avocado pears were also maintained at the Gardens, along with varietal trials on vegetable gardens.

In addition to the propagation work and distribution of livestock, the public was able to purchase new and improved varieties of fruit trees. A spraying programme was conducted from the Experimental Station and could be contracted to spray private properties. This programme played an important role in combating the fruit fly problem which adversely affected the citrus industry in the 1930s.

The facility came into existence some time during the latter part of the 1920s. The level of research technology, which was displayed at the Experimental Station depicted the esteem in which agriculture was held in the colonial Bahamas.

The principal architect in the development of the Experimental Station was Mr. L.A. Jervis, one of the West Indian Seven who came to The Bahamas in 1927. He spent 19 years at the Station, and the work programme which Mr. Jervis initiated was exceptionally outstanding in the area of plant propagation and ornamental horticulture. When he retired in 1951 as the Senior Agricultural Instructor, he was honoured by the Crown with the award of British Empire Medal (BEM), and was succeeded by Mr. Palestine Michael.

Central Agricultural Station, Gladstone Road

The Experimental Station was considered an archaic facility in the 1960s. Steps would have to be taken to bring Bahamian agriculture into the 20th century by developing a modern research facility.

In 1969, 40 years after the establishment of the Experimental Station, $2 million was allocated to construct and establish the Central Agricultural Station. Two hundred acres of prime pineland were designated for this site at the southern end of Gladstone Road in the western district of New Providence.

A wide range of research activities were undertaken at the station during the early years of its operation. However, during the late 1980s through most of the 1990s, the work at the Station deteriorated considerably.

Gladstone Road Agricultural Centre (GRAC)

During the 90s, the name Central Agricultural Station was changed to the Gladstone Road Agricultural Centre. In addition to the CAS of the facility, a Fisheries Diagnostic Laboratory was introduced.

The Food Technology Laboratory was converted to a laboratory for fisheries. The basis for the decision was to comply with an EU requirement which called on all countries exporting food commodities to EU countries food safety laboratory facilities had to be in place. Rather than expanding the agricultural infrastructure of the country, the government decided to shrink it by short changing crop producers through the elimination of an entity with the capacity to identify and create value added commodities. The EU market is a major market for the Bahamian spiny lobster or crawfish, which is a $100 million industry.

Figure 6.2   Santa Gertrudis cattle at BARTAD on North Andros

Bahamas Agricultural Research, Training and Development Project, North Andros

The Central Agricultural Station was financed entirely by the government of The Bahamas. The Bahamas Agricultural Research Training and Development Project in North Andros (BARTAD), established in 1973, was slightly different as it was funded by a $10 million grant from the US government.

Organized by two senators, the Project was a gift to The Bahamas on its independence on July 10. The US government would be represented by the US Agency for International Development (US AID) and project work commenced soon after Independence.

BARTAD was a multidimensional project because it embraced three elements– research, training and development.

Research

An elaborate research programme was organized by the Pennsylvania State

University scientists in conjunction with the Ministry of Agriculture and the project's Bahamian staff.

The research programme encompassed five disciplines from which 50 research projects were developed.

The disciplines included:

◆ Agricultural Economics and Rural Sociology—analysis on costs, enterprise analysis for crops and livestock.

◆ Agronomy—the important tropical grasses and legumes.

◆ Animal Science—chiefly beef cattle, sheep and goats.

◆ Agricultural Engineering—Specific attention was given to land clearing, ground water hydrology to monitor the fresh water lenses and maintain accurate records on temperature, rainfall, wind speed and hours of sunlight.

◆ Horticulture—specifically tropical fruit trees, winter vegetables, irrigation technology and pest management.

Training

Bahamian personnel at various professional and academic levels became eligible for training awards. Twelve individuals studied at Pennsylvania State University for B.Sc. or M.Sc. degree programmes. Twenty-three were also sent to Texas State Technical Institute, and eight others went to other institutions in the US.

Figure 6.3   Preparing a cow at the BARTAD slaughterhouse on North Andros.

Development

The Western Institute of Science and Technology in Waco, Texas was responsible for providing logistical support in purchasing machinery and supplies and supervising construction work on the project site.

A 500 acre research station was established, along with 16 pilot test farms on 900 acres of uncleared land, 260 acres offsite for distribution to members of the Andros Agricultural Cooperative, which was a new element in institutional strengthening. It also included improved land tenure arrangements and credit facilities to provide financing for the farmers. The credit aspect evolved into a national credit programme for farmers, called the Agricultural Guarantee Credit Fund.

The pilot test farms were to demonstrate the economic viability of family type farms with mixed enterprises, including livestock production. About 45 farmers completed a three-month training course to be selected for the farms.

Every effort was made for the pilot test farms to be successful. In the probationary year, farmers were supplied with inputs and technical assistance through the technical staff who were stationed on the project site. They were guaranteed an income so that they could maintain their families, and after the probationary period, they would sign a long-term lease for the use of the farm. Financing came from a guaranteed credit facility which was part of the project funding and executed through a commercial bank. By being members of the local cooperative, the farmers were able to get their machinery serviced, purchase their inputs and market their produce through the government's packing house.

A training centre with dormitories and a staff housing and apartment complex was constructed, along with an office complex and machinery, equipment and storage buildings.

The project was conducted over a five-year period and was managed by Dr. Frank Madden, a US AID employee with a wealth of experience and knowledge in implementing these types of development projects in Third World countries. His counterpart was Mr. Earl Deveaux, who was Director of Agriculture from 1993 until 1995.

In addition to Mr. Deveaux, there were several other professional agricultural pioneers who uprooted their families and moved to North Andros to participate in the creation of a new agricultural vista. These pioneers were Audley Greaves, Arnold Dorsett, Mrs. Valerie Carey-Outten, Thelmis Cathopoulis, John Hedden and Simeon Pinder.

They worked as counterpart staff with the US technical officers and after a period of attachment they were sent to Pennsylvania State University for postgraduate training in their specific areas of discipline.

Except for Messrs. Cathopoulis and Hedden who entered the private sector, the remaining officers were promoted to very senior technical and administrative positions in the Department of Agriculture.

This project brought a great focus to agriculture in The Bahamas. For the first time agriculture was on the cutting edge of science. It was finally approaching the level the Colonial Secretary had hoped to see in The Bahamas in 1930. For the first time in its history, there were two research facilities operating in The Bahamas and the future for agriculture looked bright for the 1970s.

Despite the positive aspects of this development, serious administrative problems arose when the facility was taken over by the government of The Bahamas in 1983. The facility lost its research direction and the satellite farms programme fell apart. The farmer training programmes were non-existent and eventually the whole development became an embarrassment to the government. In 1991–1992, the government decided to lease the site to a private concern. In 20 years, a $10 million project with outstanding prospects fell flat on its face, basically because of bad management and inept leadership.

Like the Millars Road Agricultural Development Project, there were lofty objectives, namely:

◆ to continue the farmer training programme and liaise with The College of The Bahamas to provide practical opportunities for agricultural students;

◆ the clearance of an additional 200 acres would generate some two man years of employment through increased farm work;

◆ establish more pilot test farms;

◆ assist the cooperatives in developing more farms;

◆ produce more farm output for the domestic and foreign markets;

◆ increase the availability of local mutton and beef for the local market.

None of the above was achieved.

Sheep In-Confinement Project, North Long Island

Over the years, The Bahamas had developed hair sheep with outstanding properties. Experts from the Food and Agriculture Organization (FAO) had determined that the features of the Bahamian sheep were comparable to those of the Barbados Black Belly which is a well-known breed of hair sheep in the tropics.

As a result of this determination a joint project was designed between the government of The Bahamas and the FAO in 1976–1977. The main focus of the project was to improve the national herd in order to establish a sustainable national mutton production programme. Northern Long Island was selected as the site because mutton production has had a long tradition in the southeastern Bahamas, especially Long Island.

Critical aspects of the programme called for the development of a bush pasture scheme, the introduction of improved animal health and husbandry techniques in sheep rearing, and the selection of the best stock from the national herd for breeding purposes.

This project began to stimulate production in its immediate locale, but its impact nationally has never been felt.

Food Technology and Animal Feeds Unit

The agricultural sector had begun to expand and new needs had to be met. In 1981 the government of The Bahamas entered a joint agreement with the European Economic Community (EEC) to conduct and develop a Food Technology and Animal Feeds Unit, which would be situated at the Central Agricultural Station. The EEC would finance this project for $1 million. The two functions of the unit were:

(1) Food technology—to develop new processed foods from indigenous fruits and vegetables; and

(2) Animal feeds—to develop feeds for animal consumption from local raw materials such as cassava, sorghum, corn and poultry offal.

This unit has developed professionals who have gained a great deal of knowledge and expertise over the years, and the unit has the capacity to make a substantial contribution to the agricultural sector. The prime mover for its establishment was Mr. Sidney Russell, a microbiologist who became Director of Agriculture in 1982.

Over the past 70 years, The Bahamas has come a long way in upgrading its scientific capability in the field of agricultural science. A conservative estimate of $15 million has been invested in providing experimental and research facilities for the agricultural sector of The Bahamas. The limiting factor has not been the facilities but properly trained and committed professionals to perform research tasks. A research capability will never develop in The Bahamas until the expertise is developed and there is a greater appreciation for the need for local research and its contribution to nation building.

AGRICULTURAL MARKETING IN THE PUBLIC SECTOR

The question of selling local produce on the Nassau market has been an issue for decades. In the Colonial Secretary's 1930 memorandum *"Agriculture in The Bahamas"* states:

"It will have been noted that most of the Out Island Commissioners commented adversely on the prices paid by Nassau buyers. It is of course a matter of opinion what are reasonable prices, but the prices quoted by various Commissioners do not appear to me unreasonably low. In some cases they are identical with those of imported products; cases could be quoted in which peasants have demanded prices exceeding those of imported produce and instances have been cited to me in which prices on the Out Islands have exceeded those obtaining in Nassau.

"On the whole the impression gained is that the Out Island producers have inflated ideas of the value of their produce.The boom spirit persists even among the peasantry and they do not realize that they must compete with imported commodities, otherwise the retailer will continue to import—which he will do with much greater convenience to himself than if he buys island produce.

"Even then the Out Islander will be at a disadvantage and this is where the real trouble lies. The points of production are scattered over a number of islands separated from each other and from Nassau by wide stretches of sea. Produce is collected in driblets shipped at random and committed to the care of the captains of vessels who sell it on behalf of the owners, receiving in return either just the freight or freight and commission.

"Under such conditions it is expected that the Out Island peasants find it difficult to disperse of their produce and the position is that of a vicious circle, the peasants producing little because they find no sale and buyers buying little because there is all too little to be of interest to them.

"A remedy suggested is the institution of a convenient Produce Exchange and the establishment of such an exchange was recommended some years ago by a committee of the House of Assembly... It is also to be borne in mind that the setting up of a Produce Exchange, whether privately or publicly conducted, introduces another middle man between the producer and consumer."

Figure 6.4   The Produce Exchange with a large supply of onions. The author is pictured with Mr. Clem Pinder, a member of The Bahamas Livestock and Agricultural Farmers Association, Mr. Fred Longley, a produce buyer from the City Market supermarket chain, and the late Mr. Cedric Smith, then Manager of the Produce Exchange at Potter's Cay.

On the basis of this report, it is apparent that the Colonial Office was aware of the problems and that the politicians of the day recognized the fact that they had to find a practical solution to this problem.

A few years later, the House of Assembly enacted legislation which allowed the Board of Agriculture to establish a Produce Exchange. This must have been a difficult decision to obtain in view of the fact that the House of Assembly was comprised chiefly of capitalistic merchants. For them to allow the Government of The Bahamas to engage in a private sector activity must have been an extreme departure from their business and political philosophies.

Produce Exchange

The Produce Exchange was set up on the premises of the Market Range to assist Family Island producers in finding an outlet for their products in New Providence. It provided a service to the producer and the consumer, but there were no storage facilities which meant that stock had to be sold immediately. Originally a wholesale entity, the Produce Exchange eventually evolved to retail sales. The original location of the Produce Exchange was destroyed by fire some time during the late 1970s, and has today been replaced by the straw market.

After World War II, The Bahamas gained an international reputation as a tourism destination. By the 1960s, The Bahamas was not only a leading resort destination in the region, but one of the leading financial centres in this hemisphere. The United Bahamian Party therefore embarked on a capital development programme to improve the harbour facilities and upgrade Bay Street in downtown Nassau.

Mailboats and small vessels were moved from Prince George Dock and Woodes Rogers Walk, and a new docking facility was constructed at Potter's Cay for inter-island vessels. In conjunction with this move, a new Produce Exchange was planned.

In 1967, a new Produce Exchange was opened on Potter's Cay. The Market Range facility reverted to a retail marketing outlet. Another retail outlet was constructed adjacent to Potter's Cay wholesale facility, and a retail outlet was established on Robinson Road to replace the one destroyed by fire.

The development of the Family Islands was an important aspect of the new government's agenda. With an increase in funding for land clearing and the construction of farm feeder roads, new acreages of land were brought into production. This meant more farm output and an increase in volume of produce being shipped to the Produce Exchange.

Seasonal production of several types of produce had created a situation where supply had outpaced demand. This led to pressure when the Nassau market was glutted with huge quantities of produce which could not be sold. Over-supply was not the only reason; poor quality and immaturity played prominent roles. The Produce Exchange being a public institution did not enforce stiff grading standards.

The Family Island farming community was becoming extremely frustrated with the system. In order to control the purchases of produce, the Department of Agriculture introduced a system of radio announcements advising the farmers which types of produce were being accepted by the Produce Exchange. Farmers who could not sell their produce directly to the supermarkets, hotels or produce vendors were experiencing heavy losses because of their inability to disperse produce which had already been harvested prior to the radio announcements.

Figure 6.5   View from the old Market Range in Nassau.

Political pressure put on the government to find a solution to the problem was turning the farmers' frustration into despair.

It was decided to expand the role of the Produce Exchange, and, therefore, deepen the public sector's involvement, by instituting and operating produce packing houses in the main farming communities in the Family Islands.

Farmers could now devote their efforts to production as the packing houses would be responsible for assembling, grading, storing and transporting the produce purchased.

The commencement of the planning and construction of the packing houses began in 1973; the first facility was finished in 1976. Facilities were built in North Andros, North, Central and South Eleuthera, North and Central Long Island, Cat Island and Exuma. A wholesale facility was built in Freeport, Grand Bahama. One million dollars was spent on this marketing infrastructure.

In addition to the facilities, about twelve staff members were recruited locally for each packing house.

Consideration was also given to refrigerated storage facilities and the production peculiarities of certain farming communities. In Exuma, for example, the packing house had an onion-drying facility as an annex, because Exuma is one of the prime onion-producing areas of The Bahamas.

The Produce Exchange along with the packing houses were established to alleviate the problems facing the small farmers in the Family Islands. As new agricultural technology became available to a number of farmers, particularly those on the Pine Islands (Andros, Abaco and Grand Bahama) where crop yields were substantially higher and acreages were larger, some farmers began to deliver substandard produce in large quantities to the Produce Exchange and the packing houses.

This created a serious financial burden for the Public Treasury, and as a result the farmers had to wait longer periods for reimbursement of produce sold to the packing houses.

The local staff became intimidated by political operatives and this led to abuses in the system. Serious modification in the operating procedures of the Produce Exchange and packing house was long overdue as the system required streamlining.

The government recognized that its deepening involvement in marketing was causing problems for certain sectors of the private sector. On August 15, 1975, the

Ministry of Agriculture informed the House of Assembly that the Ministry was withdrawing from retail marketing by closing its retail outlets on Potter's Cay and Robinson Roads.

In conjunction with the closure of the retail outlets, a new Farmers' Market was to be constructed at Jumbey Village in the Big Pond area. It was anticipated that this facility would house produce vendors and provide a location for farmers to sell their produce.

It has been established that 30 percent of all produce grown in The Bahamas passed through the Produce Exchange/packing house system in the 1970s. At one point, the annual value of produce purchased through the system was about $5 million.

The Produce Exchange and packing houses emerged as a unique tool in the development of agriculture in The Bahamas, but their role today may be considered played out. Any success in the future will depend on how the farmers and their organizations become involved in the operational aspects.

Farmers have a direct stake in how and where their produce is marketed. They can no longer sit back and allow the government agencies to take all of the responsibility for their livelihood. A new way of marketing Bahamian produce, both on the domestic and foreign markets, has to be achieved which will include all the relevant parties who participate in the marketing chain.

The Market

One of the administrative trappings of colonialism was The Market. All of the colonial powers (British, Dutch, French, Belgian) utilized the market as a socio-economic instrument to direct and control the commercial activities of their overseas dependencies, be they in Africa, the Caribbean, India and other parts of Asia.

In The Bahamas, like in other parts of the British Empire, the chief role of the market was to meet a very fundamental commercial need which was to act as a locale where the populace would obtain basic food stuffs and other consumer products. The location of the market enhanced this objective.

Being sited in the downtown area of Nassau, near the main shipping and sailing harbour, the market was the place from which the commercial life of the colony came into existence.

Functionally, the market provided an informal atmosphere and place where views and pleasantries were exchanged and encountered. It was this way because it denoted an era when the basic ingredients for daily sustenance had to be purchased on a daily basis in monetary amounts which, in many instances, represented earnings which were garnered on an hourly, daily or piece work basis.

In addition, food preservation was tied to freshness and salting, as refrigeration was limited to the ice-box for some. Electrical refrigeration was an option for the wealthy and well-to-do—the colonial class and the merchants who controlled the commercial and political life of the colony.

The standard style of the market was the warehouse type structure which was built to protect the vendors and their perishable goods from dust, rain, sun and pilferage at night. The main objective was to have a functional infrastructure to meet the elementary principles of hygiene, and reduce the proliferation of street traders selling their goods under unhygienic conditions. Daily fees were paid by the occupants of stalls, licences were issued, and public health inspectors ensured the removal of debris and the maintenance of an acceptable level of sanitation.

The British had created its administration of the colony and the colonization of the people around its political power. The colonial grand design was aimed at transforming the mental outlook of the "natives", who in The Bahamas, were descendants of slaves who either had come with their Loyalist masters or were deposited on these shores as a result of the British Navy's interdiction of slave ships on the high seas.

This notion of altering the mental outlook of the natives was not confined to the exploitation of their labour alone; the locals also had to adhere to the British model of civil behaviour in the social, political and commercial life of the colony.

The sellers in the market were primarily blacks comprising fruit and vegetable stall-holders, usually women, fishmongers, straw vendors and farmers. They came from the Family Islands, the outlying districts of New Providence like Fox Hill, and the pine barrens (coal burners), and the nearby Family Island farming communities like Spanish Wells and The Current, North Eleuthera.

Colonial business practices were adopted by the urban-dwelling native community, which participated directly in the colony's economy by acting as middle men and "petty shop" operators, with the objective of enlightening them to aspects of the market economy.

Culturally, the market had great significance for the native population. It was the place where the twice-yearly Junkanoo celebrations had taken place for decades. For the psyche of the Bahamian, the market was a cultural icon and its legacy as a cultural institution remains entrenched in Bahamian folklore.

The Produce Vendor

Produce vendors comprised a substantial proportion of the vendors who occupied "stalls" or spaces from which they sold fresh produce in the market and the market range, which was the immediate area around or near the market, usually along the wharf area which today is called Woodes Rodgers Walk.

In addition to produce vendors, there were also fishmongers, straw vendors and other purveyors of locally made handicrafts.

The produce vendors were important middlemen in the marketing chain. They bought directly from the farmers, who would accompany their produce on the mail-boats and other boats which plied between New Providence and the respective Family Islands.

Produce vendors were also large purchasers from the Produce Exchange and were responsible for the movement of large quantities of fruits and vegetables used in native dishes in Nassau households and restaurants. Their retail stalls directly impacted the cost of living of the Nassau consumer, and they devised a unique methodology for pricing their produce.

Sociologically, the vendors, both straw and produce, were women who played an entrepreneurial role in the commercial life of New Providence. Many of them were the backbone for the financial existence of their families and were responsible for funding the education of their children, the construction of houses, the purchasing of vehicles and the diversification into other business enterprises.

The produce vendor continues to play a strategic role in the agricultural sector as one of the chief avenues through which Bahamian grown produce is marketed.

The tradition of "the market women" of West Africa continues in this Bahamian element of the diaspora through the persona of the produce and straw vendors.

MILLARS ROAD AGRICULTURAL DEVELOPMENT PROJECT

One of the burning issues facing the new government in 1969–1970 was the question of land. Bahamians had felt for generations that they had been excluded from obtaining Crown Land.

For years the Department of Lands and Surveys, the agency responsible for Crown Land, had been headed by non-Bahamians who were qualified surveyors from the southern Caribbean. Bahamians differentiated themselves from the southern Caribbean during this era by referring to these individuals as West Indians.

The concept of Caribbean integration was a distant reality to Bahamians. Apart from the commonalities of being a British colony with English as the common language, Bahamians were oriented to North America.

Bahamians of African descent felt left out as chunks of Crown Land were granted to the followers of the now defunct United Bahamian Party. There was also the deep-seated feeling that the West Indians in the Department of Lands and Surveys were more sympathetic to others like themselves rather than the indigenous black Bahamian.

The Progressive Liberal Party government had little choice in addressing the issue of making Crown Land available to the hundreds of individuals who had applied.

On April 30, 1971, the Hon. Jeffrey Thompson, the Minister of Development under whose portfolio Crown Land fell, jointly chaired a meeting with the Minister of Agriculture and Fisheries, the Hon. Milo B. Butler in order to find a solution to this political problem. (PRP-1)

Approximately 500 acres of Crown Land in the Millars Road/Cowpen Road area of New Providence had been identified as a possible site for an agricultural development project. The Department of Agriculture insisted that bonafide farmers should be given priority to receive grants, followed by potential farmers with the required financial resources. Speculators with political connections numbered in the scores, along with individuals who sought land simply because they had longed for the opportunity to own more land or to obtain Crown land.

The professional officers in the Department of Agriculture established an elaborate screening procedure by setting criteria for the granting of the land. The project was divided into two phases. Phase I comprised 70 lots totalling 293.6 acres. An additional 200 acres was set aside for phase II to satisfy demand.

The land was finally earmarked for livestock production, specifically pork production, which involved small farmers. Pork production in The Bahamas was primarily a backyard activity. By encouraging the activity on Millars Road, technology could be upgraded to a capital intensive commercial level thereby reducing pork imports which, at the time, were over US$1 million a year.

By June, 1971, over 300 applicants had applied for the 120 lots, almost three applications per lot. To balance farming capability with political considerations was a difficult job for public officers. In the final analysis, political considerations outweighed farming capability. This impacted heavily on the ability of the project to meet the production expectations which were predicted by the planners.

A report on the potential of the project stated:

> "This proposed development is potentially one of the most signifi-
> cant contributions to the agricultural economy of The Bahamas to emerge
> in recent years. In terms of livestock production alone, the potential
> output is of the order of $5 million per annum from the 500 acres zoned
> for the project... But even with an initial target of $5 million worth of
> output, this represents an annual revenue of about $10,000 per acre."
> (PRP-1)

This goal for livestock production was never attained because of:
◆ the inability to enforce improved husbandry practices;
◆ lack of competent extension personnel;
◆ poor selection of farmers;
◆ lack of guidelines to administer the project area properly;
◆ lack of capital for infrastructural development; and
◆ lack of capital by farmers to develop allotments.

In 1998 the Millars Road Agricultural Development Project remained undeveloped; after almost 25 years, less than 10% of the acreage had been developed. Steps were now being contemplated to reclaim allotments from individuals who were behind on lease payments as well as individuals who had abandoned their plots, some of which were now occupied by squatters.

Despite well-intentioned objectives and goals which seemed attainable in 1971, the Millars Road Agricultural Development Project had failed.

TECHNICAL ASSISTANCE

Technical assistance programmes for The Bahamas have been few. The industrialized countries see The Bahamas as a country with a high per capita income which, to their thinking, has made The Bahamas ineligible for foreign aid. Many public officials, however, regard this as a superficial judgement and a way of keeping The Bahamas from its progressive path.

There are many professional and technical skills that are lacking as well as areas where the expertise is available but requires upgrading. Agriculture is one discipline where technical assistance will help to improve the overall capability of the sector both in manpower development and applied technology.

In the 1990s two significant technical assistance programmes were sponsored by the State of Israel and Taiwan Province, one of China's provinces.

Israeli Technical Assistance

In August, 1991, the Centre for International Agricultural Cooperation of the State of Israel held a three-week Agricultural Extension Methods and Work Planning Seminar for extension officers in the Department of Agriculture.

The Seminar was viewed as an important tool in upgrading the extension staff who were now situated in both the Pine and Coppice Islands.

The course, *The Principles and Methods of Extension Work*, was conducted by two Israeli experts. This course would assist the young professionals, who were working in the various islands and had no formal training in extension work, in communicating solutions to the farmer for his problems and to communicate the farmer's problems to those conducting research and implementing policy.

At this time, the Department of Agriculture was lacking in extension information in the form of pamphlets and brochures for farmers and farm families; organized radio and television programmes; and field days addressing specific husbandry problems.

At the opening of the seminar, the Hon. Perry Christie said, "*It is up to us to maximize on the presence of foreign expertise, technology and resources to help Bahamians who only need an opportunity… And for that transfer to properly take place and work out, extension leaders must be in place and must be there to ensure the interest of Bahamians.*"

The Israelis have conducted these types of courses all over the world and The Bahamas was fortunate to benefit on this occasion. In addition, Bahamian professional agriculturists were sent to Israel on short courses. The Jewish lobby in tourism was instrumental in persuading the Israeli government to have seminars conducted in The Bahamas.

Taiwan Province Technical Assistance

In addition to their corps of experts in agriculture and fisheries, Taiwan Province provided funding for the construction of a gymnasium and sent a number of professionals from various government departments to training courses in Taiwan Province.

Taiwan Province maintained that their model of economic development was applicable to Third World countries like The Bahamas. The people of Taiwan Province were able to transform their economy from agrarian to industrial, and they believe they can pass this know-how on to developing countries.

In May, 1990, Mr Thay-Yen Sung, head of the Taiwan Province technical panel, began their work which expanded and diversified its involvement in the agricultural sector. The work included:

(1) Research and Demonstration work—At the government's Research and Agricultural Centre (GRAC), formerly the Central Agricultural Station on Gladstone Road, trials were conducted on fruit tree propagation, vegetable production and pork production. A new piggery was constructed and stocked with an improved breed for rearing and distribution to farmers in order to expand pork production throughout The Bahamas.

(2) Botanic Gardens—Work in ornamental horticulture was undertaken to expand this aspect of the Department of Agriculture's work to assist in the development, diversification and expansion in the floriculture industry. In recent years, a number of capital-intensive nurseries have come into operation and imports on landscape and nursery plants are being curtailed.

(3) Plant Breeding and Genetics—Taiwan Province experts assisted Bahamian professionals to attain technical expertise in tissue culture work.

(4) Training—Bahamian agriculturists were sent to Taiwan Province for specialized training in various aspects of agriculture.

(5) Her Majesty's Prison—The Panel provided special assistance to this institution, particularly in the area of improving the management of the Prison's farm, improving crop output in order to help the Prison become more self-sufficient in several crop lines, and in teaching inmates some of the practical technologies of farming in order to provide them with crop and livestock husbandry skills for employment after their release.

Taiwan Province also donated a 15-feet-long and 60-feet-wide greenhouse equipped with a low-cost micro-jet irrigation system, and assisted the prison in bringing more acreage into food production. They also helped with improving the grounds with the propagation of ornamental plants.

Taiwan Province technical assistance was intended as a partnership where experts worked side by side with Bahamians, where decisions were taken jointly as partners, and where the leadership of both sides consulted one-on-one on issues of mutual concern. They based their assistance on a basic Chinese proverb which has been their tradition for centuries, *"Give a hungry man a fish and he will eat for a day. Show him how to catch fish and he will eat for the rest of his life."*

In 1997, the government of The Bahamas severed its official relationship with Taiwan Province. The government opted for the "one China" policy of its major trading partner, the US, and recognized the People's Republic of China.

PEOPLE'S REPUBLIC OF CHINA

Since 1997, the People's Republic of China has maintained a very high profile in The Bahamas. On Grand Bahama, the Chinese is a major player in Freeport. The Hong Kong based company, Hutchinson-Whampoa, owns and operates the Freeport Container Port, the international airport and the Grand Lucaya Hotel. In New Providence, the Chinese financed the two billion dollar Baha Mar Hotel/ Resort Project on Cable Beach as well as a major gateway highway from the Lynden Pindling International Airport into Nassau.

Unlike Taiwan Province, which is an integral part of China, the People's Republic of China's contribution to Bahamian agriculture has been in the form of scholarship grants for technical training in various aspects of agriculture and marine sciences, which is proved more helpful.

MINISTRY OF AGRICULTURE (INCORPORATION) ACT (1993)

From 1969–1970, the Millars Road Agricultural Development project responded to the demand for the land and, over a 25-year period, the available Crown Land on the island of New Providence was exhausted. Bahamians, particularly those resident in the islands of Andros, Abaco and Grand Bahama, continued to apply for Crown Land for farming. The bureaucracy in the Department of Lands and Surveys was burdensome and time-consuming, and this resulted in a large build-up of unprocessed applications.

Land is a factor of production and an important tool of agricultural development. It is also necessary to bring new land into production on an annual basis. This is important in the expansion of production for the domestic market and the export market.

When land on the Pine Islands was made available for production, residents on these islands began to take advantage of the opportunities which farming presented.

For a globally competitive food production system to develop successfully in The Bahamas, the following must be taken into consideration in the Pine Islands:

(1) The efficient utilization of the natural resources;

(2) The effective exploitation of the advantages of being in close proximity to the large, lucrative markets of North America;

(3) The provision of selective infrastructural improvements in the locales where high land capability is available;

(4) Research to ensure sustained agricultural progress.

Beginning in the 1950s, the Pine Islands commenced to demonstrate their potential for large-scale mechanized farming. The technology on rockland soils was perfected in the Homestead area of South Florida and transferred to The Bahamas by US offshore growers. For more than 40 years, governments of The Bahamas had seen one offshore grower after another farm for a season or two then pack up and leave.

It was within this context that a new land distribution policy was needed to address this issue. On July 30, 1993, the FNM government had parliament pass the Ministry of Agriculture (Incorporation) Act 1993. The Act would *"confer upon the Minister responsible for agriculture a corporate status with the power to acquire, hold,lease and dispose of agricultural land,to enter contracts and to sue and be sued."*

For the first time in history, the Ministry of Agriculture in conjunction with the Department of Agriculture would have control over a large acreage of high capability land.

With the Millars Road project, the Ministry was responsible for selecting farmers and the Department of Lands and Surveys was responsible for land allocation and distribution. With this new Act, all of these factors fell under the domain of the Ministry of Agriculture.

The *Land Resource Study* had already identified high capability land in the amount of 50,000 acres (20,250 hectares) on Abaco, 104,000 acres (41,600 hectares) on Andros and 30,000 acres (12,150 hectares) on Grand Bahama.

The maps of the individual Pine Islands showed the acreage and locations of the high potential land falling under the aegis of the Ministry of Agriculture (Incorporation) Act, as well as the type of farming enterprises present which were undertaken by The Bahamas and foreign offshore growers.

The population of The Bahamas in 1996 was slightly in excess of 272,000 with the majority residing on New Providence. The other urban centre is Freeport on the island of Grand Bahama where approximately 55,000 people reside. The combined population of the Pine Islands numbers about 75,000. Abaco is the third largest populated island with Marsh Harbour being the largest settlement. Besides having a sizeable population, Freeport features excellent infrastructure which has attracted tourism, industry and a modern container transhipment terminal.

The population on the Pine Islands represents a substantial market for fresh fruits, vegetables, pork, mutton, poultry and ornamental plants.

With New Providence becoming even more urbanized, the high cost for residential development makes it extremely costly to use land for farming purposes.

The serious environmental concerns and competition for water resources further eliminate New Providence from agricultural development. In the future, more farming and agro-industrial activities will take place on these large under-developed islands, particularly Grand Bahama with its burgeoning population and excellent infrastructure.

LUCAYAN TROPICAL PRODUCE AND GREENHOUSE TECHNOLOGY

The last decade of the 20th Century would usher in dramatic changes for the agricultural sector of small island states in the Caribbean like The Bahamas. These changes would come about as a result of a world which was becoming increasingly globalized. Globalization had become a reality which The Bahamas could not ignore or brush aside as just another fashion trend. It was during this decade that the General Agreement on Tariffs and Trade (GATT) gave way to a new entity, the WTO. The WTO would emerge as the institution most responsible for propelling the globalization system and creating the environment for a liberalized trading regime.

In 1995, every state in this hemisphere became members of the WTO with exception of The Bahamas. WTO membership would mean the opening of markets, adhering to agricultural trade rules and regulations as stipulated in the WTO's Agreement on Agricultural (AOA) and also the loss of preferential markets to the European Union (EU) for CARICOM states. Though not a WTO member, these factors would impact food production and marketing in The Bahamas.

The Bahamas like the rest of the Caribbean would have to address the issue of making its agricultural sector competitive if small farmers and local agribusinesses were to survive in a trade liberalized world. In order to compete in this new environment which was being stimulated by globalization, agriculture in The Bahamas would have to become technologically driven, research based and environmentally friendly. To achieve this, both the private and public sectors respectively would have to increase their investments in agriculture.

In August 2001, Lucayan Tropical Produce (LTP) was established by a group of Bahamian investors as a hydroponic greenhouse operation. The objective of this five million dollar investment was to provide competitive commodities comprising a range of vegetables, potted herbs, vegetable seedlings and native plants.

Figure 6.6   Completed Tunnel Greenhouse (30' × 16'/480 sq.ft.) for Backyard Garden.

Figure 6.7   Greenhouse under construction in New Providence: The supporting framework can be made of loops of wood, bamboo, plastic flexible tube or PVC pipes. Plastic film (polyester or PVC) for covering design. Dimensions vary. Tunnel type under construction, i.e. backyard or commercial.

LTP is making an impact on the local market as they have introduced innovative ways of marketing their products. Though its website, consumers are able to place orders.

In addition, LTP has set up several farm market-type outlets throughout New Providence.

The greenhouse was designed by Dalsean BV of the Netherlands; it is a venio style greenhouse which presented challenges originating from the tropical conditions of The Bahamas. To have better temperature control, initiatives like roof sprinklers and chilled irrigation water had to be introduced to confront features resulting from a hot house environment and high pressure fogging. In order to control pests and diseases, a bio-control strategy was employed.

In conjunction with the greenhouse operation, Bahamas Botanicals, under the leadership of Dr. Selina Campbell-Hauber, partnered with LTP to build The Bahamas' first tissue culture unit. Dr. Campbell-Hauber describes her operation and the technology utilized as follows:

> "The technology of plant tissue culture, also known as in-vitro propagation or micro propagation, was first attempted in the early 1900s, although unsuccessfully. This means of multiplying plants in a controlled environment under sterile condition is today an indispensable tool in the field of agricultural biotechnology. Plant tissue culture continues to play an essential role in the development of innumerable scientific advances from the improvement of food, textile and ornamental crops to the production of pharmaceuticals. Plant micro propagation can play a key role in the growth of agriculture in The Bahamas by making available to existing and potential producers, millions of propagules in pristine condition and of verifiable genetic integrity. It is also necessary for the development of a national bank of crops that have been developed specifically for our climate and soils by Bahamian farmers over many generations.This benefit extends further to the protection of our native flora in a time when land development and natural disasters such as hurricanes threaten the prolonged existence of our forests. The future of the agriculture industry in The Bahamas and the conservation of our environment stand to benefit immensely from this technology".

Figure 6.8   Standard single-ridge green house and (120′ × 36′/4 320 sq. ft)
for commercial production.

In my book, *The New Caribbean: A Region in Transition*, pages 47/48, the following point is made:

"Greenhouse technology is the way to go for Caribbean farmers, says FAO,… if increased productivity and competitiveness are to be realized.

"This assertion has come from sub-regional representative of the Food and Agriculture Organization (FAO). Dr. Barbara Graham, who noted that over the past three years, especially in light of the vulnerability wrought by hurricanes and other natural disasters,

"We in FAO believe that greenhouse technology is one production system, which the region needs to look toward if regional productivity and competitiveness in regional and extra-regional markets are to be achieved, she added."

In 2008/09, greenhouse construction in The Bahamas got a boost. Jamaican agro-technologist, Leroy Santiago, commenced a programme to establish a string of greenhouses in New Providence and Abaco. On North Andros, The Bahamas Agricultural and Industrial Corporation (BAIC) also constructed a couple of model greenhouses. The technology is expanding and is making an impact on food production, particularly vegetable production.

Greenhouse Technology using hydroponics has a tremendous future in The Bahamas, particularly where there is infrastructure like the availability of electricity. The system is technical and procedural in order to prepare nutrient solutions and maintain acidity levels. The output is high as studies have indicated that an acre (0.4 hectares) in a hydroponic greenhouse can produce the same output as 10 acres (4 hectares) in the field. In a high priced labour market like The Bahamas, the demand for labour is minimized for weeding, planting and harvesting as well as land preparation and water usage. Water is a scarce resource in the Southeastern Bahamas.

Bahamian agriculture, in recent years, has not attracted local or foreign direct investment; greenhouse technology can change that perception. Soilless farming is an ideal activity for investment. Another asset of this technology is that it has lifted the technical capacity of the small farmer enabling him to become a more competitive agribusiness person. He or she is now able to supply the Bahamian market with a range of high quality vegetables throughout the year. This also enhances the food security capacity of The Bahamas.

CHAPTER 7

THE IMPACT OF TOURISM ON THE AGRICULTURAL SECTOR

After World War II, The Bahamas found itself in a period of profound, and sometimes paradoxical, change. The first major economic transition since the abolition of slavery was about to take place.

Bahamians began to move from the Family Islands to the urban locales of Nassau and Freeport (see Table 7.1). Large segments of the population from the family Islands were registering for work in the United States between 1943 and 1953 as contract farm workers. Recruiting was undertaken locally, and the opportunity to work on the "project", as it was called by the locals, was embraced by both men and women. While in the United States, hundreds of Bahamians "jumped the contract" and never returned to The Bahamas.

Agriculture, as a significant sector in the economy, was approaching a state of decline in its economic importance. The new age of tourism was on the horizon as hotels were being constructed in New Providence. This also fuelled a post-war construction boom.

For vast numbers of Bahamians, the work place moved from the Family Island farm to the hotel, likewise the home from the islands to the city. As a people, Bahamians seized the new employment opportunities in the emerging hospitality industry but, as a society, the new industry introduced massive disruption and dislocation to the Bahamian way of life.

The very nature of work changed—night work, Sunday and holiday work, shift work, hotel work for mothers and fathers as maids and waiters, and the old ways of going to work in the field was almost about to disappear.

Along with all of this, communities began to change. As a result of this newly found prosperity, a new Bahamian was in the offing. This was reflected in his desire for better education, his aspirations to the professions, and his questioning of the system under which he was governed.

Even though the archipelago was firmly in the grasp of its colonial masters, the Bahamian political directorate responded by devising a an economy which would sustain The Bahamas throughout the twentieth century.

Table 7.1 Population by Island 1931–2010

Island	1931	1953	1970	1990	2000	2010
All Bahamas	59,828	84,841	169,534	255,049	303,541	351,461
New Providence	19,756	46,125	102,005	172,196	210,832	246,329
Grand Bahama	2,241	4,095	25,943	40,898	46,994	51,368
Abaco	4,233	3,407	6,507	10,003	13,170	17,224
Acklins	1,765	1,273	936	405	428	565
Andros	7,071	7,136	8,889	8,177	7,686	7,490
Berry Islands	222	327	443	628	709	807
Biminis	756	1,330	1,533	1,639	1,717	1,988
Cat Island	3,959	3,201	2,658	1,698	1,647	1,522
Crooked Island	1,329	836	689	412	350	304
Eleuthera	7,527	7,596	9,501	10,584	7,999	8,202
Harbour Is/Spanish Wells					3,166	3,313
Exuma & Cays	3,774	2,919	3,777	3,556	3,571	6,928
Inagua	667	999	1,109	985	969	913
Long Cay	144	80	26	0		26
Long Island	4,515	3,755	3,869	2,949	2,922	3,094
Mayaguana	518	615	584	312	259	277
Ragged Island	424	320	208	89	72	72
San Salvador/Rum Cay	927	827	857	518	1,050	1,039

A NEW DEVELOPMENT MODEL

During the 1950s the economic development model for The Bahamas was redefined, as tourism became a year-round activity. The architect of this was Sir Stafford L. Sands, who chaired the politically powerful Bahamas Development Board, the forerunner of the present Ministry of Tourism.

In conjunction with the development of year-round tourism, land development was encouraged and Europeans and North Americans were invited to develop the archipelago. Notable among this type of undertaking was the creation of Freeport on the island of Grand Bahama, where a 200 square-mile free trade area was developed by Mr. Wallace Groves, an American citizen. Prior to this, Canadians Sir Harry Oakes and Mr. E. P. Taylor had been involved in developing large tracts of real estate at the western end of New Providence.

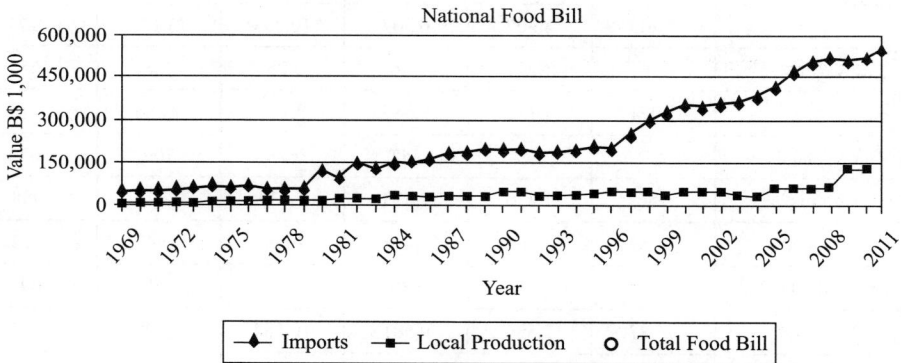

Figure 7. 1   The National Food Bill, 1969-2011

Freeport was unique as the Government of The Bahamas passed the Hawksbill Creek Agreement in 1955, giving the Grand Bahama Port Authority special powers to administer the free trade zone until August 3, 2054.

Under the Hawksbill Creek Agreement, businesses in the free trade zone were exempted from the payment of taxes on profits, capital gains, inheritance, income, earnings, distribution, and on imported and exported goods.

Sir Stafford's approach to economic development did not stop with tourism and real estate. His approach encompassed offshore banking as it was his objective to make The Bahamas the Switzerland of the Caribbean by creating a tax haven environment buttressed by a Financial Services Sector and supported by British jurisprudence. This enabled The Bahamas to establish itself as a reputable international financial centre.

With a stable political environment and a highly literate and trainable manpower base, The Bahamas was poised for sustained economic growth and development, with tourism acting as the engine of growth and the generator of foreign exchange.

AGRICULTURAL EXPORTS

As we have seen, the history of agricultural exports from The Bahamas has been checkered. Unlike its sister Caribbean countries where sugar reigned supreme, export agriculture was centred around fruits (citrus and pineapples) and vegetables for the winter markets of the eastern seaboard of the United States.

Agriculture's erratic characteristics stem from various production setbacks of pest infestations, the deterioration of the growing environment, the lack of scientific investigative facilities, and a reluctant farm labour supply. The sector did not demonstrate that it could sustain an expanding population or provide the quality of life to which Bahamians were aspiring.

Modern agricultural technology was practised by the large offshore companies on the Pine Islands, with subsistence farming taking place on the Coppice Islands of the southeastern Bahamas. There was virtually no opportunity for the transfer of technology and the practices of the indigenous farmers remained stagnant and backward.

After the 1950s, agricultural policy shifted towards a strategy of import substitution by encouraging seasonal production, with the protection of high custom duties. In conjunction with this, the government allowed agricultural inputs to be imported duty-free.

In order to facilitate farming, the sector was being subsidized at the production end through duty-free exemption on inputs, and at the output end through the Produce Exchange and the packing houses which purchased large quantities of produce from the farming communities.

Subsidies for the Produce Exchange and packing house were in the realm of $4 million annually in the late 1980s. After 1993, the government streamlined the operation of these entities and reduced the marketing subsidy substantially, with the objective of eventual elimination.

FOOD IMPORTS

By the 1990s tourism had mushroomed to a billion-dollar industry and was attracting almost 3.5 million visitors annually. The Bahamas itself had evolved into an urban society, with Nassau and Freeport accounting for more than 80% of the population.

With a per capita income statistically calculated around $10,000, an expanding visitor market, and a country whose revenue base was dependent on customs duties, food imports in the 1990s had exceeded 200 million annually (Figure 7.1).

The Bahamas had reached the point where its ability to feed itself was virtually unattainable. The dietary and consumption habits of the average Bahamian were essentially North American in content and this coincided with the dietary needs of the overwhelming majority of the visitors who were also North Americans.

In 1995, 76% of all stopovers to Nassau and Paradise Island came from the United States. This is a prime example of the influence of the US market on the largest destination in The Bahamas.

Approximately 20% of all the foreign exchange which was earned from tourism was being spent on food imports. Agriculture has been perhaps the most vulnerable sector of the Bahamian economy where the trade deficit resulting from food imports has reached the point where it may now become irreversible.

Table 7.2   National Food Bill 1969-2011

Year	Value of Imported Food Million $US	Value of Local Production Million $US	Total Million $US
1969	48,169	6,141	54,310
1970	47,682	6,823	54,505
1971	49,629	7,582	57,211
1972	51,458	8,424	59,882
1973	59,540	9,360	68,900
1974	65,618	10,400	76,018
1975	59,661	12,300	71,961
1976	69,765	14,400	84,165
1977	54,333	18,800	73,133

(to be continued)

Year	Value of Imported Food Million $US	Value of Local Production Million $US	Total Million $US
1978	53,993	18,400	72,393
1979	58,139	17,500	75,639
1980	126,244	20,200	146,444
1981	94,426	26,320	120,746
1982	147,836	22,860	170,696
1983	131,246	26,760	158,006
1984	148,597	33,630	182,227
1985	154,187	34,010	188,197
1986	163,887	28,830	192,717
1987	186,159	32,840	218,999
1988	184,230	30,270	214,500
1989	201,991	34,380	236,371
1990	195,610	48,540	244,150
1991	202,836	53,790	256,626
1992	184,285	37,150	221,435
1993	189,995	35,540	225,535
1994	196,844	42,280	239,124
1995	208,972	43,930	252,902
1996	200,000	55,070	255,070
1997	250,000	50,007	300,007
1998	300,000	47,953	347,953
1999	326,360	39,515	365,875
2000	358,530	46,933	405,463
2001	346,200	54,803	401,003
2002	360,750	50,844	411,594
2003	361,980	39,695	401,675
2004	381,480	29,596	411,076
2005	415,940	63,233	479,173

(*to be continued*)

Year	Value of Imported Food Million $US	Value of Local Production Million $US	Total Million $US
2006	466,630	61,941	528,571
2007	502,920	61,839	564,759
2008	521,560	67,830	589,390
2009	509,660	130,483	640,143
2010	520,330	137,074	657,404
2011	553,040	N/A	N/A

Food wholesalers and retailers have benefited from the openness of the Bahamian economy as the heavy reliance on food imports allowed them to enjoy healthy margins and profits which have contributed to the high cost of living in The Bahamas.

The agricultural sector of The Bahamas has not succeeded in exploiting the tourism linkages which are available either directly or indirectly to producers. The reliable supply of high quality produce has not been realised, and many hoteliers and retailers are reluctant to sever ties with overseas suppliers. The poultry industry has adapted its operation to take advantage of the linkages, while other sectors in light industries, like assembling and manufacturing as well as hand crafts, are now responding to this challenge.

Overall the model of tourism, offshore banking, and land development along with construction have generated incomes which have allowed Bahamians to purchase a wide variety of foodstuffs from aboard. Food security has not garnered enough momentum to have the government regard it as a high priority item in its agenda.

With the Free Trade Area of the Americas (FTAA) emerging as the most important hemispheric topic, a new role for the agricultural sector will have to be envisaged.

THE CHALLENGE

The challenges facing small economies like The Bahamas in the next millennium are rooted essentially in the organization of these economies, and the historical role which their vital sectors have played in the development of their societies.

The Bahamian experience has demonstrated that a small economy can coexist and prosper adjacent to the largest and richest economy in the world, while maintaining its own identity, despite the economic uncertainties and political turbulence of some of its sister economies elsewhere in the region and the hemisphere.

The development path of The Bahamas has been one of successful transformation within an atmosphere of political stability. Until 1950, The Bahamas depended on agriculture to earn its foreign exchange and provide mass employment for a people who were barely a hundred years removed from slavery.

During 1950s the foundation had been laid to transform the economy to become competitive in a post World War II times. There were no massive infusions of capital like the US Marshall Plan in Europe to modernize the economy of The Bahamas.

With very little tinkering, the Bahamian economy has matured over the last fifty or so years. It has been successful to the point where sister Caribbean countries, particularly those in the Caribbean Community (Caricom), have adopted the Bahamian model.

According to the reports from the Caribbean Development Bank, the main earner of foreign exchange in the anglophone Caribbean, with exception of Guyana and Trinidad and Tobago, is from tourism, with financial services gaining momentum.

During the post-independence era most of the Caribbean countries attempted to follow a traditional economic strategy of diversifying their economies. The objective was to redirect its manpower from the agricultural sector into activities such as light industries, or to expand industries such as bauxite in Jamaica and Guyana and oil in Trinidad and Tobago. Those without an industrial base had to choose the route of tourism. Still marginalized were the banana economies of Dominica and St. Lucia.

In 1983, The Bahamas joined the Caribbean Community but opted out of the common market and other trade related aspects of the Community. For more than a decade The Bahamas has heightened its profile in Caricom.

As a result of the EU's Lomé Conventions and the United States Caribbean Initiative, followed by the US sponsored FTAA, a common negotiation policy has been agreed upon by the heads of government of all Caricom states.

The question facing small economies like those of The Bahamas and other Caricom countries is this: are these economies equipped to function in a global environment in which trading blocs are the norm; and where the dictates of the WTO, an entity created by the rich industrialized countries whose interests outweigh the concerns of these countries with small economies, are accepted?

The challenge facing The Bahamas in this new world order of globalization is the manner in which the strategic sectors of the economy will be structured to cope with the realities of the Information Age.

Forty-five years ago, The Bahamian economy was poised to take the people of The Bahamas through colonialism, prepared them for independence, and sustained generations throughout the remainder of the twentieth century. This new world order is shrouded with challenges of unknown dimensions.

The Bahamas, like most Caribbean states (CARICOM and the French, Dutch, British and US dependencies), faces a huge food import bill. This situation stems from the growth and development of tourism in the region, and the Americanization of the Caribbean diet through the introduction of US fast food franchises like McDonald's, Wendy's, Burger King and pizza outlets like Dominos. These factors coupled with the view that it was cheaper to import food rather than to grow it led to the decline of agricultural sectors throughout the region.

The region has now become a food deficit locale as governments with the assistance of international agencies like FAO and IICA, groupings like the EU's African, Caribbean and Pacific (ACP) states and financial institutions like the World Bank, FAD and IDB have been pushing food security programmes which have called for greater investment in food production.

In 2007, the food import bill topped the half billion dollar mark. If the present trend continues, by 2013/14 when the Baha Mar project on Cable Beach is completed, the food import bill will skyrocket to a billion dollars. This is not in the best interest of The Bahamas. Food imports will become a drain on the country's foreign reserves; thousands of agricultural based jobs will be outsourced and lost to the economy.

Tourism has fueled food imports and dietary change has exacerbated the whole picture.

CHAPTER 8

AGRICULTURE'S FUTURE

The agricultural sector in The Bahamas is now redefining its growth and development while grappling to identify a farming technology which will be effective in the sector's full potential in food production. Policy makers and farmers must be aware of the possibility that poorly applied farming technology could adversely alter the delicate physical resources which make up The Bahamas.

The economy of The Bahamas has gone through peaks and valleys with wrecking, piracy, blockade running, rum running, drug smuggling on one side and tourism, banking and construction on the other. But agriculture has always been the economic activity to which government policy has returned.

Agriculture must become fully commercialised and be supported by a scientific community and manned by competent and committed entrepreneurs in order to establish itself as an integral and dependable sector in the economy.

To achieve this, the Bahamian farmer, farm labour and the environment are areas that must be addressed.

THE BAHAMIAN FARMER

The Bahamian farmer is among the most resilient business persons in The Bahamas. He works in an atmosphere where he is threatened each year by hurricanes. On the local market, foreign foodstuffs are preferred over his own. Some subsectors are under price control; insurance is either too expensive or unavailable;they face high work permit fees for immigrant farm labour along with the high costs of inputs, and the prices which he is paid for his output are not on par with inflation. Yet he continues to work the land, rear his livestock, and support his family.

All over The Bahamas, there are individuals who have been able to extract a living from the soil. Most have depended on the farming skills which they have learned from their forefathers; others have modified these skills by adopting new husbandry techniques while others have applied new technologies based on scientific investigations elsewhere.

Whereas before the Coppice Islands held the future in farming, it is the Pine Islands that now have the capacity to develop a farming system which would make The Bahamas competitive in world markets.

Another factor which has contributed to the change in the pattern of agriculture has been migration. In countries of one land mass, people move from rural areas to cities. In The Bahamas people have moved from the Family Islands to the urban centres of Freeport and Nassau.

This migration has significantly affected the decline in the number of farmers from 4,246 in 1978 to 1,780 in 1994—a decrease of 58 percent. (Department of Statistics, 1978, 1994)

Farmers in The Bahamas are also getting older. In 1976 the average age was 55 years; by 1994 it had increased to 59 years. The 1990 national population census showed the average age to be 23.6 years and in the Family Islands to be 34.5 years.Farming in The Bahamas is dominated by older people.

Academically, primary school was the highest level of education for 74 percent of the 1,780 farmers in 1994.

The three indices of the decline in the number of farmers (58% between 1978 and 1994), the average age of farmers (59 years); and the level of a farmers' education (primary); paint a gloomy picture for the agricultural sector.

The key question facing Bahamian agriculture during the remaining years of the 1990s and the 21st century is this—does the sector possess the ability to attract new, younger and better educated men and women to the field of agribusiness? Success will call for the full support and cooperation of both public and private sectors.

*Figure 8.1   Women in agriculture: Ms Audrey Cooper, Extension Officer, on
a North Andros farm with a female farmer.*

The Bahamas has an annual national food bill of approximately $300 million and
local farmers satisfy less than 20% of this demand. Because of the climatic conditions
and the close proximity to the large markets of the United States and Canada, there
is a tremendous opportunity for the development of a sustainable export marketing
programme for fruits and vegetables.

Table 8.1   Agricultural Labor Force

YEAR	LABOUR FORCE ENGAGED IN AGR.	% of TOTAL LABOUR FORCE
1970	3,099	4. 4
1973	3,320	4. 2
1975	3,797	4. 5
1978	5,561	6. 0
1994	6,435	5. 0
1996	6,445	5
1998	5,075	4
2000	CENSUS YEAR—NO DATA	
2005	5,590	4
2010	CENSUS YEAR—NO DATA	
2011	6,040	4

By directing agriculture in The Bahamas towards these opportunities, its
attractiveness as a career to intelligent young Bahamians will be enhanced.

FARM LABOUR

A distinguishing feature about Bahamian agriculture was that the plantocracy system never developed in The Bahamas.

Plantation farming had to be supported by slave labour, indentured workers, or some other cheap source of manpower. When one reviews the socio-economic implications of plantation agriculture in the development process of our neighbours to the north, the southern United States and our neighbours to the south, Haiti, Cuba and the Caribbean islands like Jamaica, Barbados and Trinidad and Tobago, the experience of Bahamians of African descent is different to that of their neighbours.

Slave labour was critical for the financial survival of plantation farming. With the abolition of slavery in 1838 former slaves had to become subsistence farmers, farm labourers or tenant farmers who worked the commonage lands of North Eleuthera, the generation properties in Exuma, or elsewhere in The Bahamas.

Freed Africans and "recaptives", who were described by Basil Davidson (Davidson,1992) as captives who were taken into slavery for shipment to America or the Caribbean, but were recaptured and set free by the crews of the British Navy, were certainly not interested in becoming farm labourers. They might become farmers as some did in Grants Town and Fox Hill in Nassau, but definitely not labourers.

This group gravitated to the trades and eventually their offspring became the professionals—teachers, priests, doctors, lawyers and ministers. Their habitats were Grants Town and Bain Town in the southern district New Providence; and Fox Hill and Freetown in the eastern district. It should be noted that throughout the 1950s and well into the 1960s, large numbers of Bahamian men were recruited to work as farm workers in the US, even though offshore farming companies from the US were growing large acreages of vegetables on the Pine Islands.

The availability of farm labour continues to be a constraint to agriculture in The Bahamas, particularly large-scale mechanized farming. As a result of the inability to attract Bahamians to farming jobs, specifically harvesting as stoop labourers and pickers, the latter part of the 1950s and 1960s saw the large illegal immigration of thousands of Haitians to The Bahamas. Large numbers of them settled in Abaco and North Eleuthera to work as farm labourers. Estimates as high as 40,000 have been given for the number of illegal Haitians in The Bahamas in the 1980s, although 25,000 was probably closer to the truth.

Farmers and large offshore operations have found Haitian labourers to be reliable, hardworking and productive employees. To demonstrate their productivity, Bahamas Citrus Growers conducted an experiment by placing four Bahamian grapefruit pickers in four different locations and a Haitian picker in another location. At the end of the work day, it was found that the Haitian picker harvested more grapefruit than the combined amounts of the four Bahamians.

Successive governments in The Bahamas have recognized the need for non-Bahamian farm labour and have cooperated with the farming community by granting work permits at a reduced rate.

There are some who believe that a commercial farming sector cannot rely entirely on imported manpower to satisfy farm labour requirements. Despite this, farming operations, both large and small, have utilized both illegal and legal immigrants as workers. This has been the situation in New Providence, Grand Bahama, Abaco and North Eleuthera. The farmers in the southeastern Bahamas have not shared this heavy dependency, and Long Island farmers have distinguished themselves by not using Haitian labour.

It has been argued that large scale agricultural enterprises in North Andros, Abaco and Grand Bahama are unable to function efficiently or competitively on the world market with expensive Bahamian labour, which is often in short supply and low in productivity. Most of the field farm labour on these islands tend to be females as the males are orientated towards the mechanical areas.

The shortage of manpower stems from the fact that the labour supply is drawn locally and not nationally. Defenders of Bahamian labourers state that Bahamian labour is not as productive as non-Bahamian manpower because there is a lack of a farming background, which leads to employment being sought elsewhere.

Housing

Large foreign farming entities in the past have understood that the provision of housing for farm labourers would have to be addressed. The question which arose was not the provision of housing but the cost of the housing and the type of housing which was acceptable to the government.

There have been examples in the past where housing was provided for foreign labourers but it was considered substandard. It is possible to provide affordable housing which could satisfy Bahamian standards, and generally foreign companies are not averse to this proposal since labour nationally is not in short supply. The provision of housing is vital to the agricultural sector if it is to absorb some of the unemployed in the country. The picture is further clouded by the fact that housing is in short supply in most of these Family Island communities.

Training

The training of manpower is essential, especially as farm labour would have to be drawn from the urban centres of Nassau and Freeport.

In too many instances, foreign companies compare inexperienced Bahamian labour working under Bahamian conditions with foreign workers, particularly migrant workers in the US. This is patently unfair given the different motivation of contract migrant labour compared with native Bahamians, and also neglects the superior infrastructure supporting US operations.

With a proper housing and training programme, Bahamians can supply the labour requirements of the farming community. Foreign companies could assist by making an investment in Bahamian human capital and in the social development of Family Island infrastructure through housing and other social amenities.

The question of productivity in the agricultural workplace is a major concern. The poultry industry, specifically the processing of broiler meat locally, makes an excellent case study to compare with broiler processing in the United States.

US poultry processing professionals state that productivity begins by implanting an attitude of pride, self respect and commitment in the work ethic of the employee. Once these prerequisites have been established, then knowledge of work, training in specific job functions, and plant organization come into play. The company is then able to develop a productive employee whose performance is measurable.

One method of measuring line-operating efficiency is by monitoring the birds per man hour and pounds per man hour. By doing this, Gladstone Farms was able to improve its efficiency, save money, and produce broiler meat at a cost comparable to the US when tariffs were factored into the equation.

The area of greatest deficiency was in absenteeism. In the US the industry norm was 8 percent; at Gladstone, it was 13 percent annually. After payday it increased to 20 percent; on a rainy day it rocketed to 40 percent.

However, Bahamian labour can be productive and produce at productivity levels comparable to any industrialized country, but the fundamental ingredients of training and motivation must be present.

The agricultural sector in The Bahamas has the potential to increase employment opportunities. Presently, the labour force is essentially employed in production. The areas of food processing, export marketing, farm equipment maintenance and the expansion of livestock production have not been exploited. With training, housing and new opportunities, unemployment can be dramatically reduced.

THE ENVIRONMENT

Farmers are on the cutting edge of environmental and developmental issues. Because of the farmer's constant and daily interfacing with the environment, it is in his interest to protect the environment by incorporating environmental concerns into all facets of his industry consisting of crop and livestock husbandry, agroindustries, all of which have an effect on the environment.

Even though The Bahamas is not a major world food supplier, it has, over the years, been able to display its food production capability in specific crop categories and livestock species. Farmers in The Bahamas, like farmers globally, have a responsibility to maintain sustainable agriculture.

The key element in sustaining agriculture comprises secure land tenure, the safe use of inputs and ongoing research into new farming techniques with heavy dependence on biological control and better on-farm management practices.

Concern for the environment was expressed as early as 1671 when Braziletto wood was thought to be endangered by over-cutting. Concern was not decreased but broadened. The Bahamas National Trust is the leading organization in the country on environmental issues and has been successful in alerting the public and the government about the environment and the measures which are needed to protect it.

The environment in which the Arawaks lived was spectacular to the Europeans, and Columbus was impressed by the rich variety of native birds along with the diversity of land mammals. Unfortunately, there have been extinctions in both of these categories.

Extinctions have been recorded for several barn owls, including the great barn owl (*Tyto pollens*), as well as a large herbivorous tortoise (*Geochelone sp.*) and a rock iguana (*Cyclura sp.*). Preventing extinctions such as these is one of the tasks which The Bahamas faces.

Legislation has been passed by the Parliament of The Bahamas over the years. Acts pertaining to the Protection of birds, flora and fauna (Statute Law) include:

(1) Penal Code 19 (Chapter 229) which affords protection for animals against cruelty and hardship;

(2) Wild Birds Protection Act;

(3) Wild Animals Protection Act;

(4) Plants Protection Act;

(5) Fisheries Resources (Jurisdiction and Conservation) Act;

(6) The Bahamas National Trust Act;

In addition to The Bahamas National Trust Act, the government of The Bahamas has long-term leases with The Bahamas National Trust affecting the establishment of National Parks; the Exuma Cays Land and Sea Park; the National Park in Inagua (for the protection of the flamingo); and the Abaco National Park (for the protection of the Bahamian parrot).

Bahamian agriculturists in the Ministry of Agriculture also have concerns about the environment and have outlined agricultural issues, such as:

Secure Land Tenure

Farmers in The Bahamas have been in a disadvantaged position because of their inability to gain title to land on which they farm. The land which is being farmed is usually of three categories: commonage land, generation property and Crown land.

Commonage land and generation property go back to the feudallike conditions of slavery. The allocation of Crown land will enable a farmer to obtain a lease which the financial institutions will not hold as collateral.

For the farmer to perform his role properly, farmers need explicit institutional rights. In The Bahamas, this has escaped the farming community and has affected investment in the sector. A secure land tenure atmosphere provides the basis for productive farming, sustainable use of natural resources and the maintenance and development of viable farming communities in the various islands of the Bahamian archipelago.

There has recently been a move to give lower lease rates for farmers who leave parts of their land in forest for wind breaks, and who maintain pesticide-free buffer zones close to forest reserves and wetlands.

The indiscriminate land clearing of large tracts of Pine and Coppice Islands will not be allowed any more. The question here is whether or not these initiatives will be enforced.

Biotechnology and Bahamian Agriculture

Biotechnology has hastened the genetic processes in which farmers have been engaged from the beginning of sedentary agriculture. Farmers have been selecting and breeding both crops and livestock for specific characteristics like productivity.

Crop scientists in Bahamian agriculture are convinced "*that some genetic diversity exists in subsistence crops such as cassava, corn, pigeon peas, sweet potatoes and beans, since these crops are grown in many agro-systems.*" Hence some effort must be made to investigate and preserve native varieties of food crops, as opposed to concentrating all their efforts on imported varieties.

Soils

The Bahama *Land Resources Study* has characterized the soils as being"*young, skeletal, free-draining and nutrient-poor.*" The depletion of the nutrients in the soil was the main reason for terminating cotton production in The Bahamas. Most soils are derived from oolitic-limestone with high alkalinity. However, there are some islands with pockets of red and black soil and others with "whiteland (sand soils) areas near the shore".

Water Resources

The freshwater lenses are, in some cases, only a few feet below the surface and the aquifers can be polluted by the leaching of fertilizers, pesticides and animal manures from farming activities.

Environmental and Natural Resource Management

On a sustained basis this is a top priority for the future growth and development of agriculture in The Bahamas. This will have to be an integral part of the planning and decision-making process for policy makers in government, farmer organizations and agribusiness.

PUBLIC ADMINISTRATION

Public administration in The Bahamas is rooted in the colonial system which was inherited from the British. It was a system based on centralized authority which was disseminated through the bureaucracy of Whitehall, London. It was deposited initially in the Colonial Office, and eventually into the Foreign and Commonwealth Office.

Policies, rules, and regulations were formulated to standardize the system of administration throughout the colonies in Africa, Asia, and the Caribbean. A colonial officer could move from colony to colony and experience no difficulties in executing his administrative responsibilities.

This was very apparent in The Bahamas. As colonies achieved their independence many senior colonial administrative officers completed their careers in The Bahamas as permanent secretaries and directors.

An elaborate system for documenting correspondence was devised. Documentation was represented as minutes, memoranda, cabinet papers, and green and white papers to name a few, along with the different types of seals to identify the hierarchy of the Colonial Service. This system of documentation, in conjunction with the legal system, called for a highly literate and regimented officialdom.

This system of public administration was designed for an empire which ruled its dominions around the world initially via the sea through its navy and merchant ships. As communications developed, other mechanisms came into use. However, the use of paper became fundamental in the administration and management of the colonial system.

This was the position in which the government of The Bahamas found itself in 1973 when Independence was gained. The government was highly centralized and this led to the compilation of volumes of paper into a filing system of enormous proportions.

With the advent of modern information technology, the need for a highly centralized public administration with paper as the focal point of communicating became obsolete. With the computer, fax machines, electronic mail, satellite transmission and the internet, new types of communication tools have come into existence since Independence on July 10th, 1973.

These new tools of communication have necessitated a different system of public administration from that of the colonial days and a new type of administrator, manager or professional to function in this system.

The Bahamas in the 21st century will have to be less Nassau centric in the manner in which its public administration is organized. It is critical for The Bahamas, as an archipelagic nation, to utilize the tools which will make decentralization more effective as the country develops its economy through greater maximization of its human and physical resources. This will enable the archipelago to take advantage of its geographical proximity to the markets of North America and its placement as a major global trans-shipment terminal to Europe, Africa, Far East, Central and South America and the Caribbean.

With a highly developed infrastructural base of roadways, Family Island and urban electrification, digital telecommunication, publicly and privately operated secondary and tertiary educational institutions, The Bahamas, with its literate and trainable manpower, is poised for sustained economic growth and development well into the twenty-first century.

In a country like The Bahamas, where the government is intimately involved in the economy, the composition and complexity of the public administration will play a critical role in determining the rate and pace of economic development. It is therefore fundamental that the public administrative system be modified in order for the country to compete and exist in a rapidly changing global environment.

Benefits of Free Trade Areas

The creation of a free trade area is based on the underlying assumption that through the removal of trade distortions, tariffs and other impediments to trade, the market will be able to allocate resources efficiently. It has been the practice of governments throughout the region and the hemisphere to put in place barriers which provide local producers with an unfair advantage over their foreign counterparts. Examples of such barriers would be the use of tariffs with tax imported goods thus making them more expensive when compared to the local products. Other examples of trade distortions would include the use of unnecessary licensing and registration requirements to discourage goods from being imported. The argument in support of free trade is that through the removal of trade impediments society gains, as consumers are able to choose between a wider range of products at lower costs. The government gains, as it withdraws subsides and grants to businesses which were inefficient and "propped up" through incentives and grants, and can now allocate these resources elsewhere in the economy.

While, from a theoretical standpoint, everyone is expected to be better off under free trade, there are countries, owing to their size, level of development, and institutional capacity that are not in a position to take advantage of the benefits under a free trade area. Realistically, one cannot expect a country like Haiti or Guyana, the poorest countries in the hemisphere, to make the same level of commitments under the FTAA as developed countries like Canada or the United States. Should we expect a country like Guyana, where 75 cents out of every dollar goes towards debt servicing, to immediately reduce or eliminate tariffs? The revenues derived from tariffs are not only critical in such cases for the repayment of debts, but are also needed to provide essential social services. These are issues which must be addressed in the context of a free trade area.

Given the diversity in size, development and institutional capacity in the region and hemisphere, the Working Group on Small Economies of the FTAA was formed to address the concerns of the small and less developed states.

Apart from the economic structures which prevent the small and less developed states from taking advantage of the benefits under a free trade area, there are also institutional weaknesses. Linked to free trade arrangements are the needs to protect intellectual property and legislation to prevent anti-competitive practices. All of which involve legislative reform at a cost to governments.

The underling assumption for the creation of a free trade area is to improve the overall level of efficiency through the removal of tariffs and other impediments to trade. However, given the diversity, size and level of development, some countries could not be expected to make the same level of commitments at the same time.

AGRICULTURE IN THE 21ST CENTURY

Small economies like The Bahamas, in conjunction with the economies of the industrialized world, will have to function within a rules-based system with an enforcement capacity. The vehicle for this is the WTO and its unique function will make economic evolution more predictable. The FTAA, which The Bahamas will eventually join, will comply with the WTO rules.

This is the economic context in which the agricultural sector of The Bahamas will be forced to compete. The factors of production, land, labour and capital, which were the hallmarks of the traditional economy, will have to embrace the factors of transformation-mechanization, biotechnology, transportation and information technologies. These are the elements which will determine the competitiveness of agricultural systems.

Globalization has introduced a borderless, knowledge-based, world economy. Information technology is not bound to any region or country, it is mobile and can be created any place. Agriculture, on the other hand, will only be successful if it combines the factors of transformation with the skills, education and knowledge (the new means of production) which are required to operate in an advanced, information-driven global economy.

This will put the small farmer at a great disadvantage. In The Bahamas, the make-up of the farming community is comprised of men and women with the most basic level of education. Because of the transformation which is taking place globally, the average Bahamian farmer will have a difficult time adjusting to the technological advances which are taking place. Essentially, technology is changing the way things are produced.

On the other hand, Bahamian agri-businesses can survive if they adopt the factors of transformation. Operations can be competitive, yet co-exist if problems are approached as an industry rather than as individual businesses. It is within this framework that unnecessary duplications of effort, manpower and equipment can be avoided, particularly transportation, which is vital in an archipelagic setting.

In this hemisphere, the FTAA is the vehicle which will drive the sector, with the WTO as the global regulator. In the FTAA process, agriculture has been given special attention and treatment which is both preferential and different from all other sectors.

This position stems from several factors, namely the nature of agriculture, the risks involved in agriculture, the importance of agriculture to countries with small economies, and the strategic importance of agriculture, i.e. food security. With this background, agriculture was given special consideration. There is the realization that innovations in traditional farming practices have brought improvements and advances in the modernization of agricultural techniques, and the movement from subsistence farming to market-oriented farming. The looming question is the cutoff period for this special treatment.

The governing factors which will direct Agriculture in the twenty-first century under the aegis of the FTAA/WTO are:

(1) tariffs will replace quotas and other market access barriers,

(2) domestic support will be quantified and will be progressively reduced,

(3) export subsidies will be cut,

(4) health and safety regulations which restrict trade will be controlled and

(5) developing countries which rely on the supply of cheap subsidized food will continue to receive assistance.

The under-pinning of this new approach is summarized in a paper of the Organisation of Americas States' Trade Unit:

> The simple answer to the question is that all countries, small or large, benefit from increased trade liberalization, and that smaller countries can benefit more than do larger countries. The reason for this lies in the theory of international trade and comparative advantage.
>
> Small size, by whatever indicator and openness, increases concentration in production and specialization in trade. Openness to trade allows small economies to specialize in a few product sectors and/or services and to derive larger benefits by overcoming the limitations of scale economies due to the small size of their domestic markets. This greater specialization should result in gains from trade which will be greater for a small country than for a large country.

CONCLUSION

The farming systems in The Bahamas have been supported by practices and programmes which have facilitated the growth and development of agriculture into a viable commercial sector making a significant contribution to the national economy. The dynamics of farming have made it possible for local food producers to assist in the drive towards self-sufficiency in locally grown produce, if only on a seasonal basis in some sub-sectors.

The policies which helped agriculture to develop were the injection of a Department of Agriculture presence (extension officers) in the main farming communities, and the introduction of the packing houses as an important element in the marketing infrastructure for fresh fruits and vegetables.

The expansion of the land-clearing programme enabled new land to be brought into production, particularly in the southeastern islands where incentives were given for the production of non-perishable crops, such as pigeon peas and hot peppers, and the development of an export marketing programme in the Pine Islands.

The research work at BARTAD in North Andros and CAS in New Providence provided the sector with information that was passed on to farmers through the extension officers in the Family Islands. Also the development of specialists in crop and livestock production, animal health, marketing and plant protection provided essential technical support. In addition, technical officers at all levels were receiving in-service awards for short and medium term training courses.

Farmers' skills were also upgraded through field days and extension meetings in their communities. The table outlining the value of local farm produce from 1974 to 1996 shows the value of local farm production over a 21-year period.

The Bahamas has the potential to become a major producer of fresh fruits and vegetables in the Caribbean region, and can be a major exporter to North America, Europe and the Far East. With the North American Free Trade Agreement (NAFTA) on the hemispheric horizon, the agricultural sector will be able to assist The Bahamas in becoming an important player in the free trade arena.

CHAPTER 9

PERSPECTIVES: WHERE GLOBAL, NATIONAL AND REGIONAL ISSUES INTERSECT

In 2003, I was appointed The Bahamas' Ambassador to the FAO in Rome, Italy. As an FAO Ambassador, I was given the opportunity to view agriculture from a global perspective. Being a specialty agency of the United Nations (UN), FAO is involved with every facet of world food production.

In addition to FAO, the UN has two other food organizations—the International Fund for Agricultural Development (IFAD) and the World Food Programme (WFP). IFAD provides funds for rural development projects in developing countries. WFP, on the other hand, specializes in delivering food on a humanitarian basis to countries which may be in crisis for various reasons, i.e. famine, drought, civil unrest, natural disasters. The Bahamas has been ratified for IFAD membership. Being in Rome enables one to see the various dimensions of food being implemented on a global scale.

In 2004/5, the Forum of Ministers of Agriculture of the Caribbean in conjunction with the Inter American Institute for Cooperation on Agriculture (IICA), "the specialized agency of the Inter-American System for the promotion of agriculture and rural well-being", felt that there should be a Caribbean representative on the board of directors of the Tropical Agricultural Research and Higher Education Centre (CATIE). This policy decision was responsible for my three year appointment as a director on CATIE's board.

CATIE is a major graduate agriculture school and research centre. It is located in Turrialba, Costa Rica but undertakes research projects for all of Central America and other Latin American states. The centre is funded by the member countries of Central America, IICA and the global donor community. As a board member, I was able to travel to member states to view on-going research projects while getting a clearer understanding of food production conditions in Latin American. In addition, one was able to interface with the donor community on funding issues, particularly global food production initiatives.

Figure 9.1 Trinidad and Tobago Ministry of Agricultural Trade Show in Port of Spain July 5, 1995. L.R. Dr. Vincent Moe, Veterinarian. Ministry of Agriculture, Trinidad and Tobago, Dr. Arlington Chesney, now Executive Director, Caribbean Agricultural Research Development Institute (CARDI) and author.

Even though CATIE's terms of reference included the Caribbean, the only Caribbean state with strong ties to CATIE was the Dominican Republic. During my tenure, steps were taken to increase the involvement of the Caribbean Agricultural Research Development Institute (CARDI) in order to facilitate greater collaboration between the institutions.

In 1995, the WTO came into existence. Every state in this hemisphere became a member with exception of The Bahamas. In my opinion this was a mistake as non-membership has retarded our economic growth and development in critical sectors of our economy, namely food production, light industry and manufacturing. An important component of the WTO is the AOA which sets out the rules and regulations for global trade in food.

Bahamian agribusinesses and small farmers have been and are being left behind in the progress which is being made in pushing the food production sector to a higher level of competitiveness, in pushing towards innovation and in pushing the sector to become more technologically driven.

Trade liberalization is driving the WTO and the AOA has been a vehicle to achieve this objective. In this hemisphere, trade liberalization has manifested itself via the proposed FTAA. Regionally, The Bahamas is classified along with other CARICOM states as an African, Caribbean and Pacific (ACP) state by the EU. The EU is seeking to have ACP states open their markets and this was displayed in the various ACP/EU agreements and conventions—Yaounde Agreement, Lome' Convention and Cotonou Agreement.

Like the US-sponsored FTAA, the EU initiated an Economic Partnership Agreement (EPA) as a scheme to create a free trade area between the EU and ACP states.

From as early as 1957, the EU embarked on an economic development policy aimed at assisting its former colonial possessions, some thirty-one former colonies, with the European Development Fund (EDF).Through the EDF, development funds have been and are being funneled to the ACP states over the past fifty some years. In the case of The Bahamas, it is EDF funds which were responsible for much of the infrastructural work in our Family Islands.

This EU/ACP arrangement has evolved into a trading bloc where ACP states were granted preferential treatment for certain commodities, i.e. bananas to the EU market. The Latin American countries appealed to the WTO on the grounds that the preferential treatment amounted to unfair competition. The WTO ruled in favour of the Latin American countries and the preferential arrangement was declared illegal. This caused substantial economic disruption and destabilization in the Agricultural Sectors of many ACP states. In CARICOM, the banana industry was devastated in the Eastern Caribbean's Windward Islands. Thousands of small farmers in St. Lucia had no export markets for their bananas.

The Bahamas must come to grips with the fact that trade liberalization is here to stay and its food production system can only survive by improving its competitiveness. The global trade agenda is being dictated to by the WTO's AOA, FTAA and the EPA. Trade is the driving force in the maintenance of an economically viable national food production system.

In conjunction with trade, the global state of the food agenda is greatly influenced by FAO and several other agencies and organization—the World Bank, IFAD and the Consultative Group on International Agricultural Research (CGIAR).

Global agenda food production initiatives influence regional and national policies and programmes; funding agencies like the World Bank, IFAD, EDF and the donor community provide the funding to implement these policies and programmes among developing countries like the ACP group. For a country to avail itself to the agenda it must be part of the network. The Bahamas does not benefit because it is not fully integrated into the hemispheric/regional consortium of institutions.

Funding for ACP states from EDF or IFAD is channeled through CARICOM. CGIAR uses CARDI as the conduit to disseminate its research or works through CARDI to identify research projects. Both FAO and IICA have identified the Caribbean as a sub-region and, at the national level, they have provided country representatives respectively.

At this juncture in the 21st century, The Bahamas will have to strive for greater involvement in the global agenda. In this chapter, essays on four subject matter areas are discussed.

GEOPOLITICS OF FOOD

We live in the era of globalization and perhaps the most propelling feature of this era is trade. International trade is a dominant factor. Two of the five most traded global commodities on the international market are food items. Food, in this context, must be viewed within the framework of geopolitics.

As a people, we take food availability for granted. We do not know famine nor do we know food rationing. Our primary sources of food are supermarkets and fast food outlets. Our chief concern is not supply; most of us are concerned about price and whether or not we could have saved by bringing it in from Miami ourselves.

The dilemma we face, however, is that few of us in this country understand or care about the mechanisms which are involved in making it possible for us to have access to food. Further, there is virtually no consideration as to whether or not our national outlook or our national perspective on food is compatible or consistent with the geopolitics of food.

Geopolitical Issues Impacting Food

The world is undergoing dramatic changes and these changes are impacting food, its production, its availability and its output. In addition, these changes are transformational as new factors have come into play. These factors include climate change, energy costs, population growth, gender and youth development, land, migration (legal or illegal), urbanism, water scarcity, biofuels, biodiversity and the decline of agriculture and the rise of services in our region and in The Bahamas.

Furthermore, there is the global economic reordering as Brazil, India and China emerge as economic powerhouses with expanding middle classes who now compete with Americans, Europeans, Canadians and Japanese for a range of food items. Annually, China and India are pulling millions out of poverty as they edge closer to a consumer-based society.

In conjunction with the above-mentioned factors, there are the power relationships which set the global food agenda and drive the policy initiatives.

Geopolitical Agencies

The three power global agencies are FAO, WTO and the World Bank. These three agencies dictate the global agenda for food.

FAO is classified as a United Nations specialized agency which has oversight for agriculture and food worldwide. Its primary goal is to work for the eradication of global hunger. Working closely with FAO in Rome, there were two other agencies, the World Food Programme, which organizes the distribution of food when there are shortages, natural disasters and engage humanitarian efforts. The International Fund for Agricultural Development (IFAD) is oriented to funding projects which are geared towards food production and rural poverty alleviation.

The WTO sets rules and regulations for international trade in food. The WTO came into existence in 1994 when its forerunner, the General Agreement in Trade and Tariffs (GATT) was dissolved.

In September 1986, at the GATT conference in Uruguay, John Block, the US Secretary of Agriculture in the Reagan Administration, made the following statement:

> "The idea that developing countries should feed themselves is an anachronism from a by-gone era. They would better ensure their food security by relying on US agricultural products, which are available, in most cases, at lower cost."

Block's statement declared that the concept of food self-sufficiency to be officially dead as it ushered in the era of cheap foods. Many countries bought this notion; The Bahamas was one of them. It is this perception that there is such a commodity as "cheap food" which has retarded food production here, Haiti and most Caribbean and Sub-Saharan African countries. Our government, like many others, adopted the policy position that it was cost effective to import food rather than to grow our own food.

This concept was pushed by the International Monetary Fund (IMF) and the World Bank. In The Bahamas, the IMF in the early 90s advised The Bahamas government to harmonize its customs tariff structure. During this exercise, tariffs were reduced and this negatively impacted agribusinesses, like Gladstone Farms, Sawyer's Food Products, P.W. Albury and Sons and, most of all, the small farmer.

In March, 2010, President Bill Clinton apologized to Haiti for the "cheap food" policy as espoused by Block 24 years ago. The point was made that decades of "cheap food" imports from the US, particularly rice, have destroyed local agriculture and left small farmers in Haiti, The Bahamas and elsewhere in the Caribbean food insecure and unable to feed their countries. In the mid 1990s it was the Clinton Administration which encouraged Haiti and other countries to drastically cut tariffs thereby giving easy access to US food exports. In The Bahamas, tariffs were decreased to less than 32%. In Europe, agricultural imports face a 30% tariff and in Japan, it is 59%.

When the WTO was founded in 1994, The Bahamas was the only country in the hemisphere that opted not to join. Last year, the government of The Bahamas sought membership, 15 years later and 15 years behind every country in this region.

Becoming WTO ready will be a formidable task for us. Trade in food is governed in the WTO by the AOA which comprises three elements: Market Access, Domestic Support and Export Subsidies. Developing countries have objected to the AOA because it is seen as being skewed to developed countries like the US, EU, Japan. An important aspect of the AOA is the sanitary and phyto-sanitary measures which deal with food safety as well as animal and plant health.

Becoming WTO ready will not be an easy undertaking as the expertise and competence in the application of AOA is lacking in The Bahamas. Where are the trade professionals? The small farmer and the agribusinesses in The Bahamas will face an up-hill task as they strive to comply with the AOA. No steps are presently in place to assist the food sector in this transitional period. For our food sector to comply, they are certain infrastructure facilities which would be required to monitor the products which are being grown or processed. Where is the Bureau of Standards?

The final power entity is the World Bank which is the international financial institution that provides loans to developing countries for a range of capital works. The World Bank along with FAO sponsors and chairs the Consultative Group on International Agricultural Research (CGIAR), which oversees 15 international centers spanning 100 countries. CGIAR has been instrumental in developing useful new production technologies for Third World countries. This has been demonstrated, for example, at the International Rice Research Institute where rice varieties were developed specifically for developing countries.

Food security is now the watch word. Those who set the agenda for the geopolitics of food have deported from the cheap food policy and have now embarked on the policy of food security.

Where is The Bahamas in This?

An effective national plan for food production must reflect the key components of the global agenda. To be successful and relevant in this era of trade liberalization, developing counties like The Bahamas cannot adopt an isolationist approach to geopolitical issues like food production. It is incumbent on governments to be cognizant of the "big picture" and, when possible, factor in those key components of the global agenda as indentified by the mega agencies like the WTO, FAO and World Bank and incorporate them into the national and regional plans.

The Bahamas, like most states in the Caribbean, is a food deficit or net food importing country. This means that the country imports more food than its produces. This makes our archipelago dependent on the state of the international commodity market as it relates to the supply and demand of critical commodities like rice, corn, wheat, meat and coffee. From this prospective, The Bahamas is extremely vulnerable to price fluctuations on the international commodities market.

In 2010, the value of food purchases by food deficit countries, like The Bahamas, was one trillion dollars. Food is a huge international business and its availability can make or break a country.

The world may be forcing another food crisis. In 1973–1974 and, more recently, in 2007–2008 the price of food on the international commodities market skyrocketed. Generally, food prices are impacted by bad weather, failing harvests or dwindling food stocks. In 2007–2008 as in 1973–1974, the price of crude oil was the determinant.

We live in an era of industrial agriculture which relies on fossil fuel to drive food production. When the price of a barrel of crude oil spiked at \$140/barrel, food prices soared causing riots in nearby Haiti and elsewhere particularly in food deficit countries like Sub-Saharan Africa.

In a February 3rd, 2011 report from the Office of the Director General of the IICA the following observations were outlined to the Ministers of Agriculture in Latin America and the Caribbean:

"Those countries of Latin America and the Caribbean that are net food-importing countries must redouble their efforts to raise productivity... At present, world markets are nervous, grain prices are volatile and there are growing concerns about the social implications of the situation, and analysts are divided as to whether this is a new separate development or the resurgence of the 2007–2008 crisis... The most serious challenge is facing those countries that are net importers of most of these products that are becoming more expensive, including tropical products such as coffee, cacao and sugar and dairy and meat products which were not affected in the 2007–2008 crisis."

The geopolitics of food is a subject we cannot ignore. As a country, we have to decide whether it is in our national interest to continue pursuing a national food policy based on imports which increase our dependence and depletes out foreign exchange position. Presently, our national food bill exceeds \$0.5 billion and with the Baha Mar project in the pipeline, this could easily escalate to \$0.75 billion when that project reaches full development.

The other option is to embark on a policy of import substitution using the comparative advantages of climate, innovative technologies, and a high value food domestic market to generate thousands of jobs which can be created out of 0.5 billion dollars as well as there are millions of dollars that can be saved by producing more at home. This will enhance the food security status of our country.

Diet

The heavy dependence on imported food has transformed the culinary orientation of Bahamians. Foods, particularly convenience and fast foods, respectively, have Americanized the Bahamian diet. This shift commenced in the second half of the 20th century when large numbers of women entered the workforce as hotel workers and took mothers out of the home. This was accompanied by the introduction of American fast food franchises.

Today, Bahamians are victims of deceptive marketing which has lead us to eating over-sweetened and highly salted foods which have been prepared with transfats, elaborately processed with preservatives and artificially colored. This has lead to a health crisis which is highlighted by an increase in the number of noncommunicable and metabolic-related diseases like obesity, hypertension and cancer. Each year heart diseases account for almost 500 deaths, deadly cancers cause another 300 deaths, and complications from diabetes another 200. Non-communicable and metabolic-related diseases are now the cause of almost 1,000 deaths per year. The Bahamas is eating itself sick.

There are several questions which have to be addressed. As a people, are Bahamians prepared to maintain the status quo by continuing on a path of total dependence of food imports or is there the desire to advance food production by investing in technologies to enhance our competitiveness? Are we encouraging a new generation of Bahamians to be satisfied with fast, convenience, processed and artificial foods rather than producing safe, nutritious, fresh and locally grown foods? Going against the status quo will call for new political thinking and a new approach to food and its production in a 21st century Bahamas.

Presently, the politics of food in The Bahamas is oriented to satisfying food importers, the fast food industry and the hotel sector. The consumer, be he or she, a Bahamian or a visitor is in the hands of those who control food imports.

Geopolitics of Food and New Realities

The geopolitics of food has created a new environment for food, particularly the manners in which food has been transformed, marketed and distributed.

The 20th century was an epoch which saw the American food industry reinvent food: supersized fast foods, energy dense snack foods, readymade prepared foods and sweetened juice beverages. The fast food fade descended on the Bahamian market like a ton of bricks. The result is an emerging catastrophic health crisis as it ushered in an obesity epidemic. The Bahamian government, as well as other governments in the region, has not been able to find a solution to this dilemma.

The new lifestyle realities in The Bahamas and in other Caribbean States where tourism dominates the economy have caused governments to alter their approach to the politics of food. Policies have strayed from the small farmer and local production to satisfy the food importer and the Tourism Sector. Food supply in The Bahamas is being driven by convenience. Hence, the processors of those products control the market which is comprised of these new food types because we, Bahamians, have become addicted to these new American food fades. The increased demand for convenience foods is directly related to the fact that women with children dominate our workforce. Working women today spend less time cooking because they have to balance home with the workplace. The end result is more than half of all meals are prepared outside the home and are purchased from fast food outlets. In far too many homes, there is heavy consumption of snack and junk foods.

The politics of food in The Bahamas has to re-orient what Bahamians eat by introducing guidelines on the types of foods which are imported into the country. This responsibility has been abdicated and left to the discretion of food importers and fast food operators. This is a 21st century challenge.

RISING FOOD PRICES

The subject of rising food prices has become a major concern to human kind. It has attracted the attention of all of the major agricultural agencies around the world.

FAO, in a statement, has explained in February, 2010 that world food prices raised again for the eighth consecutive month, with increases in all commodity groups under observation, less sugar, according to the index developed by the United Nations agency. FAO has warned that the relationship between supply and demand for cereals could tighten in the period 2010–2011.

The aim of the seminars which are being organized by FAO in the various regions

(Caribbean, June 14th and 15th, 2011 in Barbados) is to exchange experiences on the crisis in food prices of 2007-2008, and learn more about the various advantages and disadvantages of the actions outlined in the latest edition of FAO's guide policy and programmatic interventions in countries to cope with rising food prices.

"FAO considers it essential that countries review their policy options and depart from the decisions that might exacerbate the situation," warned the Deputy Director General of FAO, He Changchui. In his view, the latest food crisis aggravated the situation in some countries because they decided to impose export restrictions or made "panic buying."

The Director General of the FAO has stressed that governments should focus or "soften" the impact of rising food prices on the poor and take measures to encourage investment in agriculture.

This story does not end. Apart from the global and regional concerns, there is grave concern in the Hemisphere. In October, 2011, the Inter-American Institute for Cooperation on Agriculture (IICA) in cooperation with the government of Costa Rica will be holding a hemispheric conference dealing with rising food prices. All of the ministers of agriculture in the Hemisphere are being urged to attend this conference.

FAO has pointed out that a combination of factors is responsible for the hike in food prices. Some of these are "reduced production due to climate change, historically low level of food stocks, i.e. cereals, higher consumption of meat and dairy products in emerging nations (India, Russia, China and Brazil), increased demand for biofuels production and higher costs of energy and transport—all leading to surges in food prices."

This scenario is being acted out daily arising from competition for corn as a commodity like grits or corn flakes for human consumption, corn as an animal feed ingredient or corn for energy as the biofuel ethanol to be used as an alternative to fossil fuels. Any of these circumstances in conjunction with the escalation of fuel costs which has pushed up freight rates in The Bahamas (June, 2011) for example to $100 per ton per container for each shipment, have impacted food prices. The Caribbean has become a food deficit region with a dependence on imported food for its survival.

The Bahamas and the region are in this state because governments have fallen prey to the misguided idea that there is a commodity called "cheap foods" which is available from countries that heavily subsidize their agricultural sectors thereby enabling farmers and agribusinesses in those countries to sell on the world market at prices which Caribbean small farmers and fledging agribusinesses have difficulty competing. This has been the catalyst to liberalize markets in the region, eventually leading to destabilized and non-competitive agricultural sectors.

Caribbean Agriculture has become a victim of the "cheap foods" policy. FAO has been peddling the notion of food security and the IICA has hyped "New Agriculture", yet these pleas have fallen on the deaf ears of regional governments who have generally bought the idea that tourism and financial services were the saviours and food production could be placed on the backburner of economic importance.

This thinking has come back "to bite" governments. The Preval Administration in Haiti during the 2008 hike in food prices was a prime example as its prime minister was kicked out because the government had problems coping with the issue of high food prices. On the export side, Caribbean states have had to adjust to the loss of preferential markets for sugar and bananas in the EU. Here again, the Caribbean was a victim of the globalized trading environment that was created by the WTO.

Caribbean Agriculture has been victimized by the "cheap foods" policy on the domestic market and by the WTO on the export market with the loss of the EU preferential market. These two frontal assaults by the proponents of trade liberalization have crippled the food production system in virtually every CARICOM state. The region is now facing unprecedented levels in food prices. The situation is further exacerbated by an indigenous population, whose dietary habits have changed as a result of urbanization, rising incomes, women in the workplace and the impact of tourism. Tourism has increased food imports and Caribbean peoples have become hooked on fast or convenience foods respectively. FAO has stated that processed foods and beverages account for 80 percent of total food and drink sales.

Tourism has also fueled the demand for food, much of which is not grown in the region and where there is a supply, it is limited by seasonality and competitiveness issues.

Insights into the Food Dilemma

High food prices are not only seriously affecting the quality of life of Bahamians and those in the region but are also negatively impacting the competitiveness of the region's economic engine, tourism. This region attracts millions of visitors who are now finding that food costs are, in some cases, exorbitant. Food, as a travel expense, now rivals airfares and accommodations as a high priced item.

In Caribbean states with strong agricultural sectors like the Dominican Republic, Cuba and Jamaica, their competitiveness in food has assisted their tourism product, i.e. their food production capacity directly contributes to their tourism and economy by saving foreign exchange on one hand and utilizes local produce on the other.

For the domestic consumer, there is market manipulation as Bahamian producers and agribusinesses have had to operate under distorted market conditions. This stemmed from harmonizing the duty structure without consulting or obtaining feedback from those who would have been affected by the duty realignment. This is the case with some food importers who buy at a cheap price, benefit from a lowered duty, i.e. poultry meat and sell at one or two cents under the local producer, thereby gouging the consumer by not passing on the savings that would have resulted from the lowered duty.

Local production, if properly monitored by the government or consumer group, takes away the possibility of the food importer controlling the market. Where there is local production, the consumer gets a better deal and the food importer has less leverage in manipulating supply and the prices of products.

The Way Forward

The real solution to the high food price dilemma is to get Bahamian farmers and agribusinesses to produce more. This is a good opportunity for growers to take advantage of the demand for food in the market place. In previous years, farmers were receiving low prices for their commodities; the situation is in the reverse today.

This is a different Bahamas. We live in the age of information technology which enables farmers and agribusinesses to reach input suppliers and access domestic and foreign markets. By organizing themselves into farmer or commodity groups, they can extricate themselves from government dependency.

This is also a different global scenario from the normal supply/demand situation. High food prices are tied to high energy prices, mechanized, capital intensive agribusiness is just as dependent on fuel as any other industrial or manufacturing activity. It takes fuel (gas or diesel) to operate farm machinery, to transport product from the field to the various stages of processing and eventually to the consumer. Food production is dependent on petroleum-based pesticides and fertilizers. As a food deficit state depending on imported food, freight rates are surging as well.

There is every indication that food prices are unlikely to fall anytime soon; many factors are interplaying and energy is only one. We must face up to the fact that The Bahamas cannot continue to look to others to provide us with food. We can produce more and there are options that are open to us.

DUTY REDUCTION POLICY

A national budget provides a number of insights about a government. It outlines a government's political philosophy on the economy and the manner in which it will manage the economy. The fifteen budgets of the Free National Movement government have revealed to me the government's attitude toward food production in The Bahamas and the role it perceives the agricultural sector to play in the economy.

In a recent discussion on Love 97's Issues of The Day, a Cabinet Minister stated that duty reduction was a tool the government was using to lower cost to the consumers. This may be the government's objective. The question is: does it happen?

In this same budget the government lowered the duty on kidney dialysis equipment. Does it mean that the fees for dialysis treatments will be less? Knowing the medical community in The Bahamas, this is highly unlikely.

The Minister, if he feels that duty reduction works in lowering costs to the consumer, should present empirical data to prove his point? Statistical analysis can be done on important tools by the Department of Statistics, the research unit of the Central Bank or by economists in the Ministry of Finance to determine whether or not savings are being passed on to the consumer or are being absorbed by the importer in the case of food or by the doctor in the case of the dialysis treatment. Matter of fact, making these determinations should be an aspect of the cost of living surveys which are undertaken periodically throughout the year—that is if this is to become public policy.

The strategy of duty reduction on food products started on July 1st, 1996 when the government enacted the Traffic Act. An important element of this Act was to give effect to the harmonized system of tariffs. As a result of this Act, the duty on poultry was reduced overnight without consultation or warning, from 70% to 35% . In 2002, Gladstone Farm went out of business putting about 300 Bahamians out of work. At that time Gladstone Farms, Bahamas Poultry in Grand Bahama and Abaco Big Bird had a combined output of $17–18 million, along with layer (eggs) production; poultry was a $24 million agribusiness. In conjunction with this, imported poultry meat was worth $11 million. Poultry employment ranged between 1,000–1,200 workers.

Duty Reduction Casualty

When Gladstone closed its doors in 2002, poultry agribusiness dropped to $16 million with broiler meat production accounting for almost 50% of the output. The industry has never recovered to the pre-2002 level of output. Control of the market ended up in the hands of food importers. With a further duty reduction in the 2011/12 budget, the decline is imminent with possible elimination of commercial broiler production as an agribusiness.

Caribbean Poultry Association (CPA)

This is in sharp contrast to the rest of the Caribbean. In CARICOM, Ministers of Agriculture have made poultry a "sensitive" product as it is protected by destabilizing marketing maneuvers like dumping. Poultry production has become the largest agribusiness in CARICOM. The Caribbean Poultry Association (CPA) is recognized by CARICOM's Council of Trade and Economic Development (COTED) as the voice of the regional industry. The Bahamas is a charter member of the CPA as Bruce Hanson of Gladstone Farms was its first president with yours truly as the Executive Director. The CPA came into existence in 1999 and incorporated in 2000.

Poultry in CARICOM generates $500 million in gross output, employs close to 100,000 persons, provides close to 80 % of the nutritional protein requirement of Caribbean people and, at any point in time, provides at least three months of food security to the national economies of the states in CARICOM.

The main reason CARICOM poultry has achieved this status stems from the fact that poultry is private sector driven and has been able to integrate the small farmer into the production system. CARICOM governments have supported cost reducing technologies as these technologies have enhanced the competitiveness of this agribusiness. The integration of the small farmer and cost reducing technologies have been instrumental in growing the industry while, at the same time, improving the food security status of CARICOM states.

The Small Farmer and Crop Production

The duty reduction on local food production has now been expanded to fruits and vegetables or simply crops. Based on the 2011/12 budget, there will be no duty on crops.

The Department of Agriculture's statistics indicated that in 2010 there were 1968 small farmers throughout The Bahamas. There are 1,482 crop farmers with most of them farming on Eleuthera (334), Cat Island (279), Andros (289), New Providence (169) with the remainder scattered throughout the archipelago and producing 124 different types of fruits and vegetables.

The chief crops were bananas, grapefruits, cabbages, mangoes, limes, oranges, onions, tomatoes and watermelon. In contrast, the ten most imported crops were lettuce, tomatoes, cabbage, sweet peppers, broccoli, onion, cantaloupes, oranges and banana. There is an overlap; however, all of the top ten imported crops can be grown here. The main problem is that agriculture in The Bahamas is not research-based and technology driven, hence food production is mired in outdated technologies because research on production husbandry practices are lacking.

Over the past two or three years, Bahamians have been investing in greenhouse technology. Greenhouses are now located in New Providence, Andros, and Abaco and lettuce is one of the crops earmarked for production. The largest and most sophisticated is Lucayan Tropical which is situated in southwest New Providence. It is a multi-million dollar high tech operation utilizing the latest in greenhouse technology. A range of fresh vegetables are grown at competitive prices.

When one reviews the impact of this policy on the small farmer, he or she is endangered and could become extinct. On Eleuthera, for example, there are 334 crop farmers who have some 2,620 acres under production with an output of 50 million pounds of produce valued about $32 million, according to Department of Agriculture statistics (value seems high to me).

There are three packing houses, (North Eleuthera, Hatchet Bay and Green Castle) with the maximum payment of $9,000 per farmer. The government pays out $3 million dollars; the remaining quantities have to be sold on the Nassau market. The Family Island small farmer is essentially back to the same position he or she was prior to the introduction of the packing house more than thirty years ago. The limitations imposed by lack of investment to upgrade the agricultural infrastructure has retarded the progress of the sector.

The supermarkets, wholesalers, franchise operators, hotels and gourmet restaurants are reluctant to do businesses with small farmers for a variety of reasons. The main outlet for the small farmer is the street produce vendor possibly at Potter's Cay or on some street corner Over-the-Hill.

Export Agriculture

Intermittently during the second half of the 20th century, The Bahamas was a major supplier of fruits (citrus and avocados) and winter vegetables (cucumbers, tomatoes, okra and even strawberries) to the states of the eastern seaboard of the United States. Offshore growers like the giant food company Gulf and Western used The Bahamas as a food security reserve in the event of a Florida freeze. There were occasions when The Bahamas was the only place in North America where okra was available. In these situations, growers made huge profits as they controlled the supply. With climatic vagaries as a result of global warming, there is the possibility that The Bahamas can regain this position on the supply chain.

With reference to citrus (oranges, grapefruit, limes, lemons, tangerines, sour orange), The Bahamas had, prior to the canker outbreak in Abaco, the largest acreage of citrus in CARICOM, only Belize and Jamaica had more.

Citrus is a very versatile crop because of its export potential, its demand on the local market and as a subsistence crop for homeowners and small farmers. Most Bahamians grow up with some type of citrus tree in the backyard and this has resulted in citrus being grown from Abaco in the north to Landrail Point, Crooked Island in the southeast Bahamas. Further, citrus enjoys certain comparative advantages in the northern Bahamas on the Pine Islands where citrus can be grown commercially without irrigation. This is an important crop for The Bahamas and its production capability should not be "outsourced" as a result of a duty reduction policy.

Export agriculture has played a tremendous role in generating employment opportunities on the Pine Islands. In 1990, offshore growers pumped $21 million into the on-island economies as hundreds of Bahamians and migrant farm labourers, principally Haitians, were planting, harvesting, grading and boxing fruits and vegetables for export to America. The Bahamas had a valuable and sustainable source of foreign exchange with the potential to grow, expand and diversify. Export agriculture would have been able to assist with the enhancement of our balance of payments position because of its ability to earn foreign exchange. Policy makers and the political directorate have fumbled the ball again.

Under the United Bahamian Party (UBP) government, a policy restriction was introduced prohibiting offshore growers from marketing their produce on the domestic market. The local market was preserved for the small farmer. Local farming was seen as self-employment even though the level of technology was traditional and further, the small farmer was critical to our national security because he was the one who inhabited these far flung islands where for decades the only means of communication was the sail boat.

Canneries

To advance food production in a locale like The Bahamas where production is seasonal and subjected to gluts and scarcities there must be some form of agri-industrialization. Generally in developing countries, agri-industrialization is centered on food processing, i.e. canning and bottling. During the 60s there were three canneries in The Bahamas—one in Rock Sound, Eleuthera and the other two in Nassau. In Gregory town, Eleuthera, the Thompson brothers operated a facility which processed pineapples.

By the late 70s only two of these canneries existed—the two in Nassau. The Rock Sound cannery concentrated on tomato products in Eleuthera which was the largest tomato producer in The Bahamas. This cannery was owned and operated by the late George Baker and his brother. The advantage this cannery held was that it was located at the point of production where as the Nassau based canneries depended on some New Providence farmers but primarily on the Produce Exchange.

In '96/97 food processors would experience the same fate as the poultry producers. Duties on tomato paste and pigeon peas were reduced and some canneries switched from fresh material to imported concentrates in order to keep their businesses going. Small farmers lost a market.

The withdrawal from the processing of tomatoes put a tremendous strain on the

Produce Exchange and its network of packing houses as it became the main purchaser of tomatoes. Tomato gluts became a nightmare causing wastage, dumping and huge financial losses.

The small farmer in Mayaguana was the main supplier of pigeon peas to the canneries. When the duty dropped, the canneries began importing pigeon peas from Africa and Latin America; scores of farmers lost the canneries as a market.

Food Security and Competitiveness

Three sub-sectors of the agricultural sector are presented—broiler meat (poultry), crops and the small farmer and food processing. It seems that the agricultural sector of The Bahamas is being systematically dismantled. In an era when international agencies like the FAO, the IICA, the Inter-American Development Bank (IDB) and the World Bank are urging countries to strive for greater food security; The Bahamas seems to be heading in the opposite direction.

Enhancing the food production competitiveness among small farmers and agribusinesses will not be achieved through duty reduction if the objective is to build a sub-sector, industry or agribusiness. In this era of trade liberalization, cost competitiveness can be based on natural resources (growing conditions), technology usage and development, quality of the agribusiness environment, among other factors. A new policy framework needs to be established in order to survive in this globally competitive environment called globalization.

The Organization for Economic Cooperation and Development (OECD) defines competitiveness as "the degree to which a country can, under free and fair market conditions, produce goods and services which meet the best of international markets, while simultaneously maintaining and expanding the real incomes of people over the long term". In order to accede successfully to the WTO, The Bahamas would have to design new mechanisms to support its agriculture, while at the same time making it more competitive. There is a high level of uncertainty in the sector as a result of the manner in which food production is perceived by the government. It will be extremely difficult to attract investment.

THE STATE OF FOOD PRODUCTION

Agriculture has been a victim of lip service—a lot of fluff and no substance. The end result is that we are an extremely vulnerable people because of our heavy dependence on others to supply our food demands. This has made us a food deficit country, i.e. we import more food than we produce. The situation is being exacerbated in the face of the global policy, which encourages states to achieve greater food security by growing more. As I mentioned previously food production in The Bahamas is heading in the wrong direction.

Since the recent budget debate, there has been on-going commentary regarding the duty reduction on a range of fruits, vegetables and several household items, particularly those products that are grown or manufactured by local entities. Personally, I am not satisfied with the rationale which is being espoused by those in the political directorate and policy-making positions. From my perspective, the statistical data, which have been compiled and published by the Department of Agriculture, paint a very different picture.

The Small Farmer

In 1978, just five years after becoming an independent state, the government of The Bahamas understood that for planning purposes, data on the sector was a necessity. The first agricultural related comprehensive survey was initiated a decade (1968) earlier when a Land Resources Survey was conducted by the United Kingdom's (UK) Land Resources Division of the Directorate of Overseas Survey. As a member of the FAO, a request was made to FAO to conduct a Census of Agriculture.

The year 1978 can be considered a baseline year for agricultural statistics in The Bahamas. The outcome of the census was a revelation for public policy makers. Like most Caribbean states, small farmers dominated he agricultural sector of The Bahamas, some 4,246. The largest number of small farmers, 711 was located on the island of Andros. This was a surprise in view of the fact that the southeastern Bahamas was considered the main farming region with Eleuthera (687 small farmers) being considered for decades as the bread basket of the archipelago and Long Island closely behind with 607 farmers.

By 1994, sixteen years after the '78 census, the figures were startling. There was a decline in the number of small farmers by 69%. The overall number of small farmers had fallen from 4,246 to 1,760. Across the archipelago, small farmers became an endangered group due to aging and the lack of replacements from Bahamian youth who found this type of work unattractive. Tourism emerged as the main economic activity as The Bahamas became an urban society.

The most dramatic decrease was in Abaco where the decline was 77% and Andros 71%. These were the Pine Islands that accounted for 164,000 acres of land that is amenable to mechanical cultivation. By 2006, the sector had lost over a three-decade period, more than 3,303 farmers. In 2006, the number of small farmers had dipped to its lowest, 943; by 2010, however, there was a turn around as the number of small farmers climbed to 1,968. With the global economic meltdown, farming was the employment of last resort and served as the safety net for the unemployed in the Family Islands.

Acreage Under Production

The 1978 Census of Agriculture reported that there were 89,500 acres under some form of crop production with Cat Island having the largest acreage (29,919 acres) followed by Abaco with 20,788.

Cat Island is located in the southeastern Bahamas on coppice land where the crop production technology is based on pothole farming. There are, however, locations on Cat Island where "white land" with free moving soil which is highly suitable for onions and potatoes as well as red soils "terra rosa" on which pineapples have been grown for decades. The Cat Island small farmer was extremely productive as he or she was cultivating, on average, about 66 acres whereas the national average was only 20 acres per small farmer. The Cat Island farmer's level of productivity was three times the national average.

In comparison to Abaco, most of the land under cultivation was in the hands of large offshore agribusinesses with thousands of acres under citrus and winter vegetable production. In addition, there were the former sugar estate lands that were once under sugar cane production (25,000 acres) by The Bahamas Agricultural Industries Ltd. (BAIL), a subsidiary of the US based lumber company, Owens Illinois. The 304 small farmers were cultivating a substantially smaller acreage than the small farmers on Cat Island.

By 1994, total acreage under production had declined by 44% from almost 90,000 acres to 50,249 acres. This reduction impacted every major producing island except Grand Bahama where the acreage expanded by 217%. Large tracts of land were leased from the Grand Bahama Port Authority for orchard crops (citrus, avocados) and vegetables. Production also increased on Acklins as this small farming community, by necessity, had to turn to growing mainly non-perishable substances—crop types like corn and pigeon peas. Outside of farming and fishing, there is virtually no economic activity, apart from niche tourism for several fly-fishing lodges. The people of Acklins and Crooked Island are heavily engaged in the agro-forestry activity of harvesting Cascarilla bark as an export commodity for the EU market.

The steep decline of the sector is further reflected in 2006 when less than 6,000 acres were in cultivation. By 2010, four years later, there was resurgence in production. This stemmed from the lack of non-agricultural related employment opportunities on Eleuthera that reemerged as the leading island with 8,000 acres being cultivated by 380 small farmers.

Food Production

Food production output in The Bahamas has been erratic to say the least. In 1985, output reached 34 million, the high point since statistical data had been maintained at the departmental level. By 1988, it dropped 30 million, escalating to 53 million in 1991 and then decreasing again to 42 million in 1994. This inconsistency continued until 2001 when it peaked at 62 million. However, it again declined to 38 million in 2004. By 2008, it re-established itself at 78 million.

The state of local output was in sharp contrast to imported food that steadily increased regardless of the economic conditions or the variances in visitor arrivals. In 1995, the value of imported food was 208 million; by 2007 that figure, in about two decades, had doubled to 502 million. Food imports were now a half billion-dollar industry for food importers: wholesales, supermarket operators, US franchise holders, the hotel industry, gourmet and native restaurants.

With population growth and expansion in the tourism sector, i.e. Baha Mar project, by 2027, based on present trends, food imports will be a billion dollar industry. No wonder a major supermarket operator expressed his delight regarding the government's duty reduction policy approach to food; he felt that it augured well for his business.

The regional experience with tariff adjustment or duty reduction, up or down, is clear. When tariffs or duties are higher, local production is stimulated; when it is lowered, local production is stagnated. In the former case, food security is enhanced.

I recently circulated a paper, "The Geopolitics of Food", and my views on duty reduction, over the FAO-Carib-Agri List, an e-mail discussion medium. One of the most prominent agribusiness men in the region and a colleague in the Caribbean Poultry Association (CPA), Mr. Robin Phillips, President of the Poultry Association of Trinidad and Tobago, made the following observations:

In case anyone is in doubt about the negative impact resulting from the removal/reduction in tariffs on local producers and National Food Security, we can reference two cases:

(1) Guyana Chicken a. In 1992 the tariff on chicken was reduced to 25% Imports rose to 72% of total consumption. b. In 2003 the tariff was increased to 100%—Local production increased to 100% of total consumption—No imports for the last 4 plus years.

(2) Trinidad and Tobago: Chicken a. Prior to 2001 total tariffs 137%—Imports were less than 2% of total consumption. b. In 2006 tariffs cut to 40%—Imports as at Dec 2010—33% of total consumption and rising.

The primary product imported in both cases was US Leg Quarters, which was determined by a Chinese government investigation in 2009 to being exported at prices below the cost of production. The Chinese consequently introduced an import tariff of 105.4% on US chicken as of September 2009. We in the CARICOM region have to decide between two conflicting options:

(1) An agricultural policy in an alignment with the principles as stated by Article 39 of the EU Treaty of Rome, March 25, 1957.

Or

(2) The Block Doctrine—The recommendation of John Block, the US Secretary of Agriculture in Sept. 1986 at the GATT Conference in Uruguay.

It would appear that unfortunately Option 2 has been the preferred choice in many cases.

The erraticism in local food production output has its uncertainty in a shrinking small farmer community. Agribusinesses like those engaged in poultry production, food processing, commercial fruit orchard development, hi-tech farming (greenhouse production) and hydroponic farming and genome production (tissue culture and embryo transfer) will think twice about investing or will be unwilling to invest in Bahamian agribusiness. To date, the government does not consult with stakeholders but employs high-handed tactics to introduce policy initiates, such as duty reduction, which could destabilize an operation, i.e. canneries, Abaco Big Bird, Bahamas Poultry or even put an entity out of business, i.e. Gladstone Farms. Another factor is the dramatic decrease of farmland in production. Farming is a dynamic activity and bringing new land into production is an integral part of crop and animal husbandry.

As a result of this scenario, The Bahamas has outsourced feeding itself to America, Canada, the EU, the Latin American countries of Brazil, Mexico, Chile, Costa Rica and Argentina, Thailand in Asia and the Pacific states of Australia and New Zealand.

How Did We Get Here?

By the mid 1960s, The Bahamas had transformed its economy from an agricultural based one to one centered on services, specifically tourism. This transformation also saw The Bahamas become an urban society. Economic development in Nassau and Freeport stimulated a mass internal migration as thousands left the land and sea from the Family Islands for city life.

The Bahamas was cashing in on the post World War II economic boom that was fueled by a then dominant US economy. In the US itself, a new system of agriculture was emerging; it was Industrial Agriculture based on low cost/high volume predicated on cheap fossil fuel, synthetic fertilizers, chemical herbicides and pesticides and new hybrid seed varieties. This resulted in the US becoming the breadbasket of the world. With huge crop surpluses from this system, the US became the world's chief food exporter. Industrial Agriculture became the global model. A half century later, the question which is being asked is whether or not this model is sustainable in view of rising crude oil prices, the likelihood of environmental degradation, the concerns regarding water resources, pollution, global warming and damages to the ecosystem via chemical runoff and farm animal sewerage disposal.

The World Bank and the International Monetary Fund (IMF) pushed governments in developing countries like The Bahamas to adopt the importation of "cheep food" as a policy rather than strive for greater food self-sufficiency in order to enhance their own food security status. Like most developing countries, The Bahamas adopted this "cheap food" policy. Today, food deficit countries have become a trillion dollar market for food exporting countries like the US, Canada and the EU.

The Bahamas was now tied to competing with a growing demand for food from emerging economies like China and India where per capita incomes were on the rise. We have tied our food supply chain to the susceptibility of outbreaks like swine fever, bird flu, mad cow diseases and the recent E. coli outbreak with vegetables and beef in Europe. Dependency increases a country's vulnerability to forces over which it has no control; this is the position The Bahamas has placed itself.

The above has been the modus operandi of the global trading system for almost three decades as countries like The Bahamas and regions like the Caribbean have become food deficit enclaves where imported food has surpassed locally produced food.

By 2010, the global institutions like the World Bank, IMF, the FAO and hemisphere bodies such as the IICA began to push an agenda centered on national and regional food security.

Former US president, Bill Clinton, while in Haiti, highlighted the reality of being food insecure during the aftermath of the earthquake devastation. Clinton made the following apology:

> "Since 1981, the United States has followed a policy, until the last year or so when we started rethinking it, that we rich countries that produce a lot of food should sell it to poor countries and relieve them of the burden of producing their own food, so thank goodness, they can leap directly into the Industrial Era. It has not worked… it was a mistake…
>
> "And it failed everywhere it's been tried. And you just can't take the food chain out of production. And it also undermines a lot of culture, the fabric of life, the sense of self-determination."

This has been the context, which has caused The Bahamas to be mired in a state of food insecurity, subsequently creating a multi-million dollar industry for importing food at the expense of the small farmer and fledging agribusinesses.

Why the Decline?

Apart from the potential demise of the small farmer, the discouragement to agribusiness development and the decrease in farm production acreage; another important factor has been the lack of investment in the agricultural sector by both the public and private sectors respectively.

At the opening of a High-level Expert Forum, "How to Feed the World in 2050", the Director-General of FAO, Jacques Diouf made the following remarks:

> "Agriculture will have no choice but to be more productive... and this will require substantial increases in investment in the sector— better access to modern inputs, more irrigation systems, machinery and implements, more reads and better rural infrastructure as well as more skilled and better-trained farmers.

> "The technology gap between countries needs to be bridged, capacity building through knowledge transfer... should be strengthened to achieve sustainable increases in agricultural production and productivity."

The first decade of the 21st century has been a pivotal one for global agriculture and by extension, national and regional agriculture sectors and/or systems. In reviewing the national budgets during the first decade, the recurrent budgetary allocation for the Department of Agriculture has only increased, in the past ten years, by a mere $1.5 to $1.7 million. Most of the funding for the department pays salaries of essentially Nassau-based staff. In 2002/03 budget, the allocation for the Department of Agriculture represented 0.55% of the recurrent budget and the Ministry as a whole only 1.35% of the capital budget. This situation has not significantly changed. The entire agricultural sector received less than 2% of the national recurrent expenditure and less than 2% of the capital expenditure. To achieve the recommendations as indicated by the Director General of FAO, this couldn't be met with existing budget levels for the sector if we, as a people and our government, are serious about food security enhancement.

Investment by the private sector in food production has been marginal from

2002-2006 (\$10-15 million). In 2008, Central Bank's Annual Report indicated that commercial bank credit to the agricultural sector was \$11 million (2007) and \$15 million (2008). The 2010 Annual Report pointed out agricultural repayments to banks was a mere \$0.6 million in contrast to tourism, which was \$61.5 million and construction \$11.6 million.

In the Caribbean, the agriculture sector growth rates have been less than 2% from the 1960s to the 1990s and the sector's contribution to the Gross Domestic Product (GDP) has been less than 1% over the same period. The basis for this trend is the lack of investment in the sector by governments as they have all bought the Block Doctrine and the "cheap food" idea that has been detrimental to agricultural sectors around the region with the exception of Cuba, Guyana, Belize and Jamaica. In The Bahamas, the sector's contribution to the GDP has declined to the pint where it is less than 1%.

The Way Forward

The agricultural sector of The Bahamas is at a crossroads because of the challenges facing the sector and policymakers must determine the path of the sector will take and the strategies which will be employed to steer the sector and the stakeholders through this period. Stakeholders are and have been encountering the pressures of trade liberalization and WTO compliance, competition from the global food model, issues emanating from climate change and global warming, the demand for farm labour, access to funding and even praedial larceny.

The most immediate challenge is preparing the sector for WTO membership. How will the small farmer, the ornamental nursery, the poultry farm and processing plant, local canneries, bottling companies, food processors, local cottage industries and others become WTO ready?

Achieving WTO readiness is not a simple or inexpensive proposition. There is the aspect of manpower training and development. In conjunction with this, there is the installation of infrastructure, i.e. the establishment of a Bureau of Standards, and then there is the developing of expertise to interpret and apply the rules and regulations of the AOA like sanitary and phytosanitary measures.

We have been playing Russian roulette with our environment as we have depended on the United States Department of Agriculture (USDA) as a third party clearing house for food, plants and animals entering The Bahamas. This dependency will have to come to an end when we ascent to WTO membership. It has to be borne in mind that presently The Bahamas is the only country in this hemisphere that is not a WTO member. Also, The Bahamas is sixteen years behind every country in the hemisphere. There is a great deal of catching up which has to take place.

Another critical challenge is the issue of climate changes which experts view as the most complicated task facing agricultural productivity. Husbandry practices may have to be altered as small farmers and agribusinesses may have to adapt by shifting planting dates, switching crops and varieties and adopting new technologies. Case in point is the Caribbean Poultry Association (CPA) where poultry production in the region sought to become globally competitive in order to survive the challenge, which came with "cheap food." Today, the CPA is the largest agribusiness in CARICOM valued at half billion dollars, employing 100,000 workers and placing the region in a food secure position with four months of poultry meat on reserve.

For Bahamian agriculture to function in this technologically driven production environment research has to play a significant role. At the moment there is no research taking place in the Department of Agriculture, be it applied or basic.

Agriculture has too much to offer this country and successive governments over the past two decades have failed to unlock the potential of this great natural resource. This resource is an asset, which has been bestowed on this land through its climate, its water resources, its varied flora and fauna and most of all, its people.

The Director General of FAO is calling for a more productive agricultural sector for the 21st century. The Bahamas is in the position to meet that challenge; however, governments and the people of The Bahamas must believe that agriculture can play a meaningful social-economic role in the economy. To make this a reality, the financial commitment must be made to achieve this objective.

The world is moving away from the global model of low cost/high volume agriculture as its sustainability is being questioned in many quarters. In view of this, The Bahamas, like other developing countries who have dared to change, can design a model based on developing a competitive agricultural sector. This model must be centered on encouraging agribusiness development and the integration of the small farmer into the agribusiness network thorough technology, innovation, environmentally friendly and research based food production systems.

Food production is a hot button issue and IICA, in cooperation with the government of Costa Rica, will be hosting a hemispheric meeting for ministers of agriculture on food production in October 2011. According to Minister Abraham, "In agriculture, we talk about climate change, rising prices and marketing systems, but we have overlooked the topic of innovation, which plays a key role if we talk about food production, especially in the future." The motto chosen for the meeting "Sowing Innovation to Harvest Prosperity", calls attention to the need for governments to invest more resources in innovations that will make agriculture competitive, sustainable and inclusive.

With this new Bahamian model the benefits of food production will accrue to us as a people because we cannot continue to allow the half billion dollars annually to leave our shores without a concerted attempt to retain a good portion of these funds. Our outlook must now be that:

◆ Food production will create jobs

◆ Food production will be aligned to science and technology

◆ Food production will enable us to earn (export agriculture) and to save (domestic agriculture) foreign exchange

◆ Food production will sustain the local economies of the Family Island farming communities

◆ Food production will discourage migration from the Family Island to Nassau and Freeport

◆ Food production will enhance our quality of life and raise the standard of living for thousands.

This is an achievable objective; we need the commitment not solely from the political directorate but as a people with a mission to make a difference in a world where food availability can no longer be taken for granted.

AGROPOLITICS OF THE BAHAMAS AND THE CARIBBEAN

Bahamians are spending more that 50%-60% of their incomes on food. In a few weeks, Bahamians will go to the polls to elect a new government and, throughout the Caribbean, election campaigning is the time when politicians are apt to listen to the people. With the escalation in the cost of food and the ineffective food production policy framework which exists in many CARICOM states, food should be an election issue. For some income segments of Caribbean states, certain basic foods are unaffordable. This is the case in The Bahamas where certain income brackets are spending as much as 50 % to 60 % of their earnings on food. In The Bahamas where the commercialization of the pineapple began and its introduction on the global market goes back to the early 1800s, for thousands of Bahamians, the pineapple is unaffordable. Pineapples in the food store cost $7.00 each.

From my perspective, we are on the wrong course when it comes to public policy on food which has been, since the mid-1990s, based on the importation of "cheap foods", meaning highly US subsidized commodities, like poultry meat whose by-products are dumped on Caribbean markets, subsequently destabilizing domestic production, i.e. poultry agribusinesses. This policy is not working in the best interests of the country because:

(1) It is draining our foreign exchange;

(2) Thousands of food production and value-added jobs are being outsourced to countries like Costa Rica, Brazil, The United States, New Zealand, Scandinavia and as far east as Thailand;

(3) We have abdicated our responsibility on production inputs;

(4) We have become the dumping ground for stale dated and expired products, meats which have been frozen for years and a new group of "Export only" commodities;

(5) We are eating ourselves sick as a result of high consumption of sugar-based, processed, fast, "cheap" foods, thereby creating a health crisis of non-communicable diseases;

(6) We are not exploiting the natural resource potential of our islands through innovation, science and technology;

(7) Diversification of our economy has been stifled constraining the expansion of the economy and the development of new career opportunities.

Food and Income

I received an e-mail from a friend, Steve Dowd who is engaged in the global grain supply and transportation agribusiness, about the cost of food and its relation to wealth and health.

In 1932, Americans were spending 25% of their income on food; by 2009, the figure dropped to 10% .With the introduction of industrial farming and the decline of the family farm, greater efficiencies were achieved as a result of research and technological innovation. In a recent MSNBC show, Politics Nation with Rev. Al Sharpton, it was pointed out that 18.6% of Americans claim that food is unaffordable. This is almost 60 million Americans.The recession may have played a part. For a country which is one of the world's biggest suppliers of food on the global market, Americans find themselves in an acute situation with food. Food Banks catering to the indigent can be found all over America.

Among the BRIC countries (Brazil, Russia, India and China), Brazilians are spending 25% of their income on food and this represents the lowest among the BRICs. China, on the other hand, is spending 40% and that is the highest in that group.With the PIGS (Portugal, Ireland, Greece and Spain), the range is 10% for Ireland to 20% for Greece, the highest even with all of its financial woes and troubled economy.

The country with the lowest percentage spent on food is Denmark at 5% with France, Germany and Singapore hovering around 10% , Japan at 14% and Turkey at 30% . A number of countries like Canada, Australia, New Zealand, Argentina and others were not included in the survey.

Where does The Bahamas, along with our Caribbean sister states, fit into this argument on percentage of income spent on food? From the 80s, the US has been pushing its Cheap Food Programme on Caribbean countries. Yet in The Bahamas, households are spending on average about 50% to 60% of their income on food. In some Caribbean states, it could be higher. In 2008, Haiti had food riots because Haitians could not afford to buy the "cheap food" causing a Prime Minister, literally, to be run out of office.

Contribution to Economy

For decades, Caribbean politicians bought into this cheap food idea and paid lip service to the development of the agricultural sector. There was very little investment in the Sector. In my book, *The New Caribbean: A Region in Transition*, I point out that as a percentage of Gross Domestic Product (GDP), CARICOM governments expenditure in 2001/2 ranged from 6.8% (St. Lucia, '01) to 0.6% (The Bahamas, '02).

An aging cadre of small farmers depicts a sector which has become unattractive to Caribbean youth. The end result was a food deficit region. In The Bahamas food production became a welfare activity for the purpose of keeping a Bahamian presence on many of our islands, particularly those in the southeastern Bahamas.

As a sector in the economy of most Caribbean states, agriculture's contribution to the GDP ranges from 0.5% to 2%. In The Bahamas, the sector contributes less than 1%. In 2007, food imports for The Bahamas passed the $0.5 billion mark. By 2015/16 with the completion of the Baha Mar Project on Cable Beach and with the present approach to food production, food imports could reach a billion dollars.

Ian Ivey, publisher of the blog RIENET, provides data which shows that the agricultural sectors of African States are out performing those of the Caribbean:

Many African countries are doing well as illustrated by this year's projected GDP growth rates, e.g. Botswana—7.1%; Angola—10.8%; Côte d'Ivoire—8.3%; Ghana—7.5%; Rwanda—7.0%; Zambia—6.7%; Kenya—6.0%; Uganda—5.7%.

Urbanism and Tourism

Caribbean politicians have allowed policy decisions on food production to be influenced by urbanization and tourism. In many CARICOM states the size of the urban population exceeds that of the rural. In The Bahamas, for example, 85% of the population reside between the urban centres of Nassau and Freeport. This has resulted in governments orienting policies to the urban electorate and neglecting policy initiatives which enhance the rural (Family Island) economy like investing in activities to develop agriculture.

Tourism has become the engine which propels many of the economies of Caribbean states. In 2005, tourism became a two billion dollar industry for The Bahamas. Hotels, gourmet restaurants and US fast food outlets have played a significant role in pressuring governments to facilitate food imports. Food importers control food supplies. In some Caribbean islands like Aruba, there is no food production at all.

In response to the urban and tourism interests respectively, governments have adopted a duty reduction policy in order to satisfy an urban electorate as the voter balance has shifted to where urban voters outnumber rural voters. Tourism is comprised of a number of powerful special interests groups who have brought their lobbying weight to influence government policies in their direction; food is a huge revenue earner for hotels. Urbanism and tourism have changed the manner in which The Bahamas and other Caribbean governments view the role of domestic food production and agribusiness in their respective economies. Some governments have adopted a "negatron" outlook with respect to agriculture.

Ivey describes a negatron like this: "Some people are all about why things can't be done or shouldn't be done a certain way. They've always got reasons why something is wrong but never any good suggestions on how to do it differently or better. They're always trying to stir up trouble or a debate over nothing. Those people just suck the energy out of organizations." For too long,we have heard that Bahamian agriculture cannot compete so, import food. Well, we see the results of cheap food dependency.

New Global Agenda

The global agenda has changed. For the past twenty-five years, the US accentuated the Block Doctrine which pushed developing countries to import food from the US, thus projecting the US as a low cost producer and a provider of cheap food. Global institutions like the World Bank and the United Nation's FAO supported by the G20 countries saw this as a flawed policy based on dependency. These institutions reorganized their policies and programmes to encourage countries to achieve a higher degree of self-sufficiency in food; food security was the avenue to attain this goal.

This new global agenda was a departure from the past thereby causing many countries to re-order their food production priorities. The Bahamas is yet to make this adjustment. The situation has been compounded by the duty reduction approach to food and this has discouraged private sector investment in food production and agribusiness development.

Food supply is a challenge and will continue to present challenges for the governments of The Bahamas and other Caribbean states. A number of factors will exacerbate these challenges, i.e. the expanding middleclass in the BRIC countries thereby increasing the demand for many commodities. The sooner our politicians recognize this reality, the better positioned our agricultural sectors would be to face the impending challenges.

CHRONOLOGY

The 1994 Census of Agriculture stated that 50,250 acres (20,350 ha) were utilized for farmland which represented 1.5 percent of the total land area (3.4 million acres) of The Bahamas.

Some 500 years after Columbus's landing in The Bahamas, there has been a spectacular expansion of farming from a subsistence level during the Arawak Bahamian era, when a few ground provisions like cassava were grown along with a grainlike corn and fruits such as coconuts, to the present agribusiness atmosphere. The Pine Islands are now producing almost 70 million pounds for the local market.

A chronological list of the historical events which influenced agricultural growth and development in The Bahamas highlights the way agriculture has developed.

YEAR	HISTORICAL EVENTS INFLUENCING THE AGRICULTURAL SECTOR
1650	Brazilletto wood and cotton exported by Eleutheran Adventurers to USA
1784	Arrival of Loyalists and their slaves from the Southern United States
1785	Average annual quantity exported
1838	The abolition of slavery and poor husbandry practices hastened the collapse of cotton
1855–1864	Annual tonnage of pineapples about 2,000 tons in exports
1860–1878	In 1861, approximately 1,000 plus tons citrus/542 tons/yr/

	average; start American Civil War. Gun running era begins
1865	End of American civil war and gun running
1890	100,000 acres of sisal under production
1892	Trial shipments of sisal to UK
1906	Reports of poor cleaning of sisal
1911	Need for sisal inspection
1912	End of pineapple exports
1914	Low prices for sisal
1915	High prices as Mexico has problems with sisal production
1916	Boom in price for sisal/Blue Gray fly found in New Providence citrus
1917	Citrus industry extinction N.P., Fly reaches Eleuthera
1919	American Volsted Act (Prohibition)
1920	End of citrus exports
1925	Agriculture and Marine Products Board established
1927	Poor quality sisal and tomato placed on export market/West Indian seven arrival
1942	Burma Roads riots, New Providence
1951	Only 50% of the crop was exported because the US market collapsed and the Canadian market was depressed. Local canners purchased some £40,000 of crop at 30% export price (tomatoes)
1953	Hurricane damage tomato crop in Cat Island and South Eleuthera
1955	Prices are low because of large Florida production
1958	Local canneries purchase 80,000 bushels of tomatoes and this exceed exported quantity. General strike, New Providence
1962	Universal adult suffrage
1964	Cabinet government and the creation of the Ministry of Agriculture and Fisheries
1965	Cucumber became chief agricultural export
1966	BAIL sugar cane operation commenced. Bahamas changes currency from £ to $
1967	New Progressive Liberal Party Government came into power

	January 10th. Produce Exchange moves to Potter's Cay
1968	Bahamian agricultural graduates return. Agriculture portfolio moved to Trade and Industry
1969	Cabinet approved Land Resources Survey. In its first season, a total of 166,134 (s.t.) of cane were processed from 12,474 acres and 14,896 tons of sugar and 963,000 gallons of molasses. Special quota of 10,000 tons of raw sugar to US market and the balance to Canada
1970	Development of Central Agricultural Station started on Gladstone Road, N.P.
1971	Land clearing programme expansion—Millars Road Project
1973	Bahamas Agri. Research, Training & Development Project start. Construction of packing houses in the Family Islands begins.
1974	Cooperative Societies Act passed
1975	Hatchet Bay Farms purchase by The Bahamas Government
1976	Professional officers in Family Island
1977	Sheep-in confinement project, North Long Island
1978	Census of Agriculture
1981	Tomato Export Marketing Program organized by Dept. of Agriculture for North Andros, Abaco, New Providence. Food Tech. & Animal Feed unit started at the Central Agricultural Station
1983	Rejuvenation of exports takes place on Pine Islands
1986	B.G. Harmon citrus first planting
1990	Bahamas Citrus exports first crop of Red Grapefruit
1991	Agricultural extension seminar, conducted by state of Israel in The Bahamas
1992	New Free National Movement Government
1993	Ministry of Agriculture (Incorporation) Act
1994	Census of Agriculture
1997	FNM returned for 2nd term as Government

1998	The Bahamas becomes a member of the IICA
1999	Inaugural Caribbean Week of Agriculture—region's premier agriculture event
2000	Death of Sir Lynden O. Pindling, first Prime Minister of The Bahamas
2001	Lucayan Tropical Produce, a hydroponic facility came on stream in August; Bahamas seeks WTO membership
2002	Gladstone Farms goes out of business in November.
2003	Godfrey Eneas appointed The Bahamas' first Ambassador to FAO
2004	Death of Sir John Paul, first Governor-General of The Bahamas, in March
2005	Citrus canter outbreak in Abaco
2006	Skeletal remains of Lucayan Indian unearthed at Preachers Cave, North Eleuthera in March
2007	Declaration of St. Anne: Caricom Initiative on Food and Agriculture Policies and Obesity prevention of Non-communicable diseases
2008	European Partnership Agreement (EPA). Trade Agreement between CARIFORUM and EU in October was signed
2009	The Bahamas submitted its Memorandum on the Foreign Trade Regime in April to the WTO, Bahamas Embryo Transfer project in January at GRAC
2010	National Agribusiness Expo-comprised Mini-Expos on New Providence and nine Family Islands

A critique from *SPORE* Magazine
on *Agriculture in The Bahamas*

Before the Europeans arrived in the Bahama islands in 1492, the agricultural system developed by the Island Arawak people comprised shifting cultivation of starch and sugar-rich foods, garden plots, hunting fish and fauna, and collecting fruits. It has not stopped changing since.

In *Agriculture in The Bahamas* the author, who was Director of Bahamas' Agriculture from 1973 to 1982, reviews agriculture before Columbus and the colonial centuries, tracking social and institutional transition from subsistence to a plantation economy. Until 1950, agriculture was the major employer and export earner, but now tourism dominates a largely urban economy, and finances a massive food import bill. Diets are based on imported preferences (Florida is only 30 minutes away by plane) and agriculture strives to meet seasonal demand.

Bahamian agriculture has been compressed to a state of uncertainty and is vulnerable to the dictates of the WTO, where "the interests of rich, industrialised countries outweigh those of small nations."

This book is a labour of love, is tender and thorough with a nation's agricultural history, and is fraught for its future, "shrouded with challenges of unknown dimensions." A tale for how many ACP States?

SPORE Magazine No. 79 February 1999 edition.